SOMEBODY ELSE

CHARLES NICHOLL

SOMEBODY ELSE

ARTHUR RIMBAUD IN AFRICA 1880–91

THE UNIVERSITY OF CHICAGO PRESS

Published by arrangement with Random House, U.K., London

The University of Chicago Press, Chicago 60637
© Charles Nicholl 1997
All rights reserved. Originally published 1997 by Jonathan Cape
University of Chicago Press Edition 1999
Printed in the United States of America
04 03 02 01 00 99   6 5 4 3 2 1

Library of Congress Cataloging-in-Publication Data

Nicholl, Charles.
    Somebody else : Arthur Rimbaud in Africa, 1880–91 / Charles Nicholl.
        p.   cm.
    Includes bibliographical references and index.
    ISBN 0-226-58029-6 (pbk. : alk. paper)
    1. Rimbaud, Arthur, 1854–1891—Journeys—Africa.   2. Poets,
French—19th century—Biography.   3. Africa—Description and travel.
I. Title.
PQ2387.R5Z7178   1999
841′.8—dc21
    [B]   98–51305
                                                                          CIP

♾ The paper used in this publication meets the minimum requirements of the
American National Standard for Information Sciences—Permanence of Paper for
Printed Library Materials, ANSI Z39.48-1992.

IN MEMORY OF
KEVIN STRATFORD
1949–84

'Je est un autre . . .'

Arthur Rimbaud, 'Lettre du Voyant'

'You lose yourself
You reappear
You suddenly find
You got nothing to fear . . .'

Bob Dylan, 'It's Alright Ma'

CONTENTS

ILLUSTRATIONS

ACKNOWLEDGEMENTS

CERTAIN JOURNEYS LIE behind this book, and I wish to thank the following for help and hospitality.

In Aden: Mustapha Salem Mohamed, Ahmed Abdul Ghani Qahtan, Dr Masoud Amshush. In Djibouti: Patrick Millon, Ainalam Ngash, Thierry Merrill, Mounah Mousong, and the staff at Hotel L'Europe. In Somaliland: Gary Perkins, Garad Farah. In Ethiopia: Getachof, Nebiyat Kemer, Denis Gérard, Venus, Gerd and Christina Meuer, Dr Richard Pankhurst. In Alexandria: Valerie Teague. In France: Gérard Martin, Mark Lyons, Maryse Aubry.

I would like to make special mention of the Save the Children Fund, always helpful and sometimes invaluable: in particular Ben Foot (Addis Ababa), Andrew Hoban (Jijiga), and Don Redding and Andrew Timpson (London).

My own journeys are not the point of this book – this is Rimbaud's story: I am only following him – but it may be useful to know that I was in Aden in 1991, and in Harar, Tadjourah and Ankober in 1994, and that certain descriptions and comments in the book belong to those times. Descriptions of Djibouti and Somaliland are drawn from both journeys. This is not a book about these places, nor certainly about the wars and famines which have dogged the region in recent years. These are not subjects to use as 'background' for what is essentially a biographical study.

I wish also to thank my travelling-companion Ron Orders; my editors Dan Franklin and Euan Cameron; Jacqueline Korn, Tony Winch, Julian Sabbath, Marie Thomas, Kevin Jackson, Rob Strawson, Spike Ward, Kenny I, Bernard Samuels, and of course Sally.

I am grateful to the Arts Council of England for the provision of a Writer's Grant.

All translations from the French are my own. In the case of Rimbaud's poems I have consulted other translators, principally Wallace Fowlie and Paul Schmidt; in the case of his letters and other documents relating to his African years, they are mostly given here in English for the first time. I have used italics for the poems, mainly to distinguish the kind of quotation they are: associative rather than documentary.

I have regularized the spellings of African place-names, tribes, etc., though cannot claim to have done so on any scholarly ethnological basis. For the most part there is no standard spelling. I have indicated differences of usage between Rimbaud's time and ours – e.g. the Galla are now generally called the Oromo, the Danakil are the Afar, and so on.

It would be impossible to give a full range of conversion factors, and indeed a certain giddy relativism is intrinsic to the story. The chief trading currency in nineteenth-century East Africa was the Austrian silver thaler (*talari*) or dollar, which was then worth around five francs. The other important currency, particularly in Aden, was the Indian rupee, worth about two francs. In England the franc was worth about ten pence. Other frequently mentioned units are the *frasleh* (or *farasalah*), a trade-weight equivalent to about 36 lb (16.6 kg); and the *daboulah*, which is actually a goat-skin pannier for transporting goods by camel, but which is used as a unit of 6 *fraslehs* (100 kg) in coffee transactions.

INTRODUCTION

AT THE
EMPTY INN

I N THE YEAR 1880, IN the dogdays of August, a young Frenchman disembarks at Steamer Point, in the Arabian port of Aden. He is tall and lean-faced, with chestnut-coloured hair that the sun has faded. His clothes are shabby, his manner brusque. He carries his belongings in a brown leather suitcase fastened with four buckled straps.

He commands attention but is not a curiosity. Aden is a British protectorate, an entrepôt, a transit-camp for travellers both to Africa and to India. There are plenty of Europeans passing through – traders, explorers, engineers, clerks, cooks, all sorts. He might be any of these. He has come, as they mostly do, by steamer through the new Suez Canal, opened in 1869. He has drifted down the Red Sea, short-hauling from coast to coast, looking for any kind of work that was going; and finding none he has come by boat or ship through the straits known as Bab al Mandeb – the Gate of Tears – and along the desiccated littoral of the Yemen, to Aden.

Much of this may be guessed at a glance. The sunburnt face, the soiled cotton clothes, the scarred portmanteau: they give that sort of account of him. His eyes might suggest other, less decipherable stories. They are extraordinary: a pale, hypnotic, unsettling blue. Decades later a French missionary who knew him in Africa would say: 'I remember his large clear eyes. What a gaze!'

His eyes are all the more vivid on this particular day because he has a fever. He had it bad up in Hodeidah; he has still not shaken it off.

There are dhows and coal-barges at the wharf, and the shark-fishing boats which are little more than rafts. The eponymous steamers lie off in the glittering water, near the rock called Flint Island, used by the British as a quarantine station. Behind the docks can be seen the principal buildings of the colony: the Governor's residence, the Post Office, the agencies of the P & O and Messageries Maritimes shipping-lines, and a scattering of white bungalows, though not yet as numerous as those seen by Evelyn Waugh fifty

3

years later, 'spilt over the hillside like the litter of picnic-parties after Bank Holiday'.

As the boat prepares to dock it is surrounded by children paddling little dug-outs. They are mostly Somali, from the nearby coast of East Africa. They leap and dive and call out for coins: 'Oh! Oh! Sixpence! À la mer, à la mer! Every day, tous les jours!'

A cast-iron jetty leads him to the quayside. The heat is intense: 40° is normal at this time of year. The boat's arrival has brought people out from the shade: Somali porters, Yemeni hawkers, sun-ripened English subalterns in scout-master shorts. In the customs shed – a tin-roofed building known, in the stout parlance of British colonialism, as the Bender – he completes certain formalities.

He dislikes customs men: their pipes clenched between their teeth, their axes and knives, their dogs on the leash.

On the other side there are cabbies waiting, also Somalis, with their little horse-drawn carriages, or gharries, which another French visitor compares to American stagecoaches. Does he take one? Probably not. His destination is close by; he has learned to travel frugally; despite the fever, and the large suitcase, the *gari wallah* gets no fare from him. He is heading for the Grand Hotel, one of two French-run hotels in the colony. Its signboard, painted in letters two metres high, is visible from the wharf: GRAND HOTEL DE L'UNIVERS. This improbably cosmic name brings a momentary reminiscence of his home town, Charleville, and of a certain Café de l'Univers up by the railway station, the scene of all those drunken declamatory evenings with Delahaye, with Izambard, with . . .

But their names mean little to him now.

He is heading for the Grand because he has a contact there. Back up the coast, at Hodeidah, laid out with the fever, he was befriended by a French trader, one Trébuchet, an agent for the Marseille company of Morand & Fabre. Trébuchet has friends in Aden, furnishes him with letters of introduction. One is to a certain Colonel Dubar, currently employed in the coffee business. The other is to Jules Suel, the manager of the Grand Hotel.

The hotel is a long, low building set back from the sea. It stands on a curving street named Prince of Wales Crescent in honour of a royal visit in 1874. The frontage stretches for thirty metres, stone-built arcades on the ground floor, small wooden rooms with latticed shutters all along the first: an Indian architectural style fairly common here. To the right of the entrance is the dining room, *à la terrasse*, open to the meagre sea-breeze. To the left is the hotel shop, full of exotic souvenirs – leopard skins, oryx horns, ostrich feathers, Danakil swords, Bombay silk, Turkish delight. Behind rise the hills of scalded, dun-coloured rock that glare down on every corner of Aden, on every day that is spent here.

He climbs the broad, flint-block steps and disappears into the shadows of the vestibule.

*   *   *

This brief episode took place more than a century ago. There are no living witnesses, and it was anyway quite unremarkable. Or rather, what is remarkable about it only becomes apparent with hindsight. In this book I will try to reconstruct many such episodes, try to make them flicker into movement like a scene from a film. There was no phantom cameraman at Steamer Point on that day in 1880, but if there had been, that is approximately what he would have recorded.

The scene I am describing is the arrival in Aden of the poet Arthur Rimbaud (or as one should certainly call him by this stage, though still only twenty-five years old, the *former* poet Arthur Rimbaud). My account owes something to a visit I made to Aden in 1991, on the centenary of Rimbaud's death, but mostly it derives from documentary sources. The bare facts can be gathered from one of Rimbaud's letters, and from the memoirs of the coffee-trader Alfred Bardey, who was shortly to meet him and to become his employer. The surroundings are based on old photographs and descriptions of Aden. The suitcase can be seen at the Musée Rimbaud in Charleville-Mézières, his birthplace in the French Ardennes. The unsettling blue eyes are described by the poet Verlaine, who had looked into them often enough.

It is not, of course, a definitive account: it is more like some scratchy old home-movie. The faces around him have blurred. There are jump-cuts due to lack of information. There are guesses. The shadows of the vestibule are an area of blackness in an old photograph.

And then there are his poems, and the use one is entitled to make of them. I do not really know that Rimbaud disliked customs men. One might suppose so from his poem 'Customs Men', which according to his friend Delahaye recorded a run-in with the customs in Belgium, but a poem is not exactly an opinion, so this too is a guess. This is expressly not a book about Rimbaud the poet, but it is hard to resist using his poetry as a kind of buried interior voice: a body of images and recollections and sometimes of strangely prophetic announcements, as if he had dreamed all this up long before.

These are caveats I should enter right away. Rimbaud's African years, which are the subject of this book, and which I take to begin here with his arrival at Aden in 1880, are full of these illegible shadows. Little has been written about them and, for some periods at least, little is known about them. The sources mentioned above – letters, memoirs, etc – are tantalizingly thin. The visual record is almost non-existent: just three photographs of Rimbaud in Africa remain, self-portraits, taken within a few days of one another in April or May 1883.

These are, in the biographical convention, Rimbaud's 'lost years'. That is their fascination, and their difficulty.

*　　*　　*

Steamer Point today retains that imperturbable British stamp which it doubtless had then, though it is now a quarter of a century since the British pulled out of Aden. You are certainly in Arabia – men in turbans and skirts, goats browsing in vacant lots, hot gusts of grit blowing up off the street – but you are also in this odd little enclave of fossilized Britishness. The port building itself is dated 1919. It is not the 'Bender' that Rimbaud came through. It is built of grey flintstone, in Victorian neo-Classical style: a displaced town hall or public library. The road curves away from it like some half-remembered high street from the Fifties: a clock-tower, a tin signboard advertising Craven A cigarettes, a triangular traffic sign on a striped metal pole.

In a bookshop there are old postcards, with tinted photographs and 'Greetings from Aden' on a background of cake-tin tartan. Vintage issues of *Photoplay* are stacked on a table. My Adeni guide, Mustapha, is transfixed by a still from *One Million Years BC* – Raquel Welch in a mammoth-skin bikini.

I scented the past easily enough in Aden, but it was often a nostalgic whiff of my own teenage years rather than a glimpse back to Rimbaud's Aden. This seemed appropriate in a way, but was it history? (Appropriate because Rimbaud is a quintessentially teenage

6

poet, a 'god of adolescence' as André Breton put it; appropriate because I was a teenager when he first impinged on me via the songs of Bob Dylan; and perhaps also appropriate because it is in teenage, roughly speaking, that one is supposed to grow out of this business of having *heroes*, and yet here I was etc etc. But on this see the 'Personal Note' at the end of the book.)

From Steamer Point we head off in search of the Grand Hotel, neither by foot nor by gharry, but in the Mitsubishi Galant of Mustapha's friend Ahmed. Mustapha sits in the passenger seat, twisting round to talk, gold Rolex and amber worry-beads to the fore. The area north of Steamer Point is known as Tawahi, once a fishing village, now a coastal suburb. We arrive at the Crescent, the former Prince of Wales Crescent. The royal name has dropped off the address: an atrophied part of Aden's long history. This used to be a thriving Jewish quarter, Mustapha says. They had all the concessions – 'Rolex, Pentax, you name it' – but now they have closed down. We see an empty building once called the Tip Top Annexe. This puts me in mind of my uncle, whose chequered career included a stint as a British Forces disc-jockey in Aden.

The Grand itself has also closed down, though it was still in business when Evelyn Waugh came here in late 1930, having covered for *The Times* the coronation of Haile Selassie in Addis Ababa. It was, he complained, 'as expensive as Torr's in Nairobi'. He left this piquant description of it:

> The food has only two flavours – tomato ketchup and Worcester-shire sauce; the bathroom consists of a cubicle in which a tin can is suspended on a rope; there is a nozzle at the bottom of the can encrusted with stalactites of green slime; the bather stands on the slippery cement floor and pulls a string releasing a jet of water over his head and back; for a heavy extra charge it is possible, with due notice, to have the water warmed; the hall-porter has marked criminal tendencies; the terrace is infected by money-changers. The only compensating luxury is a seedy, stuffed sea-animal, unmistakably male, which is kept in a chest and solemnly exhibited – on payment – as a mermaid.

The Crescent is recognizably crescent-shaped, but has lost its sea-view and become a sleepy side-street. The Grand was certainly here, but Mustapha is unsure exactly where. We kerb-crawl up the street, looking for clues from the old photograph.

'I think it was this one,' he says, pointing into a shambolic apartment-block probably dating from the 1950s. 'Look, you can see the old lift.'

It took a while to pinpoint it, but there it undoubtedly was – the eleven arcades, the little shuttered windows on the first floor, the squat building on the hill above. The signboard above the entrance has gone, but I can see the nails which once held it. The Grand Hotel of the Universe has fallen on hard times. The masonry has crumbled, the lattice-work has rotted, the arcades are boarded up, but the main entrance is still open, grand in size at least. Three steps up, this leads into a tall passageway, with a sign at the end, just discernible in the sudden interior darkness: 'SMART TAILORS – Tailors & Drapers'. The shadows of the vestibule turn out to be real shadows after all.

The place has been split into tenements. What had once been a garden behind is also filled with shack-housing. The only interior trace of its former life is a broad wooden staircase, with the remains of its banister, though after the first turn this too is closed off with panels of wood and tin.

Another, smaller staircase leads to the upper rooms, in one of which Rimbaud probably stayed on this first day, and one of which he certainly used as a base a few years later.

Mustapha has melted away, as he tends to when my inquisitiveness crosses certain bounds. Having little Arabic other than courtesies, I wander round like a lost sightseer, brandishing my old photo of the Grand. The name of Rimbaud elicits no response other than the customary confusion with Rambo. (This confusion pursued me throughout my researches in these countries, where the bandannaed psychopath is still very popular. I soon took to describing Rimbaud as the 'real Rambo', or the 'original Rambo', which earned him a certain vicarious admiration.)

A young man invites me into one of the tenements. His wife stands in the front room, bows in greeting. The room is bright with linoleum, coloured glass, plastic flowers, a three-piece suite in orange plastic. A radio plays one of those racing Arab laments to the tune of an *oud*.

There is a smaller, barer room partitioned off: a mattress, a few piles of cloth or garments, the wooden walls shed-like, painted with a chalky blue wash.

I lean out of the window: Mustapha and Ahmed lounging against the flank of the Galant, yawning in unison.

Mustapha calls up, 'What's it like?'

'It's someone's home.'

Perhaps this was once Rimbaud's room. Who knows? Does it really matter if it was here, or somewhere down the corridor? Probably not. In coming to Aden I had hoped to find some clue to these 'lost years' of Rimbaud's life, had hoped perhaps to find some moment of empathy of the kind he himself expressed in his prose-poem 'Bad Blood':

> *I visited the inns and flophouses he had hallowed with his presence. I saw with his eyes the blue sky and the busy, flowering fields. In cities I sniffed out his destiny.*

He is talking of his early fascination with the figure of the criminal, but could not I also 'sniff out' the runaway poet's destiny in the dusty inns of the Red Sea?

Standing in that little cubicle at the Grand it was another of his lines that came to mind, one of his mysterious pronouncements: '*You follow the red road and it leads you to the empty inn.*'

The Grand Hotel was the first of many such 'empty inns' I would visit. There are no ghosts here, no jolts of recognition, no physical traces. There may be a neatly carved 'A.R. 1880' on some obscured wainscot, but I doubt it. This is just an old address. One comes here, perhaps, not so much to take something from the place, as to bring something back to it.

*   *   *

Jules Suel, the suave and genial manager of the Grand, was known to all the Europeans in the colony. He was a tall man in his fifties, an old hand. Alfred Bardey describes him as 'alert', a quality implicitly contrasted with the lassitude which overtook so many in Aden. He wore, Bardey notes, 'the colonial costume, which consists of trousers and jacket of thin white cotton, canvas shoes, and a very thick but light helmet'. The latter is presumably the pith sun-hat generally known as a 'topee'. This faintly comic headgear, it should be noted, was never Rimbaud's style.

So let us guess once more. Let us imagine Monsieur Suel seated among compatriots and customers on the long terrace of the Grand, which to judge by the photo is staffed by Indian waiters. His topee is on the table. He rises to greet the new arrival, the young man with the burning blue eyes, the bringer of salutations from Trébuchet.

The young man's name is familiar to him, but not in the way it is to us. It is familiar to him simply because there is another Monsieur Rimbaud already in Aden. He appears on the records as 'J-B. Rimbaud' – perhaps Jean-Baptiste – and is described as a 'conductor' working for the Aden branch of the Messageries Maritimes. Rimbaud will later complain of letters being misdirected to this namesake, and of the ten centimes surcharge this incurs.

It is the wonderful anonymity of it which catches my fancy. Rimbaud is at this moment a complete unknown. That is the keynote of the scene: what Suel does *not* know about him. He does not know that this young man is somewhat famous: a poet of the kind soon to be styled *poètes maudits*, the cursed or outcast poets; a cult figure at the least, infamous if not yet quite famous. He does not see before him the revolutionary author of *A Season in Hell* and the *Illuminations*; the brutal young man who commandeered and ultimately wrecked the life of his fellow poet Paul Verlaine; the preacher of 'a long, immense and systematic derangement of the senses'; the smoker of hashish and drinker of absinthe:

> Like a most delicate and diaphanous garment is the drunkenness you get from this sage-bush of the glaciers, this absomphe. But then afterwards to lie down in the shit.

All that is forgotten now: the poems, the debauches, 'those fine games I played with madness'. Not the least extraordinary thing about Rimbaud's poetry is that almost all of it is teenage poetry. He wrote nothing, as far as is known, after 1875. '*No more words! I bury the dead in my belly.*' For others, though, his fame was just beginning. News of it would one day reach him out here, but when asked about these poems that were causing such a stir back in Paris, he just growled that they were '*rinçures*' – slops, dregs, leavings – and abruptly changed the subject.

His unendorsed fame has continued to grow. By the time of his death in 1891 he was already hailed as a 'Master' by the Symbolists and Decadents of *fin-de-siècle* Paris, and he has continued to be acknowledged – and to some extent reinvented – by every significant modernist movement from the Surrealists to the Beats. That he was a 'major' poet does not need to be argued here. His influence is acknowledged by a whole gamut of writers: a selective list would include Stéphane Mallarmé, Paul Claudel, André Breton, Antonin Artaud, Albert Camus, Jean Genet, Henry Miller, Hart Crane, Dylan Thomas, Jack Kerouac, Allen Ginsberg, Bob Dylan, Jim Morrison and Patti Smith – not to mention *chansonniers* like Jacques Brel and Leo Ferré, and film-makers like Jean-Luc Godard, and the footballer Eric Cantona – but of the many assessments of his greatness I have read I remember best the comment of an elderly lady in a train near Charleville, who told me that she hadn't read any Rimbaud, and didn't much like the sound of him, but that he was after all '*le premier des poètes modernes*'. The first modern poet: I am happy to stick with that, even without the weasel-word 'arguably' which one feels constrained to add.

But for now he is safe, unknown, literature-free. No one on the terrace at the Grand that day would describe him, as Verlaine once did, as having 'the perfectly oval face of an angel in exile'. They see the serious-looking moustache; the flecks of grey hair on a man still young; the big, work-roughened hands. They see also, perhaps, the scar of a gunshot wound on his left wrist.

But they do not ask. Your past is your own affair: that is the law in these cross-road towns.

The only actual description of him around this time is from Alfred Bardey, who met him a few weeks later. He simply says that he found him '*sympathique*' – nice! – and describes him as a 'tall, pleasant young man who speaks little, and accompanies his brief comments with odd little cutting gestures with his right hand'. More piquantly, Bardey also records that when asked which part of France he was from, Rimbaud replied that he came from Dole. This was a lie. Dole, in the Jura region, was actually his father's birthplace. Bardey did not learn the truth, that Rimbaud was an Ardennais from Charleville, till some while later.

Standing in front of the bricked-up arcades of the Grand, I try to see him as they would have seen him. He is really nothing special: a down-at-heel young Frenchman, a bit of a drifter. He is taciturn but seems nice enough; he is no relation to Rimbaud of the Messageries.

He is *another* Monsieur Rimbaud.

* * *

So begins, with these casual yet complex anonymities, the story of

Rimbaud's African years. They have a fascination of their own – a life of dangers and discomforts, a life on the edge of the unknown – but even more they fascinate in their contrast with what went before them. They are remarkable because of who he was and because of what he left behind him. They are, in a sense, defined by what he was trying to escape from. I suppose this is a comment on our own priorities. We would not really be interested in this obscure French trader had he not previously been a remarkable French poet. We cannot allow him this anonymity he seeks. We know, as Suel and Bardey and the rest did not, who this young stranger is.

Yet also this moment of anonymity is entirely typical of Rimbaud, is classically Rimbaldien or Rimbaudish, because his whole life is a story of departures and flights, of disappearances and reappearances. His abandonment of poetry was only the most famous, the most regretted, of his departures. He is on the move, in transit, always turning up somewhere new, always the stranger:

> *Seen enough: viewed all these scenes in every possible light.*
> *Had enough: the sounds of the city at evening, or in the sunlight, or any time.*
> *Known enough. The haltings of life; the sounds and the visions.*
> *Setting out for new feelings, new noises.*['Departure']

In this sense his African years are not, as they are often taken to be, some long blank coda at the end of a brief and brilliant career, but an expression of something that was always there, in his life and in his poems and in his desire to tear them up afterwards.

In his stirring teenage manifesto of 1871, generally called the *Lettre du Voyant* ('The Prophet's Letter'), he makes his famous, syntactically improbable pronouncement: *'Je est un autre'*.

I is somebody else . . .

He was speaking of the transforming powers of the imagination, of poetry as a kind of latter-day shamanism, but I hear this phrase echoing on throughout his driven, restless, nomadic life. He is a man on the run. He has turned his back on family and friends, on the comforts of home, on his own brilliant future as a poet. He has broken the ties which bind the rest us, the ties which most of us are, sooner or later, glad to be bound by. He has seen enough and known enough; he is out in the wilderness of Africa, 'far from everywhere', hurrying on towards that last, impossible freedom, which is to lose yourself, to become somebody else entirely.

We are close here to ideas of Africa explored by Conrad in works like *Heart of Darkness*: ideas of severance from 'civilized' norms, of disappearance and loss of self, of hard-bitten heroes who have 'refined away everything except disgust'. The connection between Rimbaud and Conrad is chronological rather than literary. Conrad's years of roving, in Africa and elsewhere, are contemporary with Rimbaud's – indeed they began, like so many of Rimbaud's journeys, aboard a French vessel out of Marseille – but he did not actually begin writing until the mid-1890s, by which time Rimbaud was dead. It should also be noted that Conrad's terrain is the dark, steamy, profuse interior of equatorial Africa, whereas Rimbaud's is the dazzle of East African deserts and mountains: not a darkness but an emptiness, a silence.

I wish to restore Rimbaud's African years not just by piecing them together, by telling their story, by recovering their moments of historical intimacy; but also by seeing them as a sort of doomed existential adventure which is perhaps the true summation of his curtailed life as a poet. The French have a phrase (they always do) – *l'œuvre-vie*: the 'work of life', as opposed to the work of art. It might be argued, in other words, that Rimbaud's life of adventure and wandering in Africa was actually his masterpiece. '*After the poetry of the word, the poetry of action*' [Giuseppe Raimondi, 'Rimbaud Mercante in Africa'].

To see it in this sort of way is not to deny more down-to-earth explanations – that he could never settle down because emotionally damaged, frozen-up inside, unable to form a stable relationship, and so on. This is probably true, but it is rather like saying that Hamlet worried too much. It is a question of scale, of extremity. This is a human story, but there is also an archetypal or legendary aspect to Rimbaud, which radiates out of his poetry, which magnifies his gestures and loads his curtest utterances, and which gives to his African travels this sense of an epic trek through the outer reaches of discontent. He was, said Verlaine, '*plus libre que les plus libres*', freer than the freest: a perception one may question or qualify but hardly ignore.

One tries in a way to mediate between these two Rimbauds: between the damaged young man and the existentialist hero; between *je* and *l'autre*. I do not know if it is possible to become 'somebody else'. The upshot of Rimbaud's story is probably that it isn't, at least not by physically walking out on yourself. It is a restlessness in the heart, an impossible desire: one which all travellers in some measure feel, and which Rimbaud comes dangerously near to achieving. He sums it succinctly in the *Season in Hell*:

> *Does he have the secrets for changing life? No, I told myself, he is only searching for them . . .*

I begin with an account of his earlier years. I cannot recount them in detail – they have been exhaustively studied already, unlike the African years – but some idea of them is essential to understand the resonance of his life in Africa, to trace the route that brought him here, to see this moment of his arrival in Aden as the latest in a series of ever greater escapes.

PART ONE

THE RUNAWAY

'We will sleep on the pavements of unknown cities, without comforts, without cares . . .'

– A Season in Hell: 'Delirium 1'

1

DESERTIONS

J EAN-NICOLAS ARTHUR RIMBAUD was born in the handsome but lugubrious Northern French town of Charleville, at six o'clock in the morning, on 20 October 1854. His birthplace on rue Thiers (then rue Napoléon) is a modest three-storey town house. A rather soulless modern bookshop, part of the 'France Loisir' chain, now occupies the ground floor.

He was the second son of an army captain, Frédéric Rimbaud, and Vitalie *née* Cuif, a local farmer's daughter. His father, aged forty, was absent at the time of his birth, and would be absent for much of his infancy, and would desert the family for good in 1860, when Arthur was six. His father was all but unknown to him: a faint gallery of childhood images. In the infamous *Album Zutique*, composed with drunken friends in Paris in 1871, Rimbaud writes:

> *Sometimes I thought about my father: in the evening, the game of cards and the talk getting dirty, and the neighbour round, and me being told to go away; and the things seen – for a father is scary – and the things dreamt-of; his knee on which he would sometimes cuddle me; his trousers whose flies my finger wished to open . . .*

The absent father: there has been no lack of psychologizing on this theme. The flight of Rimbaud *père* prefiguring Rimbaud's own relentless wanderings; those wanderings in themselves a kind of covert search for that missing man. He told Bardey he was from Dole: free to invent his own biography he substitutes his father's. On another occasion – another lie – he claimed to have 'recently deserted from the 47th regiment of the French Army'. This was the regiment of his father, the original deserter.

His father had served in Algeria, first as a soldier and then an administrator. (He was head of the 'Arab Bureau' at Sebdou, near

Oran.) He was something of a scholar of Arabic: in this too Rimbaud followed him. He left behind certain 'Arab papers' which remained in the family, and which Rimbaud refers to in a letter from Africa:

> Tell F to look in the Arab papers for a notebook entitled 'Jokes, Puns, etc' in Arabic; there should also be a collection of 'Dialogues', or 'Songs', or something of that sort, useful for someone learning the language. [15 February 1881]

'F' is Frédéric, the elder brother, named after the father. Never much liked by the younger, wilder Arthur, he lived out his days in provincial obscurity, finally becoming a bus driver.

Rimbaud's childhood was spent with his mother and Frédéric, and his two younger sisters, Vitalie and Isabelle. In 1860 – the year of Isabelle's birth, the year of the father's last desertion – they moved to rented accommodation on rue Bourbon, in one of the poorer quarters of Charleville. This was the lowest point of their social standing.

In an autobiographical poem entitled 'Seven-year-old Poets', written in May 1871, Rimbaud evokes this sombre chapter of his childhood – the shabby, depressing town house; the little garden out back with its scabbed fruits *en espalier*; the chill of his bedroom, 'a bare room, tall and blue, with the shutters closed, and the sour smell of damp over everything'. Amid these gloomy oppressions come the first awakenings of rebellion and poetry and sex:

> *And the Mother, closing up the exercise book, went off well pleased and very proud, without seeing in the blue eyes beneath the pimpled forehead that the soul of her son was filled with revulsion.*
>
> *All day he sweated obedience; such a bright child, except for those little dark tics, something you'd glimpse in him which suggested certain bitter hypocrisies. In the shadow of the corridors with their mouldy hangings he stuck out his tongue as he passed, and pressed his two fists into his crotch, and in his closed eyes saw spots . . .*
>
> *In the summertime, defeated, stupefied, he liked nothing better than to shut himself up in the cool of the privy. There he meditated, at peace, with his nostrils opened wide . . .*
>
> *For company he chose only those children who were sickly and bare-headed, whose eyes watered all down their cheeks, who hid their thin, yellow, mud-darkened fingers underneath worn-out*

*clothes that smelt of diarrhoea, who spoke with the gentleness of
idiots. When the Mother found out these filthy sympathies, she
took fright . . .*

*Then the daughter of the workers next door came over: crazy girl,
brown eyes, wearing a calico dress. She was eight years old. This
little wild-cat got him in a corner, and jumped on his back, and
pulled his hair. He was underneath her. He bit her on the bottom
– she never wore any knickers – and bruised by her fists and her
heels he took away the taste of her flesh to his room.*

The baleful presence of his mother is an obsessive theme. She
was a peasant's daughter, proud, strict, rigid, with fierce if limited
ambitions for her children. There is a sketch of her by Rimbaud,
aggressively scribbled. She is long-faced, hair scraped back and
partly covered with a headscarf, dress tightly fastened across her
bosom; she is writing a letter. In 'An Old Idiot's Memories' (from the
Album Zutique) we hear her climb 'noisily into bed, like some
labourer's son'. Her nightdress is 'frayed at the bottom and yellow
like a fruit' and 'exudes a sour smell'.

To his poetic cronies she was the overbearing 'Mère Rimbe', or
'La Daromphe' (a formation from the slang word for a mother,
daronne). Rimbaud styled her 'La Mother' – '*La Mother m'a mis là
dans un triste trou*', he wrote to his friend Delahaye, the 'sad hole'
being his home, and she his gaoler there. Another phrase he used
was 'La Bouche d'Ombre' – the Mouth of Shadow – an ironic
borrowing from a poem by Victor Hugo.

One can certainly sympathize with Mme Rimbaud, a single
mother with four children to care for, but one cannot quite forgive her: Rimbaud's childhood was cold, loveless, traumatic. His
mother's '*inconscience*', said his friend Izambard – her sheer
unawareness of her son – was 'quite extraordinary'.

And yet it is to La Mother that the vast majority of his letters
from Africa are written (they are usually addressed to the whole
family – to his 'dear friends' is the typical phrasing – but it is to his
mother that they speak). It is as if that rage against her could only
be healed at this great distance. It is also an irony of these letters that
at his most exotic and far-flung, Rimbaud is most like the good
Ardennais peasant she wanted him to be, with his constant talk of
money and work, of profit and loss. He has learned how to please
her. (This aspect of his letters home – this residue of deep family

tension – has to be taken into account when using them as a documentary source. They are a narrow window onto his life in Africa.)

The psychologist might take this further, and find in this rejecting mother – as in the vanishing father – another deep-seated clue to the mystery of Rimbaud's African adventure. In *Love, Guilt and Reparation* (1975), the psychoanalyst Melanie Klein writes of explorers:

> It has been found that phantasies of exploring the mother's body, which arise out of the child's aggressive sexual desires, greed, curiosity and love, contribute to the man's interest in exploring new countries . . . In the explorer's unconscious mind, a new territory stands for a new mother, one that will replace the loss of the real mother. He is seeking the 'promised land', the 'land flowing with milk and honey'.

*   *   *

In 1862 the family moved to more salubrious surroundings. In 1863 our first picture of Arthur, aged nine, chubby and serious, in a row of schoolchildren. Another, a couple of years later, shows him at his first communion, next to Frédéric, an image which reminds me once again of 'Seven-year-old Poets':

> *He feared those washed-out Sundays in December, when he sat with his hair slicked down, on a stool of acajou wood, reading from a Bible whose pages had cabbage-green edges.*

In 1865 he is enrolled at the Collège de Charleville. He is a star pupil. *'Tu vatis eris'*, he writes, in the course of one of his prize-winning Latin compositions. 'You will be a poet . . .'

At college he forms the two most important friendships of his youth: with his fellow pupil, Ernest Delahaye; and then, early in 1870, with his twenty-one-year-old schoolteacher, Georges Izambard. They would later be deserted, as was everyone, but their intimate knowledge of Rimbaud's youth (Delahaye over many years, Izambard over just nine months) is the raw stuff of future biographies.

In 1870, aged fifteen, Rimbaud's first publications, in magazines: 'The Orphans' New Year Gifts' and 'Three Kisses' (later retitled 'The

First Evening'). This is a time of change, of adolescent frustrations, of dreadful clashes with La Mother. Charleville, he tells Izambard, 'is the most supremely idiotic of all little provincial towns'.

On 19 July 1870 the Franco-Prussian War is declared. The conflict laps around northerly Charleville: soldier boys (*pioupious*) in the streets, jingoism in the air. The adolescent responds cynically:

> A dreadful sight: aged grocers dressed up in uniform. It's amazing how they leap into action, the notaries and glaziers and taxmen and carpenters, all the fat-bellies patrolling round the gates of Mézières with their breech-loaders up against their hearts. My country rises up!! Personally I'd prefer it to stay sitting down. Don't stir your shoes – that's my motto. [25 August, 1870]

The Empire totters, there is revolution in the air – but not here, not in Charleville, 'this province where the people feed on flour and mud'. And so Rimbaud runs away, to Paris: *la première fugue*, the first escape, at the age of fifteen. 'Paris hypnotized him,' Izambard said. The date was 29 August 1870.

* * *

The direct railway line to Paris was no longer open, so he travels north, across the Belgian border to Charleroi. The small sum of money in his pocket (the result of having sold off some of Izambard's books) is soon exhausted; he travels from Saint-Quentin to Paris without a ticket.

On 31 August, arriving at the Gare du Nord, he is arrested. Izambard narrates as follows:

> He went to see a revolution. But he didn't see it, having no ticket to show. Picked up by two policemen, he was taken down to the station, thoroughly frisked, deprived of his papers – suspicious papers, covered with those hieroglyphics in uneven lines – taken for a thief, for a spy, for anything except what he said he was, and finally banged up in the Black Maria [*le panier à salade*, or salad-basket] and thence – don't spare the horses! – to Mazas.

Mazas prison (on what is now rue Diderot) was a notorious hole, full of dangerous criminals. He is a penniless teenage truant in a wartime city. 'He tries to explain everything, but is not heard, is not understood, this being no time for musicians or rimesters.'

The stirring revolutionary poem 'You Dead of Ninety-Two' is inscribed 'done at Mazas, 3 September 1870' (in fact it was probably copied or rewritten there: according to Izambard it had been written some weeks earlier). On 4 September, the Empire collapses; the Republic is proclaimed. In Paris the crowd surges around the Hôtel de Ville. Rimbaud is behind bars and sees none of this.

On the 5th, a chastened Arthur writes in desperation to Izambard: 'Today I'm awaiting the verdict in Mazas. Oh, my hope rests in you, as in my mother . . . I love you as a brother, I will love you as a father.'

The liberal, myopic and somewhat exasperated schoolteacher Izambard bails him out, pays the thirteen francs owed to the railway company, and invites Rimbaud to cool his heels in Douai with him and his three 'aunts' (so Izambard calls them: he had been brought up in their family after the death of his mother) the Misses Gindre, who are very *sympathiques* and not a little *érotiques*, and who are very probably the attentive ladies celebrated in Rimbaud's gorgeous poem, 'The Seekers of Lice', in which 'two tall and charming sisters' seat a boy beside an open window and browse through his hair with their 'silvery fingernails'. (Izambard himself believed they were the Gindres: on a folder of letters he wrote: '*Caroline: La Chercheuse de Poux*'. Caroline was the eldest of the three *tantes*: she was about thirty-eight when Rimbaud was there.) Their fingers run through his heavy chestnut-coloured hair, removing the lice he has brought from the Paris jailhouse:

> He hears their black eyelashes beating in the perfumed silence, and their soft electric fingers make the little lice crackle as they die beneath their regal nails, and in the midst of this misty indolence there is the wine of idleness coursing through him, and the sigh of a harmonica which might just send him mad, and inside him the boy feels, ceaselessly rising and falling to the rhythm of their slow caresses, a desire to weep.

On 26 September he returns to Charleville, summoned by La Mother. For a few days he kicks around in Charleville. 'I am decomposing among platitudes and nastiness and greyness,' he writes to Izambard. 'Whatever you say, I am wildly determined to worship free freedom.'

La liberté libre . . . A key Rimbaud phrase, much heard on the streets of Paris during the *événements* of 1968.

After about ten days back home, he is off again. 'Hat on, coat on, a fist in each pocket, and let's go.' This time he travels on foot to Brussels via Fumay, Vireux, Charleroi. He knocks on schoolfriends' doors, is sometimes fed and sheltered. He visits, and swiftly offends, the editor of a local newspaper. He dines on beer and ham at an *auberge* called Le Cabaret Vert, served by a flirty waitress 'with enormous tits'. He commemorates the occasion in two sonnets. Scholars have confirmed the existence of this truck-stop (actually La Maison Verte), and even the name of the pneumatic waitress, a Flemish girl called Mia.

The hapless Izambard, summoned by Mme Rimbaud and clearly deemed culpable in the matter, sets off in pursuit. He follows Rimbaud's footsteps, and he cannot catch up. He is the paradigm of all future biographers.

Rimbaud arrives in Brussels, presents himself at the house of a friend of Izambard's, Paul Durand, on rue Fossé-aux-Loups, but by the time Izambard arrives there in search of him he has gone again. Yes, 'little Rimbaud' was here, Durand says. 'He looked like he had walked for miles. He was dusty, muddy, his collar filthy, his necktie twisted.'

In mid-October Rimbaud arrives once more on the doorstep of the bewitching *tantes* in Douai. 'It's me,' he says sweetly, 'I've come back.' Izambard, returning from his fruitless search, is astonished to find him there, calmly copying out his new poems, dressed up to the nines on the money that Durand had given him: 'a fashionable collar with the corners clipped, a necktie of burnished silk: the effect was dazzling; a real *dandy*.'

On this second stay with the Gindre sisters Rimbaud completed the 'Douai Notebooks', essentially his first collection of poems (though never published as such). This he sends to the poet Paul Demeny, another acquaintance of Izambard. The *cahiers* contain twenty-two poems, among them such gems as 'The Sleeper in the Valley', 'Winter Dream' (written on a train on 7 October 1870), 'At the Cabaret Vert' and 'The Tease' (both written at Charleroi), 'Nina's Replies' and 'My Gypsy Life'. They have a wild sparkle but this is not yet the deranged poet of legend: Izambard calls them 'those very clever, very refined, very strong and completely intelligible verses of his first period'. They are about sex and romance (much of it, perhaps, imagined), about life on the road in the last days of summer 1870, striding through the countryside with his fists thrust down into the torn pockets of his overcoat – '*mon paletot aussi devenait idéal*': his coat was so lacking in substance it had become a Platonic 'ideal'.

> *. . . My inn was the Great Bear,*
> *My stars rustled like silk above me,*
> *And I listened to them, sitting on the roadside,*
> *On those sweet September nights when I felt*
> *The drops of dew on my brow like strong wine,*
> *And rhyming among the fantastic shadows,*
> *I plucked like lyres the elastic*
> *Of my wounded shoes, one foot close to my heart!*

On 20 October he celebrates his sixteenth birthday.

He left Douai again at the end of the month; it was the last time Izambard saw him. Rimbaud passes through his life like a meteor: nine months of acquaintance, decades of reminiscence thereafter. As Alfred Bardey would say of Rimbaud in Aden, many years later: 'I could no longer hold onto him' – here in the commercial sense of retaining him – 'any more than I could hold onto a shooting star'.

* * *

He ran away again early in 1871. The circumstances are shadowy, the mood rather different from those first truancies. It appears he made two brief excursions to Paris. The first was in February. He arrived at the Gare de Strasbourg (now the Gare de l'Est) on the 25th. The city was in a state of unrest, the government near collapse. The displaced of the war slept under bridges beside a frozen Seine. We know nothing of this trip except that the artist André Gill, whose address Rimbaud had got somehow, came home one night to find this unknown *gamin* asleep, fully clothed, on his bed. Gill (whose name is punningly remembered in the famous Montmartre cabaret, Le Lapin Agile) gave him ten francs and sent him on his way. He slept rough, ate out of dustbins, read pamphlets on the bookstalls, offered his own poems to the Librairie Artistique, and on 10 March, less than two weeks after his arrival, set off home on foot – a journey of 150 miles, lasting about a week.

It is perhaps this harsh journey that he remembers in the *Season in Hell* –

Those winter nights on the road, no shelter, no clothes, no bread, a voice clutched my frozen heart: 'Weakness or strength? Of course, choose strength. You don't know where you're going, or why you're going. Enter everywhere, respond to everything. They won't kill you, any more than they'd kill a dead man.' In the morning I looked so lost, my face so dead, I don't think the people I met could even see me. In the cities the mud seemed to me suddenly red and black, like a mirror when the lamp sways in the next room, like treasure in the forest . . .

He was scarcely home before news came of the establishment of the Paris Commune on 18 March.

It is always said that Rimbaud took part in the Commune, but his involvement must have been brief. He was in Charleville on 17 April, and again on 13 May. The brutal suppression of the Commune by loyal troops began on 21 May and was mostly accomplished by the 28th – *la semaine sanglante*, the Week of Blood.

According to Delahaye, he walked to Paris in mid-April, and joined up with the *franc-tireurs* or 'Irregulars of the Revolution' who were based at the Babylone barracks. A hotchpotch of soldiers and adventurers had thrown in their lot with the insurgents. There were National Guard and Algerian *zouaves* and disgruntled infantry-men back from the front. Among them (this is again only from Delahaye) Rimbaud was befriended by a soldier in the 88th Infantry Regiment, of whom he afterwards spoke 'with a tender sadness, thinking it certain he was shot during the Versaillais victory'.

This tenuous anecdote is all that remains of Rimbaud's brief days as a Communard. Verlaine and others, including some later police reports, confirm the general belief that he was there, but add no details. (Verlaine actually contradicts Delahaye's version, and says he was at the Château d'Eau barracks.) Nor do Rimbaud's Communard poems – 'The Hands of Jeanne-Marie', 'Paris Repopulated' etc. – offer any biographical purchase. It is a curious lacuna: a formative experience of which he makes no mention in his letters, of which he leaves no actual record, only rumours and guesses, and behind them a sense of something unspoken or indeed unspeakable. (His poem 'The Stolen Heart' is perhaps a record of his experiences in the Babylone barracks: I will look at this in the next chapter.)

*   *   *

Rimbaud's first taste of life on the road changed him profoundly. 'I abandoned ordinary life more than a year ago', he informs Paul Demeny on 28 August 1871. It would be guessing to say this was the first of Rimbaud's alterations and reincarnations, but it is the first to be biographically noticeable. The shy, prize-winning scholar has disappeared. This is somebody else: a dirty, long-haired, loutish young man who 'scandalizes' the locals with his new 'romantic hairstyle coming halfway down his back', his workman's *brûle-gueule* or clay pipe, his obscenity-filled harangues against Church and State. He scratches 'Merde à Dieu' on the municipal benches. He tells Izambard: 'I dig up any old fool from my schooldays, I dish up all the dirty and ugly things I can think of, and they pay me in beer and liquor [*bocks et filles*, the latter not girls but shots of brandy].'

College reopens, after the hiatus of the war, but he refuses to go back. He hangs around outside the school gates, making faces at the pupils, the old alumnus ostentatiously turning out bad. La Mother is 'absolutely resolved to put him in a *pension*', but instead he spends his days and sometimes his nights living rough in an old workman's hut in a quarry near town.

In these ways 'this *gamin* with the pink cheeks and the little felt hat' – Delahaye's description, borne out by Verlaine's famous sketch of him a year later in Paris – terrorizes Charleville with visions of beatnik degeneracy.

There is a literary French pun about Rimbaud which plays on *voyou* and *voyant*. The *voyou* is precisely this sneering, lounging figure. The dictionaries give the word an Artful Dodger twist – urchin, rascal, scalliwag, etc. – but it is better to transpose it to a more modern landscape. The *voyou* is a hooligan, a thug, a punk. The *voyant*, by contrast, is a prophet or visionary – literally a seer, as in 'clairvoyant' – and is Rimbaud's own coinage for the poet, as outlined in his famous manifesto addressed to Paul Demeny in May 1871, and generally referred to as the 'Lettre du Voyant':

> I tell you: the poet has to be a seer, to make himself a seer. He makes himself a seer by a long, immense and systematic derangement of all the senses. All forms of love, of suffering, of madness. He searches himself, he drains down all the poisons so that only the quintessences are left. . . .

It is an idea he would return to in his *Season in Hell*, where he is the deranged 'master of phantasmagoria' weaving poetic magic:

Listen! I have all the skills. There is no one here and yet there is someone. I don't want to squander my treasure! Do you want negro chants? Houri dancers? Do you want me to vanish? To dive into the deep to fetch the Ring? What do you want? I'll make gold. Medicines. Trust me . . .

Thus by the summer of 1871, at the age of sixteen, Arthur Rimbaud of Charleville has virtually created the 'Rimbaud' of legend: the evil teenage genius, the hooligan poet, the most terrible and yet most poignantly child-like of enfants terribles.

2

MY BALLERINAS

THERE WAS A GIRL with violet eyes . . .

Or was there? On the subject of his youthful amours Rimbaud achieves early on that veiledness of which he will become a master. The poems tell us something, though how this can be translated biographically is another matter.

According to Delahaye, writing over fifty years later [letter to Louis Pierquin, 1922], Rimbaud was in love with a dark-haired Charleville girl whom he nicknamed Psukhé, after the exotic heroine of a poem by Catulle Mendès. Delahaye remembered a few fragments of a lost Rimbaud letter about her – her bourgeois origins, 'her brother has the soul of a magistrate, her mother the soul of a Catholic'; her coming to a rendezvous complete with chaperone, and treating him haughtily, whereupon he became 'as timid as thirty six million new-born puppies'. The story reverberates on, unsourced, in the early biographies: that she was going to run away to Paris with him, but didn't; that he was heartbroken for a long while and would refuse to talk about her; that he even spoke of her on his deathbed.

And that he wrote his poem 'Vowels' with her in mind, which gives her the 'violet eyes' of the last line, if not a 'hairy black corset' also.

Then later there was – according to a throwaway remark of Verlaine's – the girl he courted in London. She has been sought in vain among the *Illuminations*, some of which date from his spells in London. Was she the 'Hortense' of the poem called 'H' – 'her solitude is erotic mechanics, her lassitude the dynamics of love' – with whom he associates the 'terrible frissons of inexperienced love'? Or was she 'Henrika', who wore an old-fashioned cotton skirt with a brown and white check, and who (to stretch the biographical point) walked with him in the suburbs of London on an unseasonably warm morning in February 1873? Or was she the 'lady' in whose house he became 'a big blue-grey bird fluttering up to the mouldings of the ceiling', and then 'a fat bear with mauve gums', and finally an ass? (This poem was at first titled 'Metamorphoses', and then 'Bottom' after the transmogrified weaver of *A Midsummer Night's Dream*.)

The uncertainties multiply. There is no single piece of biographical data on this most tantalizing of subjects: the loves of Rimbaud.

* * *

The power of sexual desire is signalled early on. There is that crazy girl in the calico dress, and the early fascination with the female members of his family—

> *Back home from school, with her clogs worn-out from walking on the ice, my little sister pissed, and watched the thin thread of urine coming from her lower lip, tight and pink . . .*
>
> ['An Old Idiot's Memories']

—and he felt the 'cruder and calmer shame' of watching her. He is the young penitent trembling with guilty desires: 'No one was aroused so often, as if astonished!' He is full of sexual self-doubt, a late developer – 'Why puberty so late . . . why the shadow so slow at the base of my belly?' – and prone to masturbation: 'my insistent and too often consulted gland'. The poem ends, 'And now let's jerk off'. Another poem (also from the *Album Zutique*) ends: 'Poor young man, he doubtless has the *habit*' – i.e. masturbation.

These solitary satisfactions shade into another vein – one that might be related once more to La Mother – in which girls are associated with rejection and humiliation and tongue-tied longings. 'To Music', which is specifically set in the Place de la Gare in Charleville, is typical:

> *Dressed in my ragged student clothes, I follow those sparky girls under the green chestnut trees. They know what I'm doing; they turn and laugh at me, their eyes full of indiscretions. I don't say a word, I just keep staring at the skin of their white necks bordered with tumbling hair. I follow beneath the bodice, beneath the skimpy blouse, the divine curve of the back down below their shoulders. Soon I have flushed out the little boot, the stocking. In a beautiful burning fever I reconstruct their bodies. They find me*

funny; they whisper together; and my brutal desires fasten onto their lips . . .

In the joyous 'Novelette', his hymn to being seventeen (though actually written when he was just sixteen), a girl goes by, 'under the glow of the pale street light', but she too finds him 'incredibly comic'. And there is the witty vignette entitled 'Nina's Replies' in which the poet covers several pages of high-flown romantic propositions about taking off together, only for Nina to reply with the words, *'Et mon bureau?'*

She can't, in other words: she has to get back to the office.

The 'Deserts of Love', a fragmentary prose-poem thought to date from 1871, is described by Rimbaud as 'the writings of a young man, a very young man, whose life has unfolded in no particular place; without a mother, without a homeland, careless of everything people count as familiar'. Of this young man he says: 'having never loved a woman – though full of passion! – he found his soul and his heart, and all his strength, raised in sad and strange errors.'

The piece is a kind of erotic reverie: 'the following dreams – his loves! – which came to him in his bed or in the street'.

This time it is the Woman: the one I saw in the city, the one I talked to, the one who talks to me.

I was in a room without light. They came to tell me she was waiting for me, and I saw her in my bed, completely mine, without light. I was very excited, especially because this was the family home; anxiety also gripped me. I was in rags, and she, a woman of the world who was offering herself: she would have to go. A nameless anxiety: I took her, I tumbled her from the bed almost naked, and in my unspeakable weakness I fell upon her and dragged the two of us over the carpets, without light. The family lamp reddened the neighbouring rooms, one after the other. Then the woman vanished. I spilt more tears than God could ever have asked for.

I went out into the endless city. O weariness! Drowned in the mute night, in the flight from happiness. It was like a winter's night with a snow that completely suffocated the world. I shouted to friends – where is she? – and they answered with lies. I stood in front of the windows of where she goes every evening. I ran into a buried garden. I was chased away. I wept enormously over all of this . . .

She did not come back, she will never come back, that Adorable One who came to my room . . .

I was abandoned in this rambling house in the country: reading in the kitchen, drying the mud on my clothes in front of my hosts, amid the drawing room chatter, moved to death by the murmuring of the morning milk and of the night of the last century.

I was in a very dark room: what was I doing? A maid came up close to me: she was a little dog, I can tell you, but she was beautiful, with what seemed to me an inexpressible maternal nobility: pure, known, quite charming! She pinched my arm.

I cannot even remember her face any more: this is not just so I can remember her arm whose flesh I rolled between my two fingers; nor her mouth, which mine seized on like a small desparate wave, endless probing something. I tumbled her in a busket of cushions and ship's canvases, in a dark corner. All I can remember is her lacy white knickers.

Then, despair. The partition wall merged vaguely into the shadows of the trees, and I sank down into the voluptuous sadness of the night.

Prosaic secretaries, compliant maids, sparky girls under the chestnut trees, unattainable older women hunted through skeletal city landscapes; a mood of romantic disappointment, of unrequitedness, of snatched and unsatisfactory consummations. He is a teenager in love with an idea of women, a sexed-up young man lying alone at night:

I turn down the flames of the lamp, I throw myself down on the bed, and turning towards the shadows I see you, my sweethearts, my queens . . . ['Phrases']

But then he becomes the despiser and humiliator of women:

> *One evening you crowned me poet,*
> *   O ugly blonde:*
> *Get down here so I can whip you*
> *   Across my lap . . .*
>
> *Ugh! My dried-up spittle,*
> *   O ugly redhead,*

Still infects the trenches
Of your round breasts.

O my little sweethearts
How I hate you!
Cover those ugly tits of yours
With nasty pimples!

Tread all over my old dishes
Of sentiment;
Up you go! Be my ballerinas
For just a moment.

['My Little Lovers']

*   *   *

Difficulties of dating and interpretation make these poetic escapades tenuous, so it is hard to say whether Rimbaud's first homosexual experiences happen alongside these teenage embroilments, as part of a general sexual omnivorousness – 'experimenting', as headmasters like to gloss it – or are the result of a particular self-awakening, a conscious identification of himself as 'gay'. It is certain that Rimbaud's relationship with Verlaine (which dates from September 1871) was sexual, but how much experience had Rimbaud already had, and how much did it mean to him?

The missing father and the domineering mother; the adolescent years in the all-male college – these provide a plausible backdrop. His friendship with the eccentric homosexual Charles Bretagne is also important. Rimbaud was introduced to him, by Izambard, some time in 1870. A large, copiously moustached man in his mid-thirties, Bretagne combined the respectability of a minor *fonctionnaire* at the local sugar-factory with what would nowadays be called a 'colourful private life'. He was a scholar, a musician, a cunning caricaturist; his bibulous harangues against the Catholic clergy delighted the rebel teenager. Bretagne was a breath of intellectual freedom in dreary Charleville, but there is also a faintly cloying air in his cluttered, velvety room on the Cours d'Orléans. A young man, excitable and vulnerable, enters there at his peril.

Bretagne was passionately interested in the occult: the caballistic tomes of Dom Pernety and Éliphas Lévi that line his shelves are undoubtedly a source for Rimbaud's 'Lettre du Voyant' – the poet as

32

magus – and there may be sexual aspects to that 'systematic derangement of the senses' urged by the young *voyant* of mid-1871.

Izambard was also a bachelor. There is perhaps an overtone of physical attraction, of 'crush', in his relationship with Rimbaud. (This would only be a guess: there is no evidence of it.) One recalls Rimbaud's letter from the Paris prison: 'I have loved you as a brother and will love you as a father.' One recalls the frisson of intimacy in his sign-off of another letter [November 1870] – '*ce "sans-cœur" de A. Rimbaud*': your 'heartless' Rimbaud – with the quote-marks suggestive of some secret little catch-phrase between them. Izambard wrote, many years later: 'He was, I think, a homosexual – yet despite my invincible disgust for that lot [*cette engeance*] he himself did not disgust me because I saw through to the noble motives he was obeying.'

This covers Izambard himself, as does his presenting of the case as a matter of opinion ('*je crois*') rather than personal knowledge. Those 'nobler motives' which Izambard discerned are apparently that homosexuality was a way to 'mortify himself'. It was, says Izambard, Rimbaud's 'catharsis, or at least his hell'. This may say more about Izambard's attitudes than about Rimbaud's, though the shorthand allusion to *A Season in Hell* is interesting, suggesting that Izambard saw in the poem a refraction of Rimbaud's ruinous affair with Verlaine.

Delahaye, it should be noted, expressly denies that Rimbaud practised any such '*inversion*' – a favourite euphemism – at college or afterwards. 'At college . . . he never had that reputation', and never in conversation did he show 'the slightest tendency that way'. This contradicts other evidence, and here too one senses an over-protestation. A deeply physical admiration of Rimbaud – his 'eyes of forget-me-not and periwinkle', his 'strong, supple' body – runs through Delahaye's reminiscences. Delahaye was short, stocky, incipiently plump: there is an element of hero worship, at the least, of his rangy, loose-limbed friend.

And then there is the strange, disturbing poem which first appears in Rimbaud's letter to Izambard of 13 May 1871, in what must be the immediate aftermath of his Commune adventure. He calls it 'Le Cœur Supplicié' (the Tortured Heart); it was later called 'Le Cœur du Pitre' (the Clown's Heart), and was finally published as 'Le Cœur Volé' (the Stolen Heart). It begins:

My poor heart drools at the poop,
My heart is full of tobacco spit:
They spurt jets of soup at it,
My poor heart drools at the poop.
Beneath the jeers of the soldiers,
When they all burst out laughing,
My poor heart drools at the poop,
My heart is full of tobacco spit.

Early biographers say that the poem describes an 'intimate degradation' – in other words, a homosexual rape – which Rimbaud underwent at the Babylone barracks in Paris. This sort of reading has become unfashionable but seems in this case quite persuasive. The opening line suggests seasickness, but this seems a brutal metaphor, a choreographic parallel between someone retching over the side of a boat and someone being forcibly buggered. Phrases such as *'ithyphalliques et pioupiesques'* – i.e. men with 'soldier-boy hard-ons' – confirm this. The 'jets of soup' and 'tobacco spit' are images of semen, as are the *chiques* – quids or wads of tobacco – of the last verse:

How my stomach will heave if I must
Swallow my poor heart back down.
When they have used up their wads
What shall I do, O stolen heart?

*   *   *

The clues are scattered, kaleidoscopic. Did something *happen* to him? Was the ardent young seducer whose kisses are like 'little spiders' on a girl's neck ['Winter Evening'] in some way different from the jaded voyeur who watches an old balding tart with an ulcerated anus climbing out of a coffin-like bathtub ['Venus Anadyomene']? And if so, do we take heavy pettings *chez* Bretagne or the rough trade of the Babylone barracks to be the cause of this alteration? Psycho-biographical studies have announced Rimbaud as a mother-fixated homosexual, as a pathological misogynist, as impotent, as schizoid, and much else besides, but these seem no more than clinical-sounding additions to the elaborate smokescreen of contradictory hints and undigested emotions which

34

the poems offer. Those who knew him cannot agree; their reminiscences seem faintly untrustworthy; indeed the poems have in themselves – as do the later African letters – a curious timbre of rumour, as if the young man who wrote them cannot be trusted either, as if these experiences he recounts are momentary reveries, hoaxes, *fumisteries*. It is hard to reconstruct Rimbaud because he was himself so unconstructed, so much in flux; *'there is nobody here, and yet there is somebody'*.

His sexuality remains, like everything about him, elusive. It does not quite add up – should it? – and it is wrapped in biographical obscurity. Of all these hinted encounters of his teenage years only one can be fastened to a particular name: the fat Flemish waitress named Mia, who was perhaps the waitress he kissed at the Cabaret Vert in Charleroi.

3

VERLAINE

I N THE SECOND week of September 1871, Rimbaud set off across the
Place de la Gare in Charleville, with its 'measly lawns' and its
bandstand echoing to the tune of the *Valse de Fifres* (but not yet
its neatly-coiffed statue in honour of him, erected in 1901) and
boarded once more the southbound train to Paris. He had an
invitation to meet a Parisian poet he admired: one of the few to
escape the scattershot of his execrations. The poet's name was Paul
Verlaine.

He had written to Verlaine sometime in August, sending poems.
(This was one of a few letters he wrote at this time to established
poets, half-begging, half-bragging letters: one to Théodore Banville
he signed 'Alcide Bava', a name suggestive of *baver*, to drool or
slobber.) Verlaine wrote back, appreciative of the 'prodigious talent'
of the poems, though also taken aback by their intensity – 'Your
lycanthropy makes me feel as if I'd caught a whiff of the sewer' –
and invited him to town.

Verlaine and Rimbaud. Their names are indissolubly linked: the
great Bohemian double-act, the existentialist Laurel and Hardy.
Their story, says Wallace Fowlie, 'is one of the literal epics of our
age, in which the myth of the modern artist is related'. The 'epic' is a
saga of obsession and destruction, of nervous breakdown and
alcoholic burn-out, but it begins as a kind of black comedy of
manners. Verlaine goes to meet Rimbaud at the Gare de Strasbourg;
goes to the wrong platform and misses him; comes back to the well-
appointed house in Montmartre where he is living with his in-laws;
and there finds him, in the pompous little drawing-room with its
Louis-Philippe furniture, very ill-at-ease, under the increasingly
tight-lipped scrutiny of Verlaine's young wife, Mathilde, and his
mother-in-law, the snobbish and affected Madame Mauté de
Fleurville.

Mathilde later described Rimbaud as she first saw him, in the drawing room on rue Nicolet:

> He was a large sturdy lad with a reddish face: a peasant. He looked like a young schoolkid [*potache*] who had grown too fast. His trousers were too short for him, and you could see his blue cotton socks, clearly his mother's handiwork. His hair was tousled, his necktie stringy, his clothes untidy. His eyes were blue, rather beautiful, but they had a shifty look which, indulgently, we took for shyness.

Verlaine was astonished. He had expected – well – a poet: a man perhaps in his twenties or thirties, a frustrated provincial, a man of culture. His mouth gapes as he takes in this scruffy, mumbling, long-legged *kid* . . .

Nearly thirty years later ['Nouvelles Notes sur Rimbaud', *Beaux Arts*, 1 December 1898] Verlaine recalls his own first impressions. The childish face – 'chubby [*dodue*] and fresh' – on top of a 'tall bony body'; the clumsiness; the heavy Ardennes accent, peppered with impenetrable idioms; the voice going up and down like a voice when it's breaking.

It's the Angry Young Man scenario: the boy genius from 'up North' bursting into the appalled surburban drawing-room. He is red-faced from the sun, the road, and from embarrassment. His hands – people always noticed his hands – are big, and have dirt under the nails.

Dinner is served: the tinkling of cutlery, the polite questions, the supercilious gaze of Madame Mauté. The musician Charles de Sivry is there, Verlaine's brother-in-law. Also Charles Cros, who will later preserve from oblivion the unique copy of the *Album Zutique*. One imagines the sardonic glances among the friends, the sophisticates. What has poor Paul let himself in for this time?

Rimbaud scoffs his food, pushes his plate aside, rests his elbows on the table and lights a pipe. The thick blue smoke of the cheap tobacco called '*scaferlati*' eddies impolitely among the diners. The only thing he said that Verlaine could afterwards remember was – eyeing Madame's little lap-dog, Gatineau, busy at their feet picking up scraps – '*Les chiens, ce sont des libéraux*'. Dogs are liberals. (Meaning no one is quite sure what. That dogs are free to do what they please? That in this impeccably bourgeois household even the dog votes Liberal?)

And Verlaine is enchanted: his divine rent-boy, his *gamin*, his walk on the wild side – '*mon grand péché radieux*', as he later put it: my great and radiant sin.

Verlaine was twenty-eight, more than ten years older than Rimbaud. He was a published poet, a minor civil servant, a radical sympathizer, a dilettante homosexual. His thinning hair and droopy moustache made him look older than he was. He suffered from a conviction that he was physically repulsive: one acquaintance describes his face as ape-like. One will feel sorry for him in this story, but also be maddened by his absurd melodramatics. He has a weak-chinned aspect; his lip trembles easily. He was already drinking a lot, and was suffering an acute post-nuptial crisis. Mathilde was pregnant with their first child.

Verlaine found Rimbaud seductive both in a sexual sense and as an impish incarnation of the freedoms he was himself losing – the Bohemian bachelor's life, the daily round of poetry, inebriation and dalliance in the louche café-set of writers and artists who called themselves Les Vilains Bonshommes (the 'bad lads' or 'nasty chaps': the name is hard to translate). With Rimbaud it seems simpler, or at least more opportunistic. Verlaine offered him everything he wanted: money, freedom, ideas, contacts. He offered him, in a word, Paris. Yet also one sees that reaching out for older male companionship, for that elder brother to replace the witless Frédéric, for that missing father. Izambard, Bretagne, and now Verlaine. In the aftermath of the affair Rimbaud will write of Verlaine: 'My pathetic brother! What dreadful nights he caused me.' ['Vagabonds']. This brings a note of obscure vulnerability into the mix of emotions. Verlaine was an oppressively selfish man, prone to outbursts of violence; he was in a position of power over Rimbaud; he held the cards. In the same poem Rimbaud calls him 'that satanic doctor'.

That night Verlaine read the manuscript Rimbaud had brought. If he had any doubts about the strange young creature in the spare room, they dispersed as he drifted off down the twenty-five quatrains of 'Le Bateau Ivre':

> *As I drifted off down the uncharted rivers,*
> *It seemed that all of my boatmen were gone;*
> *Whooping redskins had taken them for targets,*
> *Had nailed them naked to painted stakes . . .*

> *Sweeter than the flesh of sour apples to children,*
> *The green water penetrated my pinewood hull,*
> *And washed away the stains of blue wine and vomit,*
> *And carried off my rudder and my grappling hook.*

Did he already have inkling, as he read, that his own life was about to slip its moorings, and head off into some torrid tropical zone of the soul?

*   *   *

They become inseparable, a double-act in the bars and cafés where the poets and radicals congregate (the dilettante radicals at any rate: the more committed had fled after the suppression of the Commune, many of them to London).

They are au Rat Mort, au Gaz, au Delta; they are in the Café de Madrid and the Café de Suède; they are at the brasserie of 'Baptiste le Garçon'. They drink *bistouilles* (coffee with a slug of liqueur) and *gn'niefs* (genevas or gin) and *curaçao bleu*, and the concoction they called the *trois couleurs* (rum, cognac and kirsch), and of course absinthe, that bitter-tasting firewater composed of eau-de-vie and wormwood (specifically the leaves and tops of the French worm-wood, *Artemesia gallica*, 'that sage-bush of the glaciers', as Rimbaud puts it). They called it *absomphe*, part of their little private lexicon ('Rimbe' for Rimbaud, 'Delahuppe' for Delahaye, 'Charlestown' for Charleville, 'La Daromphe' for Mother Rimbaud, and so on).

In September or early October Rimbaud makes his first appearance at one of the bibulous poetic soirées of the Bonshommes. Hervilly cries: 'Behold Jesus in the midst of the doctors!' De Maistre, less enamoured, retorts: 'The Devil more like'. The poet Léon Valade describes the scene in a letter to an absent member:

> A most alarming poet, not yet eighteen, was introduced to the company by Paul Verlaine, his inventor . . . Big hands, big feet, a real baby-face which could belong to a thirteen-year-old, deep blue eyes, his temperament more savage than shy. Such is this kid [*môme*] whose imagination, full of power and unheard-of corruptions, has fascinated and terrified all our friends.

One notes he says Rimbaud is 'not yet eighteen': in fact he was not even seventeen yet. One notes also the sardonic reference to

Verlaine as his 'inventor': this makes one think of Frankenstein, with Rimbaud as the monster he is creating.

Valade concludes: 'Were it not for the millstone which Destiny keeps in store for our necks, I would say we are witnessing here the birth of a genius.'

*   *   *

All is not well, however, *chez* Mauté. Mathilde and her mother grow alarmed at Rimbaud's drastic influence, especially with regard to Paul's drinking habits. They are sick of this loutish young house-guest who just sniggers when they speak to him. They dislike his habit of stretching out on the neat gravel drive, sunbathing and smoking in view of the neighbours. They suspect him of stealing things. His bed is found to be infested with lice. Then comes the news that Monsieur Mauté is returning to town – he has been on a country hunting-trip. He is an overbearing man, with a predictably low opinion of his arty, feckless son-in-law.

Shortly before or after his return – accounts differ – Rimbaud leaves rue Nicolet. The *voyou* slips out the back way, down the steep, cobbled street. He disappears. Verlaine found him a week or two later, 'pale and wretched', selling key-rings and other trinkets in the street: our first glimpse of Rimbaud the trader.

Verlaine fixed him up. He persuaded his friends to club together to provide Rimbaud, as if their mascot or fool, a daily stipend of three francs a day. And he found him new lodgings. This was an attic on the rue de Buci, just off the Boulevard St-Germain. It was kindly provided and furnished by Théodore de Banville, a leading literary figure. (Rimbaud had written to him the previous year.) Soon after his arrival he is spotted standing naked at his window, hurling his clothes down into the courtyard. The police are called; the Banvilles are embarrassed; Rimbaud explains that his clothes seemed too filthy for this nice new room.

He was next billeted on the musician Ernest Cabaner (real name François Matt). The biographers tend to describe Cabaner as 'dreamy' or 'absent-minded' – permanently bombed on absinthe and hashish is probably more accurate. He attracted anecdotes and vignettes, for instance that at his father's funeral, when everyone raised their hats, he remarked: 'I never knew I was so famous'. There is a gouache portrait of him by Manet. Verlaine said he looked 'like Jesus Christ after three years on absinthe'.

Cabaner lived at the Hôtel des Étrangers, a rambling apartment block on the Boulevard St-Michel. (It is now a smartly refurbished hotel, the Belloy St-Germain.) Here the Bonshommes often met – Cabaner is described as their 'barman' – and here some of the poems of the *Album Zutique* were composed, among them various pastiches and scatologies by Rimbaud.

It was here at the Hôtel des Étrangers that his friend Delahaye found him, on a day in November 1871. He had not seen Rimbaud for about nine months. He discovered him lying on a sofa, in a shabby room where people drifted in and out. His eyes were shut, oblivious to everyone. He was huddled in an old overcoat too big for him, and he wore a grey felt hat. He had been smoking hashish. When he woke and drowsily greeted Delahaye, he said it was not good hashish. There had been no 'beautiful visions', he said, only a monotonous reverie in which 'black moons were chased across the sky by white moons'.

Delahaye was alarmed by Rimbaud's life in Paris. He was also astonished at how tall he was. He reckoned Rimbaud had grown an incredible twenty centimetres in the nine months since he had last seen him.

*　　*　　*

Rimbaud liked Cabaner. He called him 'Tronche', a slang word for the face: 'Mug' perhaps. He learned from him the rudiments of musical composition, which he later pursued (he played on a piano at Roche and on an Abyssinian harp in Harar). Another of his friends was the diminutive poet Jean-Louis Forain, nicknamed 'Gavroche' after the street-wise urchin in Hugo's *Les Misérables*. Forain's sketch of Rimbaud caricatures him as baby-faced, and is captioned *'Qui s'y frotte s'y pique'*. Stroke him and he'll scratch you. He also liked the novelist Jules Claretie. Rimbaud thought him a *'bon garçon'*, says Delahaye, and 'in the mouth of Rimbaud that was no slight praise'.

But mostly he held these well-to-do *littérateurs* in contempt; and mostly they disliked him in return. A particular enemy was Verlaine's future biographer Edmond Lepelletier. He was an old friend of Verlaine's: there was doubtless jealousy, but also Lepelletier was well-placed to see the havoc that Rimbaud was causing. They were quickly at odds. Rimbaud called him an 'inkshitter' and a 'saluter of the dead'; when Lepelletier told him to shut up, Rimbaud threatened him with a table-knife. Lepelletier got his revenge. Reviewing the first night of a new play, he mentioned various literary celebrities who were there, among them Verlaine, 'who had on his arm a charming young thing, a certain Miss Rimbaud'.

There is a mass of jest-book stories about Rimbaud's appalling behaviour in Paris. He calls Banville an 'old cunt'; he stabs the photographer Carjat with a sword-stick; he repays Cabaner's hospitality, in an infamous folkloric incident, by masturbating into his cup of milk. This story is often bowdlerized as Rimbaud peeing into the cup. The only source for the story is Rimbaud himself, who told Delahaye: 'I went into Cabaner's room when he wasn't there, and I found a cup of milk that had been left for him, and I jerked off over it, and I ejaculated into it.' *'Je me suis branlé dessus'*: the phrase is fairly impolite and quite unequivocal. The peeing version misses the essential reverberation of the anecdote, which is that Cabaner may well have drunk this confection, unaware of its extra ingredient.

The biographer Jean-Luc Steinmetz sums up this period of Paris escapades thus:

> It is less interesting to repeat these anecdotes by rote than to find in them a certain character, or rather a certain resolution. Rimbaud seeks to displease. . . . He is intent on shocking those who help him. He is like the zen master, who uses violence or apparent absurdity to awaken others from their sleep.

There are two famous portraits of Rimbaud at this time – the photograph by Étienne Carjat, and the painting by Henri Fantin-Latour. Both reveal a typical story of confrontation and violence.

Carjat was one of the leading photographers of the day (see his marvellous portraits of Dumas and Rossini). A cartoon shows him with a big nose and a little goatee beard and pince-nez. He was of an older generation, a successful Bohemian: it was something of an accolade to sit for him.

The famous photo is dated October 1871: around or perhaps even on Rimbaud's seventeenth birthday (20 October). It catches the beauty, difficulty and charisma of the young Rimbaud. Here is the tousled hair, the lop-sided tie, the hooded frightening eye, the sulky mouth: here is the 'hoodlum poet' of the Rimbaud legend.

There is another portrait by Carjat, from around the same time but not, from the look of it, from the same session. It shows him neater, more composed, but with the same sultry, abstracted air, looking through rather than at the photographer. (It was this, rather than the other, which Izambard described in 1898 as the 'best likeness'.)

A few months after these sessions, in January 1872, Carjat and Rimbaud had a fight at a brasserie near Saint-Sulpice. There was a poetry reading. Rimbaud was sitting at the back, drunk as usual, and punctuating every verse with a shout of '*merde!*'. He was eventually hustled out by Carjat and others. Carjat called him *petit crapaud*: a little toad. Rimbaud waited downstairs, furiously pacing the lobby, and when the others came down he launched himself on Carjat. He got hold of a sword-stick – Mérat's? Verlaine's? The accounts differ in the heat of the scuffle – and wounded Carjat in the hand. He was escorted, still ranting, back to his dingy lodgings at rue Campagne-Première.

As a result of this, Carjat smashed the photographic plates from his sessions with Rimbaud, whom he called his 'assassin'. The pictures we have are the only two to survive.

Fantin-Latour's group portrait, *Coin de Table*, first exhibited at the Paris salon of 1872, has a similar sub-text. The painting was originally intended as a homage to Baudelaire, featuring 'Les Trois' – the three main poets of the Baudelairian school: Leconte de Lisle, Théodore de Banville and Albert Mérat – and their colleagues, among them Verlaine. Verlaine insisted that Rimbaud should be included, as a major new disciple of Baudelaire. De Lisle and Banville thereupon refused to sit. Mérat was in the original version of the painting, but later withdrew in protest after Rimbaud's assault on Carjat. He may also have objected to Rimbaud's sonnet, 'The Arsehole'—

> *Dark and wrinkled like a violet carnation*
> *It breathes, modestly snuggled amid the moss*
> *Still moist with love . . .*

—which is a satire on Mérat's insipidly sensual sonnets in praise of the female body.

Reluctantly, Fantin-Latour painted Mérat out of the picture: the vase of white flowers on the far right replaces him. Thus by the time the painting was finished, in April 1872, not one of the 'Trois' was in it. They have called for their tall hats and top-coats, and left the canvas in a huff.

The portrait now centres on Émile Blémond, the editor of the magazine *La Renaissance Littéraire et Artistique*. (This magazine Rimbaud recommended for use as lavatory paper. However, it later published his wonderful poem 'Crows'; no manuscript of this poem survives, so Blémond's magazine rescued it from oblivion.) Standing beside him are Pierre Elzéar, in top-hat, and Jean Aicard; and seated at the table, from left to right, are Verlaine, Rimbaud, Léon Valade, Ernest d'Hervilly and Camille Pelletan.

Verlaine and Rimbaud sit slightly apart, at the edge of the group. Rimbaud turns his shoulder away from Valade. Verlaine is cadaverous, balding, stiff-looking. Rimbaud sits with his chin resting on his left hand, his gaze insouciant, his nose a little *retroussé*. His face has a pale shine suggestive of too much hashish. Nothing here of that ruddy country complexion which they had all remarked on a few months before. He has the city pallor now.

*　　*　　*

Rimbaud left little direct comment about his life in Paris. There are fragments in the *Album Zutique*: a Paris in the edgy aftermath of war and revolution, where

> *Despite the curfew, and the delicacy of the time,*
> *And despite the omnibus returning to l'Odéon,*
> *A drunkard rants lewdly at the dark crossroads.*

There is the cryptic comment in 'Lives':

> *In a wine-cellar I learned history. At some dance-night in a northern city I met all the wives of the old painters. In an old backstreet in Paris I was taught the classical sciences.*

And there is that profound empathy he had with the poor and dispossessed of the city; that 'charity' which is one of the abiding social themes of his poetry, and which is an often-remarked feature of his life out in Africa. He knows hunger and homelessness from the inside:

Black in the snow and the fog, at the grating which is all lit-up, down on their knees, their bottoms in a circle, five of poverty's children watch the baker making thick golden bread.

They see his strong white arm work the grey dough. They listen to that good bread cooking. The baker with his fat smile mumbles an old tune.

Not one of them moves as they snuggle into the breath of that red vent, which is as warm as a breast . . . And when the bread is brought out, when that warm hole breathes life, their souls are in rapture underneath their rags.

They feel themselves alive again, these poor Jesuses covered with frost. They press their little pink snouts up against the grille, they mumble through the holes, they utter their stupid prayers, and crouched before this light as if the heavens had opened up for them, they bend so low that they split their trousers, and their shirt-tails flutter in the winter wind. ['The Frightened Ones']

Of his actual circumstances in Paris his only comment that remains is the wonderful letter to Delahaye, datelined '*Parmerde, jumphe 72*' ('Parishit, Joon 72'). Here he is, in his garret on rue Monsieur le Prince, writing deep into the night:

> At three in the morning the candle sputtered; all at once the birds start squawking in the trees; it's over. No more work. I had to sit looking at the trees, at the sky, caught in this first, unspeakable hour of the morning. I saw the dormitories of the lycée [Lycée Saint-Louis], absolutely mute. And already, the jerky, sonorous, delightful noise of the carts on the boulevards. I smoked my hammer-pipe, spitting down onto the tiles, for it was a garret, this room. At five o'clock I went downstairs to buy bread: it is the time. The workers were up and about everywhere. This is the time, for me, to get soused in some wine-shop. I returned to the room to eat, and went to bed at seven in the morning, when the sun brings the woodlice out from under the tiles. The early morning in summer, and evenings in December: these have always thrilled me here.

In June, in the heat of the 'oppressive summer', there are dreadful scenes *chez* Mauté, where the birth of Verlaine's son, Georges, had brought a new crisis. On 8 July 1872, Rimbaud and Verlaine left Paris, self-styled fugitives from normality. They wound up in Brussels. Verlaine writes to his distraught, uncomprehending wife:

'Don't be sad, don't cry. I'm in the middle of a bad dream! Someday I'll return . . .'

Mathilde follows them to Brussels, accompanied by her mother. Verlaine sees her in his hotel-room, alluringly stretched out on the bed.

> *I stood at the half-open door. You were lying on the bed as if tired out. But then, with that lightness of the body which love brings, you jumped up: naked, tearful, gay . . .*
>
> *If I could keep just one memory, it would be of your smile and your lovely eyes as they were at that moment; it would be of you, whom I should curse, and that exquisite trap you laid for me.*

But after they have made love, the mood changes. He sees her once more in her summer dress, 'yellow and white with a pattern of flowers like a curtain'. She is dull and suburban again:

> *The little wife and the eldest daughter reappeared when you were dressed, and it was our destiny I saw looking out at me from under the veil of your hat.*

This poem, 'Birds in the Night', was published in *Romances sans Paroles*, where it is dated 'Bruxelles-Londres, Septembre-Octobre 1872'.

Mathilde believes she has got him back. She is full of plans. They will go away, just the two of them. They will take a long therapeutic vacation in Nouvelle Caledonie – the French Pacific: Verlaine on Mururoa! Her mother will look after the baby while they're away. Verlaine agrees to return with them to Paris; he is actually on the train with them. In some accounts Rimbaud is on the train as well, a malign presence in the next carriage. Whatever the truth of that, it is certain that at the Belgian border town of Quiévrain, when they left the train to complete customs formalities, Verlaine slipped away from the two women. They searched the station for him, but had to reboard the train without him. This was the last time Mathilde Verlaine saw her husband. He was standing on the platform at Quiévrain as the train pulled out. Madame Mauté put her head out the window and yelled at him to jump aboard. There was still time. But he just stood there shaking his head.

His wife returns to France, and he returns to Rimbaud: his 'bad dream'. The following day, back in his hotel room in Brussels, he wrote a letter of sordid abuse to Mathilde:

Pathetic little orange-haired housewife! Princess mouse! Flea to be squeezed between the fingers and chucked in the pisspot! You have done all you can do; you have probably broken my friend's heart. I am going back to Rimbaud . . .

A few weeks later they boarded a steamer at Ostend, and after a rough crossing they landed, late in the evening, at Dover.

4

'DEUX GENTLEMEN'

THEY ARRIVED AT Dover on the night of 7 September 1872, a Saturday. The following day, having toiled around the town in search of breakfast, they took the train up to London, a four-hour journey, arriving at Charing Cross. Rimbaud is, for the first time in his life, a foreigner, the incarnation he would choose over all the others. It begins here, in what they jokingly called 'Leun 'deun'.

They probably took a room in Soho, the haunt of many French Communard exiles at this time. The first glimpse we have of them, however, is in Langham Street, at the studio of Verlaine's old friend and erstwhile *vilain bonhomme*, the artist Félix Regamey. They appeared unexpectedly, Regamey recalls. Verlaine was as charming as ever, 'though somewhat lacking in the linen department'. Rimbaud – 'his mute companion', as Regamey styles him – 'didn't exactly sparkle with elegance either'. They looked, in other words, like a pair of tramps. There is a sketch of them by Regamey. Verlaine has a cane, a handful of books, a cigarette, and that dotty-looking walrus moustache. He looks round at his sullen companion in the inevitable overcoat, with the spiky, greasy-looking hair and the pipe held between his fingers. Both of them wear the soft, low-crowned hats that will soon be called 'trilby' after the eponymous Bohemian heroine of George du Maurier's novel, published in 1894. (Rimbaud has not yet bought the famous *haut-de-forme* or top-hat – price ten shillings – which becomes his trademark.) A London bobby is in the background, pointedly looking the other way.

Another of Verlaine's contacts in London was the radical journalist Eugène Vermersch, now under sentence of death in France. He had edited a revolutionary newspaper, *Père Duchêne*, which Rimbaud had admired, and he was the author of *La Lanterne en Vers de Bohème*, which inspired some passages in Rimbaud's caustic parody, 'Things to say to a Poet on the Subject of Flowers'.

He was now a leading figure among the French exiles, and had founded a short-lived journal, the *Qui Vive?*

Vermesch, they learned from Regamey, had just got married (to the daughter of the printer of the *Qui Vive?*). 'Insane,' mutters Verlaine. But also convenient, as it meant his room was going to be free. Within a week or so they had moved in.

This is Rimbaud's first London address: '34, Howland Street, London W.' It was an eighteenth-century house with tall ornamental windows, in the style of Adam. It was owned by a Frenchman. Dingy behind its rather grand façade, it was partitioned into small furnished rooms.

The street runs west from Tottenham Court Road, close to Fitzroy Square. This is the seedy, rooming-house London of George Gissing, who himself lodged round here in 1878, as described in his autobiographical novel, *New Grub Street*:

> From a certain point of Tottenham Court Road there is visible a certain garret window in a certain street [i.e. Charlotte St], which runs parallel with that great thoroughfare . . . He paid only three-and-sixpence a week for the privilege of living there; his food cost him about a shilling a day; on clothing and other unavoidable expenses he laid out some five pounds yearly.

These are broadly the economies of Verlaine and Rimbaud a few years earlier – or, rather, of Verlaine, who was paying for them both, out of the allowance his mother was sending him.

This is the area which would later be dubbed 'Fitzrovia'. It was not yet the 'artists' quarter' it was to become, but there is a kind of continuity from Rimbaud's presence in 1872 through to the days when George Orwell and Dylan Thomas were drinking at the Wheatsheaf on Charlotte Street. (In his early years of poetic rebellion in Swansea, Thomas the 'no-good boyo' styled himself the 'Rimbaud of Cwmdonkin Drive'.) On Fitzroy Square itself lived the painter and critic Ford Madox Brown. They may have met his son, Oliver Madox Brown, something of an enfant terrible himself. He wrote a self-consciously scandalous book, *The Black Swan* (1873), and died of food-poisoning the following year, aged nineteen. But the refined, middle-class Bohemianism of the Madox Browns was a long way from Verlaine and Rimbaud in their shabby lodgings, 'full of dirty daylight and the noise of spiders'.

The house has gone, as has all of nineteenth-century Howland

Street, though other nearby streets retain the authentic Fitzrovian air. It was demolished in 1938 to make way for the new central telephone exchange; the London County Council declined to mark the spot with a plaque. The site is now dominated by the giant plinth of the Post Office Tower, which covers the entire block. Thus the precise location of Rimbaud's first dwelling in London can be seen from all over the city though the house itself has vanished.

*   *   *

This was mid-Victorian London – the London of Dickens, who had died two years earlier; and of Whistler, whose controversial 'Nocturnes' were exhibited at the Grosvenor Gallery in 1877.

In his first letters home Verlaine affects dismay at this fogbound city 'as black as a crow and as noisy as a duck'. He disliked its surly air, its pompous policemen and blowsy barmaids. They were, one should remember, of a kind of underclass. They were assumed to be refugees – probably 'communist' ones at that – and their behaviour together hinted at further heinousness.

Their stamping-ground was Soho, virtually a 'French quarter' of impoverished exiles. They took a leisuredly breakfast at the Café de la Sablonnière on the corner of Leicester Square. They attended militant meetings at an upstairs room on Old Compton Street. Here Vermesch delivered a stirring lecture on the Communard Blanqui, and read out Verlaine's revolutionary poem, 'Cloître de Saint-Merry'. This may be the 'Communist club-room near Leicester Square' which features on the cover of an *Illustrated London News* of 1872. It is now the West End Tandoori restaurant, with a peep-show next door; the tiny, steamed-up windows above the restaurant are perhaps authentic. Other French meeting-places were the Duke of York pub off Gray's Inn Road, and the Cercle d'Études Sociales in Francis Street.

They found some 'tolerable' eating houses, though Verlaine's opinion of English cuisine was as one might expect – the 'so called oxtail soup'; the ersatz coffee which was nothing but chicory-essence and milk; the slippery fish 'which always looked like octopus'. The beer is warm, the gin tastes like 'concentrated sewage water', the tobacco is dirty, and the matches – 'Oh God, the matches. They never light. Never, you understand, *never!*'

But soon they began to get the feel of it, to see the beauty behind

50

the shabbiness, the warmth behind the rudeness. They drank grog and punch, pale ale and porter. They listened to Offenbach and Hervé at the Alhambra, Shakespeare at the Queen's Theatre. They heard the barrel-organs playing the serenade from Coppée's *Passant*. They went to café-concerts at the Alhambra, 'where jigs are danced between two *God Save's*', and to the popular 'minstrel shows'. At one of these the clowns performed a skit on the Jesuits and Verlaine said they all looked like the pompous poet Leconte de Lisle.

Visiting a French art exhibition they were surprised to see their own faces staring out from Fantin-Latour's *Coin de Table*, and Verlaine caused a stir by shouting out, in his newly acquired English, 'Fantin forever!'

All this comes from Verlaine's irrepressibly chatty letters. Of Rimbaud's impressions we know nothing. If he wrote home, the letters are lost; there are only a couple of letters to Verlaine, during a spell of separation, and these are emotional (and pecuniary) rather than informative. He certainly left no journal or diary. All we have is the *Illuminations*, individually undated and problematically collected, but some of them certainly composed in London. For instance this:

> *Over pink and orange sands washed by a wine-coloured sky, great avenues of crystal have risen up, criss-crossing, inhabited by a swarm of hard-up young families who buy their food at the fruit stalls. Don't expect riches. This is the city.*
>
> *A straggling line of helmets, wheels, little boats and horses' rumps hurries away from the wilderness of asphalt. Sheets of fog hang in hideous layers in the sky, which unbends and hovers and descends, composed of black smoke . . .*

These teeming, fogbound, city-of-the-future streets appear in the prose-poem 'Metropolitan'. The title almost certainly refers to the newly opened Metropolitan line: these are glimpses from a train-window, on a winter's evening, transformed by Rimbaud's exotic, mythologizing eye. 'City' is also suggestive of London:

> *I am a transitory and not at all discontented citizen of a metropolis thought to be modern because every known taste has been avoided in the furnishings and façades of the houses. . . . From my window I see new phantoms floating through the thick,*

unrelenting coal-smoke, our woodland shade, our summer night . . .

And 'Bridges' is probably a view of the Thames:

Grey crystal skies. A strange pattern of bridges, some straight, some arched, others descending at oblique angles . . . Some of these bridges are still covered with shacks. Others support masts, signals, frail parapets . . . You glimpse a red jacket, perhaps other costumes and musical instruments. Is it some street tune, or the tail-end of a nobleman's concert, or the remnants of public hymns? The water is grey and blue, as wide as an arm of the sea.

A white ray falling from the top of the sky blots out this comedy.

* * *

For a while they were happy. They were full of plans; they were writing poetry. They studied at the British Museum: Rimbaud's application for a Reading Room ticket is extant, untruthfully stating he is over twenty-one. They learned English. Rimbaud's hand-written list of English phrases attains the gnomic status of what was known in the 1960s as 'concrete poetry':

I was taken all aback – abaft – to be abashed
The fever begins to abate – to be abed
We will abide by this – What is this about
What remains over and above
Tell one where about I shall find it
I will bring it about
The thing was blazed abroad and failed
You must learn to abstain from these indulgences . . .

Back a little – Background – Backslider
He will not be Backward to undergo –
Backward fruit, children, season
Walk read backwards – This is not so bad
They baffled all our designs
The skin bagged . . .

Howitz – Hucklebacked – Hucksteress
to huddle up work – set up a hue and cry
I huff this man – to hug a sin – a huge eater
The hulks – it is all a hum – humdrum

> *You humour him – hunchbacked – Hurl*
> *this matter is hushed – Hythe . . .*

And, above all, they walked. In a letter to Blémond Verlaine writes: 'Every day we take enormous walks in the suburbs and in the country round London . . . We've seen Kew, Woolwich, and many other places . . . Drury Lane, Whitechapel, Pimlico, the City, Hyde Park: all these have no longer any mystery for us.' The suburban walks recall another of the *Illuminations*, the elusive vignette called 'Workers' – a certain 'warm February morning', the blowing of 'an unseasonable south wind':

> *We took a turn in the suburbs. The day was dull and that southerly wind stirred up all the foul smells of those ravaged gardens and desiccated fields . . . The city, with its smoke and the noise of its trades, followed us all the way along the paths.*

Verlaine also notes Rimbaud's fascination with the London docks: the babble of languages, the mongrel faces, the bales of exotic merchandise. He examined the cargoes with their strange languages and alphabets, and talked with the sailors. Here, it has been suggested Rimbaud's exotic imagination found a focus in the idea of far-flung trade and commerce: in these dark Victorian dockyards, in other words, lie the seeds of the African adventure.

The relationship was fraught but powered by the sense of adventure, of rootless freedom: they are outcasts together. They have the desperate camaraderie of the marginalized: of gay lovers, which they were; of junkies, which their alcoholism almost makes them.

For Verlaine the affair was agonizingly tinged with guilt and regret for the life he had left behind, for the deserted Mathilde and for the son he hardly knows. In November Lepelletier writes that Mathilde is initiating proceedings for divorce, and that one of the grounds is to be Verlaine's 'immoral' relationship with Rimbaud. Verlaine replies full of fraught exculpation, even offers to undergo medical examination: 'We are ready, Rimbaud and I, to show, if we must, our (virgin) arseholes to the assembled company' [23 November 1872]. It would be naive to take him at his word. In a later letter to Rimbaud [18 May 1873] he writes: '*Je suis ton* old cunt ever open *ou* opened' – as if English were some code private to them alone. Mathilde claimed to have in her possession several letters from Rimbaud to her husband – '30 to 40 of them' – which offered 'conclusive proof of their monstrous immorality'. (These were not shown in court, as the grounds of physical cruelty were enough to win the divorce; she later destroyed them for fear they would one day be seen by her son; the number and nature of them may well be exaggerated. 'There were many things in them,' she said, 'that I will not repeat'.)

There were also police reports, for the French security services had the exile cliques under surveillance. An anonymous informer writes of the 'unnatural relationship' between Verlaine and 'the young Rimbault'. The latter is described as 'a young man who often comes to Charleville, where his family is, and who joined the *francs-tireurs* of Paris during the Commune'. (This report, dated 26 June 1873, was discovered in the archives at the Préfecture de police in the 1940s: a residue of notoriety.)

*   *   *

Rimbaud returns to France in December 1872. Verlaine spends a solitary Christmas of self-pity and illness: 'I am *dying* of grief, of illness, of boredom, of loneliness', he writes. His mother hurries across to nurse him back to health. Back in France Rimbaud comments acidly, 'He is like a child left in a room without a light, sobbing with fear', but he accepts the train fare sent to him by Madame Verlaine, and in late January he is back in London, where the pair resume their walks, binges and studies.

In April 1873 they both returned to France, Verlaine to patch up for the umpteenth time his domestic affairs, Rimbaud to the family's new home, the farmhouse at Roche, in the canton of Attigny about twenty miles from Charleville. The moment is caught in the diary of his sister Vitalie, now thirteen. It was Good Friday; she was in the front room at Roche with her mother, Frédéric and Isabelle: 'There was a quiet knock at the door. I went to open it and – imagine my surprise, I found myself face to face with Arthur . . .' The daemonic Rimbaud is suddenly human: the prodigal son returning, the innocent delight of his sister, the day passing in 'the intimacy of the family'. They explore the property, 'which Arthur hardly knew'. On Easter Sunday they celebrated Mass at the little chapel at Méry.

The farmhouse at Roche is gone – it was burned down by retreating German troops in 1917 – and Roche itself is a hamlet so small you are out of it before you know you're in it. Pictures show a steep slate roof, four tall chimneys, dun walls and shuttered windows: a typical French farmhouse. A single ruined wall remains, with the characteristic ventilation slats which can be seen in Paterne Berrichon's sketch of the house (1897). The local Tourist Board has tried to make something of the nearby *lavoir* – the village washing-place – though the logic of its connection with Rimbaud eludes me. What remains is only the silence, the flat plainish landscape, the enormous ploughed fields mobbed by crows:

> *Lord, when the meadow is cold,*
> *When in the huddling village*
> *The sound of the angelus fades,*
> *Over a nature deflowered*
> *Bring swooping down from big skies*
> *The dear delightful crows . . .*

Here Rimbaud began *A Season in Hell* (dated at the end 'April–August 1873'). In May he writes to Delahaye that he is working 'fairly regularly':

> I'm doing some little stories in prose, under the general title: The Pagan Book or Negro Book. It's foolish and innocent . . . My fate depends on this book, for which I still have half a dozen horror stories [*histoires atroces*] to invent. How can one invent horrors here? I won't send you any stories yet, although I already have three of them.

This is the first we hear of the *Season in Hell*. It is possible but not certain that the three 'stories' he had already completed are the three sections of the poem that exist in an early draft, namely 'Bad Blood', 'Night in Hell' and 'Alchemy of the Word'.

Vitalie adds her own innocent confirmation: 'Arthur did not share at all in our farm-labours; for him the pen was too important to permit his involvement in manual labours.' (Ironically Rimbaud was arriving at the opposite idea: 'The penman's hand is worth the same as the ploughman's hand,' he writes in *A Season in Hell*.)

* * *

In May Verlaine persuades Rimbaud to go with him again. They head once more towards London. They are at Liège on 26 May; then '*wagonnant*' (i.e. by train) through Flanders to Antwerp. Here they embark for England, and after a fifteen-hour crossing they are once more in 'Leun'Deun'.

A new start: the beauty of London in May. Sometime between 28 and 31 May Verlaine inscribed his manuscript of *Romances sans Paroles* with the following dedication:

À Arthur Rimbaud
Londres, mai 1873
P.V.

This was suppressed before publication the following year: the MS survives with the dedication violently scored out.

They found lodgings this time in Camden Town, at No. 8 Great College Street (now Royal College Street). Their landlady was a Mrs Alexander Smith. This is the only one of Rimbaud's London lodgings still to survive. It stands next to the Royal Veterinary College (which gives the street its name): a single short block of original houses in an area almost entirely redeveloped into housing estates in the 1960s. This gives it a precarious air, as if it were a Dickensian film-set. The house is as dingy as it probably was then, with its flaking white paint on the ground floor, its mauve-grey London brick on the three upper storeys (the top no doubt the servant's attic room), its narrow arrangement of railings and door-steps, its fuse box visible through the glass above the front door, its shabby lace curtains. To the south is the great Victorian hangar of St Pancras Station, and its nocturnal under-the-arches workshops (car valets, furniture makers, etc.) still redolent of Rimbaud's *randonnées* around the city.

Vermersch lived nearby, in Kentish Town. Verlaine liked the area, with its cottage gardens and leafy squares. 'One might almost be in Brussels,' he writes to Blémond. The Alexandra Theatre opened a few days after their arrival.

On 21 June an advertisement appears in the *Daily Telegraph*:

Leçons de français, latin, littérature, en français, par deux gentlemen parisiens; prix modérés. Verlaine, 8 Great College Street, Camden Town.

Little did the readers of the *Telegraph* know, on that midsummer morning in 1873, what dangers lurked behind this innocuous announcement.

5

HELL

IN THAT SUMMER of 1873 things fell apart. There were drunken tantrums and tearful remonstrances. Verlaine could no longer support 'this violent life', nor the 'pointless scenes', nor the 'fantasy' which governed Rimbaud's life. Rimbaud's poem 'Vagabonds' dredges up the mood of edgy, nightmarish and ultimately pointless intensity (Verlaine acknowledged that he was indeed the 'satanic doctor' of the poem):

> *My pathetic brother! What dreadful nights he caused me. 'The whole business never meant much to me; I was playing on his weakness; it was my fault that we would return to exile, to enslavement'. He thought that I was strangely jinxed, that I was strangely innocent, and he had other unpleasant ideas as well.*

> *I answered this satanic doctor with a sneer, and ended up leaving by the window . . .*

> *Almost every night, as soon as I fell asleep, my poor brother would get up, his mouth stinking, his eyes on stalks – it was just as he dreamed it – and drag me out into the room, yelling in the idiotic anger of his dream . . .*

Verlaine's 'Crimen Amoris' is also an epitaph for his affair with 'the most beautiful of all the bad angels':

> *You knew that there is no difference at all*
> *Between that which you call Good and Evil,*
> *And that at the heart of each lies only suffering*

*   *   *

Then, in the first days of July 1873, *la rupture*. The anecdote is that Verlaine arrived back at College Street with a fish and a bottle of olive oil for their lunch, to be greeted by Rimbaud sunning himself

57

on the window-sill and sneering: 'If only you knew what a cunt you look with that fish.' Verlaine has had enough. He packs his bags and leaves. Rimbaud follows but arrives at St Katharine's Dock as the Antwerp steamer pulls out. Verlaine is up on deck. He turns away to avoid seeing the wildly gesturing figure on the wharf.

Letters flew between them. Verlaine threatens suicide in the letter written 'at sea' [*c.* 3 July 1873], which concludes:

> I have to inform you that if in three days from now I am not back with my wife, with conditions perfect, I'm blowing my brains out. 3 days in a hotel, a *rivolvita* – it's going to cost me: you know my terrible '*stinginess*'. You'll have to forgive me. If, as seems very likely, I have to perform this last idiocy, I will at least do it like a brave old bastard [*en brave con*]. My last thought, my friend, will be for you, for you who called to me from the pier, you who I couldn't go back to, *because I have to shoot myself* – AT LAST!
>
> Do you want me to hold you while I'm pegging out?
>
> Your poor
P. Verlaine

Rimbaud received the letter on the 5th, at Great College Street, and replied instantly in his most sceptical, lucid vein:

> Dear friend,
>
> I have your letter dated 'at sea'. You are wrong this time, very wrong. First: nothing positive in your letter. Your wife won't come or she will come, in three months or three years, who knows? As for shooting yourself, I know you too well. While you're waiting for your wife, and your death, you'll work yourself up into a frenzy, and go around annoying everyone . . . you think life would be better with other people than with me? *Think about it!* – No! Definitely not. Only with me can you be free.

Next, from Brussels, Verlaine telegrams:

> VOLUNTEERING SPAIN COME HERE HOTEL LIÉGEOIS LAUNDRY MANUSCRIPTS IF POSSIBLE

The latest drollery: he is joining up as a mercenary!

On 8 July Rimbaud arrives in Brussels. Verlaine and his mother are in rented rooms on rue des Brasseurs. Verlaine is wild, drunk, maudlin: he begs Rimbaud to stay with him. Rimbaud is in pacificatory mood, but refuses. He is going to Paris.

Verlaine says: 'Go then – and see what happens!'

On Thursday 10 July, Verlaine quits the house on rue des Brasseurs early. He had drunk himself into a stupor the previous night, but is up and out by 6 a.m. Around midday he returns, drunk again. He has purchased a hand-gun – the *rivolvita* he had spoken of in the letter written 'at sea'. He bought it at the Galeries Saint-Hubert; together with a priming tube and a box of bullets it cost him twenty-three francs. He loaded it in a bar on rue des Chasseurs.

Rimbaud asks him what the gun is for. He replies with a wild laugh: 'It's for you, for me, for everyone!' He was, Rimbaud later said, 'extremely over-excited'.

They went out for some liquid lunch, and were back in their room at about two o'clock. The argument continues: Verlaine begging him to stay; Rimbaud 'immovable' in his desire for Paris. True to form, he plans to touch Madame Verlaine (glad to be rid of him) for the train fare.

They are alone in their room together. Verlaine locks the door that leads out to the landing, sits with his chair against the door, issues dark ultimatums. Rimbaud is standing, he later estimated, about three metres away from Verlaine. He is leaning with his back against the wall.

Verlaine pulls out the revolver. He shouts: 'This is for you since you're going!' (Or, alternatively: 'Here! I'll teach you to try and leave me!' This is from Rimbaud's *déclaration* of 10 July; the former is from his longer *déposition* two days later.)

He levels the gun at Rimbaud and fires. The bullet strikes him just above the left wrist. A second shot follows, 'almost instantly', but the gun is no longer aimed at Rimbaud and the bullet ricochets off the floor.

Verlaine – 'pathetic brother' – runs sobbing into his mother's room next door. He was like a madman, Rimbaud says. He throws himself down on the bed; Rimbaud, shocked and bleeding, follows him. Verlaine pushes the gun at him. He begs Rimbaud to finish him off, to put a bullet through his head (the phrase he probably used – it appears in his tragic-gestured letter 'at sea' – is *brûler la gueule*, burn my face out.)

That night Verlaine was in threatening mood again. Somewhere near the Place Rouppe, he turned on Rimbaud. 'I saw his hand reach into his pocket to get hold of his revolver,' Rimbaud later deposed. 'I turned round and went back the way I had come. I met a policeman and explained to him what had happened.'

Verlaine is arrested and spends the night in the cells; Rimbaud tosses with fever back at the rue des Brasseurs. The bullet is still lodged in his wrist. The following morning he is admitted to the Hôpital Saint-Jean. There, on 12 July, from his hospital bed, he gives a detailed deposition to the *juge d'instruction*. The latter notes Rimbaud's attitude as 'rather unpleasant' [*peu aimable*], and takes the opportunity to search through his papers, finding among them some poems and letters of Verlaine's which he confiscates.

The bullet was not extracted till 17 July: his fever had been too high to allow this before. He left the hospital on the 19th, and on the same day filed an *acte de renonciation*, formally stating that he had no wish to press charges against Verlaine. But by now the Brussels police had their teeth into the case, and into this poetic undesirable, Paul Verlaine, who is a filthy queer and a commie sympathizer to boot. The case was not dropped, though the charge was reduced from attempted murder to criminal assault. The prosecution of Verlaine has a sour note of political vindictiveness, and was unfairly coloured by a seepage of moral outrage from the concurrent divorce proceedings. On 8 August Verlaine was tried and convicted. The judge handed down the maximum sentence: two years' hard labour and a fine of 200 francs.

It was less than two years since Verlaine had first seen Rimbaud, slouching up to greet him in the Mautés' drawing-room, and now as the summer of 1873 drew to a close, he contemplated the debris of his life. His marriage was finished, he was sequestered for life from any contact with his son, he was an outcast and a criminal.

*   *   *

Rimbaud, meanwhile, returns to Roche by foot, appears at the door grey-faced and dirty, with his arm in a sling, in a state of imminent collapse.

There he completes, by the end of August, the *Season in Hell* – a catharsis, if not a convalescence: 'a few pages torn from my notebook of the damned'. By tradition it was written in one of the outbuildings at Roche; by tradition his family heard strange 'yellings' coming out; by tradition the table on which he wrote was later found scored deeply with a knife, scored in the shape of a cross.

In part, at least, the 'hell' was his affair with Verlaine. In 'Delirium 1' (subtitled 'Foolish Virgin, Infernal Bridegroom') he mines deeply into their doomed relationship. He does so with this twist: it is written as if through Verlaine's eyes. The text is essentially a dramatic monologue by Verlaine. One might think of it as Verlaine's prison reminiscence: an unburdening, a haunted confession. This is, in other words, Rimbaud's version of Verlaine's view of Rimbaud, and of the ruinous affair between them. Verlaine is the 'foolish virgin', obsessed and enslaved, and this is some of what he says:

> *Before this I was someone of substance. You wouldn't think I was about to turn into this skeleton.*
>
> *He was almost a child. His mysterious delicacies had seduced me. I forgot all my human duties just so I could follow him. What a life! Real life is somewhere else. We are not of this world. I go where he goes: I have no choice. And often he rails at me – at me, poor soul that I am! The demon! You must understand: he is a demon.* He is not a man.
>
> *He says: 'I do not like women. Love is to be reinvented, we know that. All women are after is security, and once they've got it, their hearts and their beauties are pushed aside. Only cold scorn is left, which is what marriages feed on nowadays. And then there are women bearing the signs of happiness, women I could have turned into trusted friends, who are devoured in an instant by brutes with the sensibility of a log.'*
>
> *I listen to him turning infamy into glory, cruelty into charm. . . .*
>
> *Many nights his demon seized me, and we rolled together, and I struggled with him! Sometimes at night, when he's drunk, he hangs out on the street, or in certain houses, just to scare me to death – 'I'll probably get my throat cut. Won't that be* horrid*!' And then, oh, those days when he tries to act like he's some kind of criminal!*
>
> *Sometimes he talks, in that melting brogue of his, about death bringing repentance, about the unhappy lives people lead, about punishing labours and heartbreaking departures. In the dives where we went to get drunk he would weep for the people around*

us, for the herd of poverty. He lifted up drunks in the dark streets. He had the sort pity a cruel mother has for her little children . . .

I followed him: I had no choice. I saw the decor of his mind, all that he surrounded himself with: the clothes, the sheets, the furnishings. I lent him weapons, and a new face. Everything he cared about, I saw it just the way he would have created it for himself. When he seemed to be depressed, I followed him into strange and complex actions, further and further, come what may: I was sure I would never enter his world. What hours I lay awake in the night, with his precious sleeping body beside me, wondering why he wanted so much to escape from reality. No one ever desired this more. I realized he could be a real menace to society, but this did not make me fear for him. Does he have, perhaps, the secrets for changing life? No, I told myself, he is only looking for them. . . .

Everyone sees his own angel, never the angel of another. I was in his soul, as if in a palace where everyone has been cleared out so they won't have to see such a miserable creature as yourself. That's the sum of it. I counted on him, alas. But what did he want with this dull, cowardly existence of mine? He did not improve me, but he did not quite kill me either.

Sometimes, sad and desperate, I said to him: 'I understand you!' He just shrugged his shoulders . . .

*   *   *

For many, *A Season in Hell* is Rimbaud's masterpiece. It has neither the shimmering complexity of the *Illuminations* nor the poignant sparkle of the early poems, but it is quintessential Rimbaud. He takes the Baudelairean medium of the prose poem and makes it wholly his own, a skittering, angry, adolescent voice, peppered with slang yet blossoming into sudden images of arcane beauty.

For the student of his 'African years' it is also a curious mine of themes and motifs and indeed *voyant*-style prophecies of his life to come: *'the march, the burden, the desert, the boredom and the anger.'* The renunciation of poetry is foreseen (though this farewell is sometimes erroneously taken as literal: in fact Rimbaud continued to write at least until the end of 1874). Poetry is a game, a delusion, an inertia. In its place there is a new and 'very severe' idea of rigorousness and physicality, of 'hard life, simple brutishness':

> *And I, I who called myself magus or angel, exempt from all morality, I am returned to the soil, with a duty to seek, and rugged reality to embrace. A peasant!*

This idea of the 'peasant' in place of the effete and degenerate poet is extended into the poem's powerful motif of the *pagan*. (One recalls the working title of the poem: the 'Pagan Book' or the 'Negro Book'):

> *I am dancing the sabbath in a red clearing, with old women and children . . .*

> *I understand, and not knowing how to explain myself without pagan words, I prefer to be silent . . .*

> *My eyes are closed to your light. I am a beast, a savage; but I can be saved . . .*

> *No more words. I bury the dead in my belly. Cries, drum, dance, dance, dance, dance . . .*

In these lines one might glimpse an underlying motive of the African years – to recover something elemental and primitive, an 'ancient feast', a mythologized childhood, an antidote to a Europe corrupted by sophistication and pretence; an escape from this hell he's in, because 'Hell has no power over pagans'.

There is, of course, an irony in Rimbaud's identification with the 'savage' or 'negro' who is the victim of European settlement—

> *The whites are landing. The cannon! We will have to submit to baptism, and wear clothes, and work. I have been shot through the heart by grace. Ah! I had not foreseen this . . .*

—because he was himself to become a settler, a disembarking white man. His cynicism about the colonial enterprise is pungently expressed in one of the *Illuminations*, 'Democracy', where these 'conscripts of good will' travel 'to the peppery, dried-up countries in the service of the most monstrous industrial or military exploitations'; where the flag is raised in some 'squalid landscape' and 'our speech drowns out the drum'.

In the contradiction between these two versions of himself, perhaps – between the imagined savage and the actual settler – lies

something of the brooding self-disgust which is a feature of his
African life (or, at any rate, of his African letters).

And so he scribbles and paces and yells, in that old outhouse at
Roche, and imagines himself setting off for a new life:

> *And now here I am on the Breton shore. Let the towns light up in*
> *the evening. My day is done. I'm leaving Europe! The sea air will*
> *burn my lungs. Lost climates will tan me. To swim, to trample the*
> *grass, to hunt, and of course to smoke; to drink liquor as strong as*
> *molten metal, like those fine ancestors did around their fires. I will*
> *come back with limbs of iron, a dark skin, a burning eye. To look*
> *at me you'll think I'm a superman. I will have gold; I will be lazy*
> *and brutal. Women nurse these fierce invalids back home from the*
> *tropics. I'll get mixed up in politics. I'll be saved!*

He will find these 'lost climates' in Africa; he will trample the pallid
grasses of the Somali plains; he will hunt and sit around the fire at
night – and then there is that curious adjustment, as if something
had clarified in this vision of the future, and he sees that the
bronzed, weather-beaten, brutal-seeming voyager who returns will
also be an 'invalid', to be nursed by a woman, one whom by then he
will scarcely know, though she is physically close to him as he writes
these lines: his sister Isabelle.

But all this is in the future. *'For now I am cursed. The best thing*
now is to get drunk and fall asleep on the beach.'

*   *   *

Apart from the magazine printings of his earliest poems, *A Season in*
Hell is Rimbaud's only literary work to have been published by his
own volition and effort. All his other poems appear in what are,
essentially, unauthorized editions.

The edition was financed by his mother. It was printed in
Brussels, in October 1873, by one Jacques Poot, whose company, the
Alliance Typographique, otherwise dealt in respectable legal tomes.
How or why Rimbaud chose this printer is uncertain; various
misprints suggest he did not correct the proofs. Five hundred copies
were printed. He visited Brussels to get his author's copies: the
Brussels police, still keeping an eye on him, noted his 'furtive'
departure from the city on 24 October. A few of these copies found
their way to friends – to Delahaye, to Forain and, of course, to

Verlaine. The latter received his copy by mail at the Petit Carmes prison; it bears the curtest of inscriptions: 'À P. Verlaine, A. Rimbaud'. Others, it seems, were burnt by Rimbaud at Roche sometime in 1874. The remaining copies mouldered at the printer's warehouse in Brussels, where they were discovered, in 1901, by a Belgian lawyer, Léon Losseau.

His mother was totally baffled by the poem, and asked him what it all meant. He told her: 'It is to be read quite literally'.

6

SOLES OF WIND

RIMBAUD REMAINED AT Roche for most of the winter of 1873–74. There are a few sightings of him in Paris, but he was shunned by former acquaintances, who held him responsible for Verlaine's demise. In early November, at the Café Tabourey, a minor poet called Alfred Poussin tried to converse with him. 'Rimbaud was pale and even more silent than usual,' he recalled. 'His face, indeed his whole bearing, expressed a powerful and fearsome bitterness.' For the rest of his life Poussin 'retained from that meeting a memory of dread'.

In March 1874 Rimbaud crossed over to England once more, this time with the young Provençal poet Germain Nouveau, whom he had met a few months before. A letter from Nouveau signals their presence in London on 26 March. They have a room south of the river, near Waterloo station: 178 Stamford Street (the block was demolished in 1945). The reaction of Nouveau's friends in Paris indicates something of Rimbaud's reputation at this time. 'This sudden departure *à l'anglaise* [i.e. without saying good-bye] seemed very like a kidnapping. Subjected to the direct influence of Rimbaud, in a foreign country, without any counterbalance, we feared Nouveau lost.' [Memoir by J. Richepin, *Revue de France*, January 1927].

Their existence was precarious. It is said that at one point they were working in a cardboard factory in Holborn, owned by a certain Mr Drycup. The London trade-directories of 1874 do not confirm the latter's existence.

What – or if – he was writing is not certain. The chief memento of this visit is a flush of advertisements in the Classified sections of the newspapers, offering services as French tutor or (in one case) as 'travelling companion'. A total of eight small ads have been unearthed, dating from 10 April to 28 July, though not all are definitely by Rimbaud. The 'G.R.' (a 'French Gentleman, age 20', contactable through the Foreign Registry Office in Macclesfield Street) and the 'N.A.' (of Southwark Bridge Road, offering to teach two afternoons a week) are probably a composite of the initials of Germain Nouveau and Arthur Rimbaud. The duo 'Tavant' and 'Nouveau' appears to be them again; 'Le Licencié Silvy' (Silvy was the name of Nouveau's maternal family) also points to them. Nouveau seemed to have a penchant for nicknames: their landlady at Stamford Street, Mrs Stephens, he christened 'Madame Ponchinelle'. The mysterious 'Mr Drycup' may be another such chimera.

Two advertisements are certainly Rimbaud's. The first appears in *The Times* on 8 June 1874:

A FRENCH GENTLEMAN (25) most respectably connected, of superior education, possessing a French diploma, thorough English and extensive general knowledge, wishes EMPLOYMENT as PRIVATE SECRETARY, Travelling Companion or Tutor. Excellent references. Address, A.R., 25 Langham-street, W.

And then the following day, and for two days after, in the *Echo*:

A YOUNG PARISIAN – speaks *passablement* – requires conversations with English gentleman; his own lodgings, p.m. preferred. Rimbaud, 40 London-st, Fitzroy sq, W.

The former, smarter address is perhaps the Langham Street studio of the artist Félix Regamey, whom Rimbaud and Verlaine visited on their arrival in town in 1872. 40 London Street is presumably, as the advertisement states, Rimbaud's 'own lodging' at this time. This is just a stone's throw from Howland Street; both Verlaine and Nouveau would lodge on this street in 1875 (Verlaine in March, at no. 10; Nouveau the following month, at no. 26a).

In July Rimbaud's mother and his elder sister Vitalie, then fifteen, arrived in London. He meets them at Charing Cross station, and installs them in lodgings in Argyll Square, not far from his old Fitzrovian haunts. He takes them sightseeing: to the Houses of Parliament, to the Duke of Northumberland's palace on the Strand, to the Alhambra on Leicester Square, to St Paul's. They watch the Changing of the Guards. They walk through the new Tower Bridge subway under the Thames. He is their voluble guide and translator ('impossible to buy anything without A,' notes Vitalie.) When La Mother wants to do some window-shopping, he 'lends himself to the task with great goodness and willingness'. She wears her best clothes (grey silk dress, Chantilly lace mantle) so that everyone will know how respectable they are.

Vitalie's journal of her stay in London gives us this tantalizing glimpse of a normal, familial, obliging Arthur, and is an antidote the daemonic legend:

> *Thursday 9 July*: Today we ate some gorgeous strawberries and then some redcurrants. At 6 in the evening, A returns from the British Museum, and takes us to some new streets, all of them splendid ... The heat being oppressive I nursed a desire for an ice-cream or some lemonade. Arthur is so kind: he guessed my wish and granted it – a cream ice. Absolutely delicious!

One entry in Vitalie's journal has a prophetic edge:

> *Monday 27 July*: We spend the afternoon at the British Museum ... What interested me most are the relics of the King of Abyssinia, Theodoros, and his wife: tunics, one of which is decorated with little silver bells; his crown, with real diamonds on it; his weapons; various hats; the queen's shoes, in silver studded with precious stones; some wooden combs; and some very large wooden forks and spoons.

These were a new exhibit. The Abyssinian emperor or *negus* Theodore killed himself in 1868, after his defeat at Magdala by British troops; these 'relics' first went on show at the British Museum in 1874. Looking through this journal much later, after Vitalie's early death, Isabelle Rimbaud intercalated the following comment: 'There is no doubt that the objects singled out by Vitalie were brought to her attention by Arthur ... Her notes suggest, indeed make certain, that Arthur experienced deep emotion at the sight of Theodoros's relics.' It is perhaps too much hindsight to say that Rimbaud was '*appesanti avec émotion*' by these Abyssinian curios, but it is certainly a glimpse of an earlier interest in the region which would one day be his home.

By the end of their stay the effort was beginning to tell:

> *Wednesday 29 July*: At 9 o'clock Arthur, sombre and tense, suddenly announced that he was going out and wouldn't be back at lunchtime. But at 10 he is back and tells us that he is leaving London tomorrow. What news! I was dumbfounded ... After tea I repaired Arthur's trousers and overcoat; afterwards he went out.

Thursday 30 July: Arthur did not leave today, as the laundry-woman hadn't returned his shirts.

Friday 31 July: Arthur left at 4.30 this morning. He was sad.

*   *   *

With this mysterious dawn departure in the summer of 1874 Rimbaud exits from Vitalie's journal and enters one of those shadowy periods which will increasingly predominate in his life.

It used to said that he left to take up a teaching post in Scotland. There is no evidence of this: it is based on a statement by Charleville acquaintances [Houin and Bourgignon, *Revue des Ardennes*, Sept-–Oct 1897] who had no precise knowledge of him in this period; and one might question why he left Argyll Square at 4.30 a.m., when Euston Station was only ten minutes away, and the earliest train left for Scotland after 6.00?

There seem to be two alternatives. One is that he went to Scarborough, and that his stay there is recalled in the poem 'Promontory', which refers to 'the circular façades of Royals and Grands in Scarbro'. The orthography is particular: it is found in local newspapers like the *Scarbro' Record* and *Scarbro' Mercury*. There was both a Royal and a Grand Hotel at Scarborough, more or less opposite one another. Their façades were indeed curved, if not quite 'circular'. The Grand – which opened in 1867, and claimed to be the largest hotel in Europe, with 340 rooms on ten floors – was indeed built on the promontory. Other details in the poem are also suggestive. It is not impossible he had a job working at the Grand – the hotel manager was a Frenchman, Auguste Fricour – but perhaps more likely that he was working for one of the French language teachers whose advertisements are found in the local papers (a Monsieur de Meilhac, who lived on Westwood Street; a Madame Berthelot; and others).

The other possibility is that he went to Reading. He was certainly there by November 1874, for on the 7th he inserted a new advertisement in *The Times*:

A PARISIAN (20), of high literary and linguistic attainments, excellent conversation, will be glad to ACCOMPANY a GENTLE-MAN (artists preferred) or a family wishing to travel in southern or eastern countries. Good references. – A.R., No. 165, King's-road, Reading.

This is an unexpected location for the errant poet, but the 'A.R.' is definitely Rimbaud, as there is a rough draft of the advertisement in Rimbaud's hand. (This turned up in a Paris sale of autographs in 1937. The catalogue stated, erroneously, that it was corrected by Verlaine. It was therefore dated between September 1872 and July 1873, the *termini* of their period together in England; the later discovery by Starkie of the printed advert in *The Times* put the matter straight.)

In the autumn of 1874, therefore, we find Rimbaud in the salubrious suburbs of Reading, in the large detached residence on King's Road called Montpellier House. The house was leased, since July of that year, to a French teacher, Camille Le Clair, who described himself as a 'graduate of the University of France' and 'Professor of French language and literature'. From July 1874 Le Clair offered 'morning and evening classes held at his residence' and a 'finishing class for advanced pupils', and it is almost certain that his *assistant* in this was Arthur Rimbaud.

Nothing, it seems, came of Rimbaud's advertisement, but the new tone is set: he wishes to travel to 'southern or eastern countries'. The English winter is setting in – 'I distrust winter because it is the season of comfort', he wrote in *A Season in Hell* – and as he sits in his bedroom in the draughty, laurel-shaded villa in suburban Reading he is dreaming of distant lands, of heat and exoticism: 'the peppery, dried-up countries'.

*   *   *

Nothing further is heard of Rimbaud until 29 December, when he turns up at Roche. Vitalie announces in her journal, 'A returned at 9 o'clock in the morning': no indication of where he had spent Christmas.

Six weeks later he was off again, to Stuttgart, to learn German and to work as a tutor. He lives first on Wagnerstrasse, and then in a family *pension* at 2, Marienstrasse. He teaches a certain Herr Lubner.

In March, Verlaine (released on 16 January after serving eighteen months of his two-year sentence, first at the Petit Carmes prison in

Brussels, and latterly at Mons) visits him. He is full of a newly acquired religiosity which does not endear him to Rimbaud: 'I will say nothing about the latest vulgarities of our Loyola, and I have no energy left for any of that stuff now' [letter to Delahaye, 14 October 1875]. There are ugly scenes; rejection and humiliation for Verlaine; he will not see Rimbaud again, though he will continue to write and think about him.

Rimbaud's life now takes on a new timbre of relentless, drifting travel – further and further, obscurer and obscurer – with spells of inactivity and *ennui* at home in between.

Verlaine called him *'l'homme aux semelles de vent'* – his feet, or shoes, had 'soles of wind': a Mercurial imagery. Delahaye styled him *'le voyageur toqué'*, the 'crazed traveller'. (This phrase is an echo of Hervé's popular operetta, *Le Compositeur Toqué*). Another nickname they gave him was *'l'œstre'*, the gad-fly. It is largely due to the faithful Delahaye, and to the letters and ditties and cartoons that pass between him and Verlaine, that we know anything about these obscure years of Rimbaud's life. The biographer Steinmetz says:

> It is impossible, from this moment on, to reconstitute a *'Rimbaud tel qu'il fut'*[Rimbaud as he really was]. It seems preferable to accept a construction desired by Rimbaud himself and realized by his acolytes. The Rimbaud of the years 1875–1879 (up to the beginning of his African adventure) is woven out of multiple strands: voices, private writings, letters, sardonic little poems, satirical drawings. His friends, those who were bound to him by erotic or literary ties – Verlaine chiefly, but also Nouveau and Delahaye – have constructed him, imagined him, while he himself retired into the silence of his actions.

*   *   *

In May 1875, shortly after his last dealings with Verlaine, Rimbaud leaves Stuttgart and heads south into Italy. A fragment of a letter to Isabelle survives, undated:

> I am in a beautiful valley which will bring me to Lake Maggiore and old Italy. I slept in the heart of Tessin [i.e. Ticino], in a solitary barn, to the ruminations of a bony cow who graciously permitted me to share her straw.

He is in Milan on about 5 May, penniless, but lands on his feet, finds a 'very charming widow' (*una vedova molto civile* – the phrase is Verlaine's) who takes him in. He lodges with her, in a third floor apartment in the Piazza del Duomo. He writes to Delahaye, asking him to send the widow his copy of *A Season in Hell*.

He leaves Milan and the merry widow, and walks through the beauties of Liguria, but on about 15 June, somewhere near Siena, he suffers acute sunstroke. He is brought down to Livorno – haunt of the English poet and revolutionary Shelley, whose influence is perhaps felt in Rimbaud's teenage manifesto of the *voyant* – where the French consul (not the last to deal with him) undertakes to repatriate him. On 17 June he boards a steamship, the *General Paoli*, for Marseille, where he is hospitalized.

This is, as far as is known, Rimbaud's first visit to Marseille, where he would die sixteen years later.

He remains there a little. According to Delahaye, writing to Verlaine: 'Rimbe is at this moment in Marseille . . . He announces his intention of going to join up with the Carlists!' (Germain Nouveau had apparently referred to this plan in a letter to Verlaine in May, saying that in Milan Rimbaud was 'awaiting money for Spain'.) The 'Carlists' were supporters of the Spanish pretender, Don Carlos II, whose father had been ousted from the throne after the first Carlist Wars (1833–40). Pro-Carlist intrigue continued until the death of Don Carlos II in 1909.

It seems unlikely that Rimbaud really intended to go off soldiering in Spain. More likely he intended to '*toucher la prime*' – in other words, to get his hands on the recruitment money, and then desert. He may possibly have done so, prefiguring the Java adventure of the following year. At any rate, he was back in Paris by mid-July 1875.

A slow and frustrating second half of the year. He is briefly employed as a tutor for the Maisons-Alfort (a tutorial college or crammer: the Parisian equivalent of London's Gabbitas Thring), then returns to Charleville. He works on the farm, he socializes once more with Delahaye and others, he learns the piano, he learns languages, he even considers becoming a missionary teacher, a Christian *frère des Écoles*, so they can send him to the Far East.

Verlaine, who comforted himself with news and thoughts of 'Rimbe', has left a comic sketch of Rimbaud at the piano, driving his mother and his neighbours crazy. He is sketched as a kind of

Lisztian concert-pianist pounding the keyboards, but the sound I hear when I think of Rimbaud the pianist is a kind of wild proto-jazz.

On 18 December his sister Vitalie dies of a tubercular synovitis: a foreshadowing of the condition which would later cripple Rimbaud himself. She was just seventeen years old; the warmth between them shines out of her poignantly naïve journals: 'Arthur is so kind' . . . 'Arthur smiles at me' . . . 'I think of Arthur, and his sadness'.

Rimbaud attends the funeral with his head shaved.

*   *   *

One might hear Rimbaldien jazz in the mind's ear, but what of poetry? We do not know for certain, but it seems very likely that the great renunciation had taken place, as prefigured in the *Season in Hell* – 'no more words: I bury the dead in my belly'. Isabelle claims there was an actual frenzy of manuscript-burning, though her reminiscences were not written down till some twenty years later, and are somewhat moulded into clichés. Claims are sometimes made for certain references in the *Illuminations* being later than 1875, but the latest strictly dateable poem by Rimbaud is contained in a letter to Delahaye dated 14 October 1875, a week before his twenty-first birthday. Entitled 'Dream', it is scarcely a poem at all, more a ditty. Its chief subject is farting:

> *We're hungry here in the barracks –*
> *That's for sure.*
> *Emanations and explosions. A genie says:*
> *'I'm Gruyère!' . . .*
>
> *The soldiers carve up their bread –*
> *'That's life!'*
> *The genie says: 'I'm Roquefort!*
> *This one'll kill us all'*

With this questionable little coda, it seems, the great pioneer of modern poetry lays down his pen. Steinmetz sees in it 'the last degraded replica of the famous *Cœur Supplicié* of the first Lettre du Voyant'. The surrealist André Breton called it Rimbaud's last 'testament', and included it in his *Anthologie de l'Humour Noir* (1940).

Chronologically, at least, one can relate this period of ceaseless travel in the later 1870s to his disillusioned abandonment of writing. 'Poetry makes nothing happen,' wrote W. H. Auden. 'It survives in the valley of its saying.' Something similar is perhaps in Rimbaud's mind. In the *Season in Hell* there is an opposition between the vaunted magical powers of the poet and the world of 'duty' and 'soil', the 'peasant' world. Rimbaud the wanderer – immersed in physical landscapes, in the preoccupations of travel, in the tactile closeness to people and things which travel brings – is in some measure the poet 'returned to the soil, with a rugged reality to embrace'. In this same letter to Delahaye, Rimbaud says: *'Je tiens surtout à des choses précises'* – my interest is only in precise things.

It was a complete break, a severance. Delahaye recalls Rimbaud's reaction a few years later when he broached the subject with him.

'Mais la littérature?' Delahaye asked.

Rimbaud seemed 'puzzled, even astonished, as if by the image of a word which had been completely absent from his head for a very long time', then simply said: *Je ne pense plus à ça'*. (Or in a subsequent version recounted by Delahaye: *'Je ne m'occupe pas de ça.'*)

The tone is one of utter dismissal, as of some pursuit or hobby or even some romantic entanglement now considered in hindsight to be rather embarrassing.

Oh *that*. . . .

*   *   *

The year 1876 saw a very strange adventure. It begins erratically. In April he travels to Vienna, but on arrival at the station, probably drunk, he has all his luggage and money stolen by a coachman, and is back in Charleville a few days later. This period strikes me as one of intense divestment: everything is stripping away from him. The last poem, the burned books, the dead sister, and now this last, almost literal fleecing.

But it is spring. He cannot stay in Charleville. He hits the road once more, striding through the fields and forests of the Ardennes. Delahaye has left this marvellous description of walking with Rimbaud at about this time:

Rimbaud was then still robust. He had the strong, supple look of a

74

resolute and patient walker, who is always setting off, his long legs moving calmly and very regularly, his body straight, his head straight, his beautiful eyes fixed on the distance, and his face entirely filled with a look of resigned defiance, an air of expectation – ready for everything, without anger, without fear.

He heads – as he had done on that first truancy five years earlier, one jump ahead of the pursuing Izambard; as he had done in the peregrinations with Verlaine – for Brussels. It is perhaps just habit or instinct that takes him that way, and it is perhaps pure chance that led, in this free-falling mode of 1876, to what happened to him there. This is one of the strangest incarnations of his career: the mercenary soldier.

In May 1876, in Brussels, he is recruited by certain *racoleurs* – army touts, recruiting agents – for the Dutch Colonial Army. There is some trouble in Indonesia; new men are in demand. He is enrolled at the Dutch consulate, is sent by train to Rotterdam, and thence to the garrison port of Harderwijk, '*dépôt de recrutement colonial*'. He arrived there on 18 May.

The recruits are quartered in an old monastery. It is a kind of apotheosis: Rimbaud among the delinquents and fugitives and outcasts, the *hommes perdus* he has hymned in his poetry. The contract stipulates six years of service: this is a Foreign Legion of sorts. There are a few Frenchmen among the recruits: Durant, Brissonet, Dourdet, Monnin, Michaudau. The records reveal nothing except their names and their ages, and that Michaudau died of a fever shortly after their arrival in Java.

After three weeks of basic training at Harderwijk, the company assembles at Niewe Diep: ninety-seven foot-soldiers bound for Java. On 10 June they set sail aboard a requisitioned steamship, the *Prins van Oranje*. Twelve days later they are at Naples. They enter the Suez Canal, and now Rimbaud sees for the first time the desolate shores of the Red Sea, like blank pages on which his future life will be written.

They arrived at Padang, in Sumatra, on 19 July 1876. '*The white man is landing . . .* ' From there to Batavia, the capital of Java; then, on 30 July, to Samarang, Java's second city; and then by train and foot to the Dutch garrison of Salatiga. They are there by the evening of 2 August.

His active service as a soldier lasts just thirteen days. On 15

August, the Feast of the Assumption, the soldiers attend a Mass: Rimbaud is not there. At evening roll-call he is absent. The following day he is listed as a deserter. Here, once more, he disappears from all record: a physical disappearance into the jungles of Java. A last footnote – that the goods he left behind at the camp raised the sum of 1.81 florins, which was donated to the orphanage at Salatiga – and he is off.

Rimbaud in the tropics: a 'child of the sun' at last, a furtive figure glimpsed amid the lush, intricate foliage of a Douanier Rousseau painting. We know absolutely nothing about what he did or saw except in as far as he had already imagined it:

> I have touched the shore of incredible Floridas,
> Where among the flowers you see the eyes of panthers with
> Skins like men, and rainbows stretched like the bridle-reins
> Of glaucous beasts beneath the horizon of the sea.
>
> I have seen the enormous swamps fermenting, the fish-traps
> Where a whole Leviathan rots among the reeds . . .
> And brown gullies where giant serpents, eaten by insects,
> Tumble from the twisted black-scented trees.

> ['The Drunken Boat']

Within a couple of weeks, it seems, he was on the coast at Samarang.

Early the following year, writing in English, Rimbaud stated that he had served for 'four months as a sailor in a Scotch bark, from Java to Queenstown, from August to December 1876'. Assiduous detective work by Starkie and others has established that this vessel was the *Wandering Chief*, registered at Banff and commanded by a Captain Brown. She sailed from Samarang with a cargo of sugar in early September 1876 and docked at Queenstown, in Northern Ireland, on 6 December. Among the sailors recruited by Captain Brown for this return voyage was a certain Edwin Holmes. Holmes's claims of previous crewmanship are not backed up in the extant shipping registers of the period. Under this alias, it is now thought, the deserter Rimbaud made his clandestine exit from the Dutch East Indies.

After a three-month voyage via the Cape, Saint Helena and the Azores, he arrives at Queenstown on 6 December. He takes the train to Cork, crosses by ferry to Liverpool, joins a boat to Le Havre, and

76

is back in Charleville on 9 December. Delahaye comments breathlessly in a letter to Ernest Millot:

He's back!

Back from a little excursion, almost nothing really. Here are the stages – Brussels, Rotterdam, Le Helder, Southampton, Gibraltar, Naples, Suez, Aden, Sumatra, Java (two months' stay there), the Cape, St Helena, Ascension, the Azores, Queenstown, Cork (in Ireland), Liverpool, Le Havre, Paris, and finally – as always – to Charlestown.

The whole series of scrapes and yarns which he underwent on this adventure would be too long to explain.

Enclosed with this letter is one of Delahaye's little cartoons. It shows him and Rimbaud drinking and smoking in some *auberge*. The captions read –

Delahaye When will you leave again?

Rimbaud As soon as possible.

* * *

In what is becoming an increasingly familiar rhythm, a parabola of going and returning, he rests up through the winter of 1876–77 at Charleville and Roche, and then in the spring he is on the road again.

In early May he is in Cologne, where it seems he has himself become a *racoleur* or army-tout, signing up young men for the Dutch army, working on commission. Delahaye sums up this new plan with the phrase: '*on l'a racolé, il racolera*'.

His knowledge of German enables him to get into conversation, in some brasserie in Cologne, with some recruits. He charms them, they introduce him to their friends, and soon there's a dozen Prussian soldiers on their way to Holland. Bonuses for them, a nice commission for him.

On 14 May, now at Bremen, he writes a curious letter to the United States Consul, apparently seeking to join up with the American navy. His 'application' is in English, full of the little nuanced slips of someone who thinks they speak the language better

77

than they do; full also of curious rewritings, indeed the 'John Arthur Rimbaud' of Bremen is like another of his aliases, like the 'Alcide Bava' of the early poems, and the 'Tavant' of the London classifieds, and the 'Edwin Holmes' of the *Wandering Chief*. The following is verbatim [OC 302–3]:

The untersigned Arthur Rimbaud

– Born in Charleville (France)
– Aged 23
– 5 ft. 6 height
– Good healthy
– Late a teacher of sciences and languages
– Recently deserted from the 47 Regiment of the French army,
– Actually in Bremen without any means, the French consul refusing any Relief.

Would like to know on which conditions he could conclude an immediate engagement in the American navy.

Speaks and writes English, German, French, Italian and Spanish.

Has been four months as a sailor in a Scotch bark, from Java to Queenstown, from August to December 76.

Would be very honoured and grateful to receive an answer.

John Arthur Rimbaud

Nothing came of this. Its fascination lies in the striations of fiction that run through it. The lie about his age (he was twenty-two) is typical; the fluency in Spanish is a pardonable exaggeration; the height he gives (he was actually 1.9 metres tall, about 5 ft 11 ins) is probably an error rather than a falsification; but his description of himself as a deserter from the 47th Infantry Regiment is fascinating, for this was his father's old regiment.

We glimpse him next in Hamburg. There, according to Delahaye, he blew all his money at a casino.

The tone of these years is of a young man drifting around the underbelly of Europe – mercenaries, touts, deserters, riffraff. And next . . . the circus! Sometime in June or early July, probably in Hamburg, Rimbaud signs up with the Cirque Loisset. This was a popular French travelling-circus, famous for the 'Haute École' horsemanship of François Loisset and for the beauty of his two daughters. (One of them later married a Russian prince, and the other died in an accident in the ring.) According to Delahaye,

78

Rimbaud worked as the circus's cashier: 'having already seen so many countries, he is very familiar with different currencies, knows how to count in them, to explain them, and to bargain with them in various languages'. The circus moves on to Copenhagen and Stockholm. A Delahaye cartoon shows Rimbaud in Eskimo furs, holding cordial converse with a polar bear. 'The most learned geographers suppose him to be somewhere near the 76th parallel,' he writes to their mutual friend Millot. Verlaine adds Norway to this itinerary, though he was not a learned geographer, and later confused Abyssinia with Afghanistan.

This is a shadowy episode. Isabelle later denied it: he was working at a saw-mill in Sweden, she said. Handing out tickets in a circus box-office did not accord with her heroic idea of her brother. It is said he was repatriated penniless from Sweden, though no trace of this is found in the consular archives. He was back in Charleville towards the end of the summer.

7

ALEXANDRIA & BEYOND

THESE NORTHERN EXCURSIONS were short-lived. Rimbaud tends towards sun and heat: *'sea air will burn my lungs, lost climates will tan me'*. This will become a physical necessity. It is one of the constant themes, or rationalizations, of his letters from Africa that he could no longer survive in the chill and gloom of the Ardennes.

His thoughts now turn, in the late summer of 1877, to Africa, and to the fabled port of Alexandria, which was still – though already somewhat marginalized by the opening of the Suez Canal – considered the 'gateway' to northern Africa.

Let us consider his situation at this point. He is twenty-three years old, a young man with no job, no prospects – *'he'll never work: he wants to live like a sleepwalker'* – and virtually no means. His family was not exactly poor but their wealth resided in land, in bricks and mortar, in farm produce. La Mother's purse strings are tight: this errant son has no allowance.

'I will have gold!' Rimbaud promises himself in the *Season in Hell*. The African years will be marked by this desire for physical cash, for massy silver thalers, for gold bars to carry sewn in your belt (in Cairo in 1887, very paranoid, he was carrying eight kilos of gold, the weight and irritation of it giving him dysentery).

But for now he has nothing. It is as well to remember what this means in practical terms. When Rimbaud travelled down to Marseille, en route for Alexandria, in September or October of 1877, it is pretty certain that he did so mostly on foot. This is nowhere stated (the whole journey is very shadowy, and rests on Delahaye's testimony) but it would certainly explain the sequel, which is that once embarked on the steamer to Alexandria Rimbaud was so ill or exhausted that he was forced to abandon the journey after a few days. Delahaye specifies the condition: 'gastric fever and inflammation of the stomach-lining caused by rubbing of the sides against the abdomen in the course of excessive walking: this was, textually, the doctor's diagnosis'.

He is put ashore at Civitavecchia, former haunt of the great French novelist Henri Beyle, known as Stendhal, a writer whose obsessive disguisings prefigure Rimbaud's. He recovers, makes a brief visit to Rome, and returns to Marseille, and Charleville.

A year later – a bitty year: mostly at Charleville and Roche, briefly in Paris – he is off again. This time he decides to embark for Alexandria at Genoa, and once again he resolves to travel the overland part of the journey on foot.

He leaves Charleville on 20 October 1878, to walk through the Vosges, and to cross the Alps by the Saint-Gothard pass. The journey will take him four weeks. In these short paragraphs of Rimbaud's itineraries he covers hundreds of miles: 'the tramper of the highway'.

His crossing of the Alps is related in a long letter, written at Genoa on 17 November. This is the first real indication of a new documentary vein of writing: letters are virtually all that can be salvaged from Rimbaud's years of poetic silence, the only texts. The keynote is brusque, informative:

> All this area, so fierce in aspect, is heavily worked and very productive. Sometimes you see steam-driven threshers at work in the valley, and more or less everywhere you hear the sound of saws and axes above the treeline. It goes without saying that the produce of the area is mostly logs. There is also a lot of mining works. The hoteliers offer you mineral specimens of varying quality. They say the devil buys them up the top of the hill and sells them down in the town.

This is not yet the pared, sardonic narration of the African years, but in its deliberately practical, product-orientated view of this 'fierce' Alpine landscape one sees a kind of correlative to his own tamed and straitened wildness.

His account of his near-fatal journey across the Alps is wonderful: wading through snowdrifts, hunched into blizzards of hail, pitting himself against danger and exposure –

> Here you are, not a shadow above or below or around you, even though surrounded by enormous objects; there is no more trail, no more precipices and gorges, no more sky: there is nothing but

whiteness to think of, to touch, to see or not to see, it being impossible to raise your eyes from the white pointlessness [*l'embêtement blanc*] which you take to be the middle of the trail; impossible to raise your nose into the raging of the north wind; your eyelashes and moustache forming stalactites, your ears nearly torn off, your neck swollen. Without your own shadow, and the telegraph poles which follow the supposed trail, you'd be as hopeless as a sparrow in the oven.

Now you're wading through snow more than a metre high. You can't see your knees any more. You're getting worked up now. Panting away, for in half an hour the blizzard could bury you without any trouble, you shout encouragement to one another. (You never make this ascent alone, but in groups.)

Then, at last, a little hamlet, where they charge you 1.50 for a bowl of salt water. On we go. But now the wind gets angrier, the trail fills up in front of our eyes. Here is a convoy of sleighs, a fallen horse half-buried. The trail now disappears completely. Which side of these telegraph poles is it? (The poles are only on one side.) You lose your way, plunge up to your waist, up to your arms.

Finally, not a moment too soon, he discerns the Hospice de Gothard, 'a charmless structure of pinewood and stone with a bell-tower'. Here he is fed and sheltered, and weathers the stormy night on a thin straw mattress, 'listening to the monks intone, in sacred canticles, their pleasure at having conned for another day the governments who subsidize their shack'.

Contemporaneous with this Alpine drama, curiously parallel to Rimbaud's own brush with death in the Saint-Gothard Pass, his long-lost father Captain Frédéric Rimbaud lies dying at Dijon. He died on 17 November 1878, the day that Rimbaud arrived at Genoa.

Two days days later he embarks for Alexandria, grumbling at the cost the ticket. He arrives at the end of November, over a year after his first abortive attempt to get here.

Alexandria was then – as it had been for two millennia, and still is today – a strangely evocative city. Founded by Alexander the Great in 322 BC, its position on the Mediterranean coast of Africa made it a crossroads of Greek, Turkish, Arab, Levantine and European influences: a place with a chequered history and a louche, cosmopolitan air. The novelist Lawrence Durrell, whose *Alexandria*

Quartet captures this rich atmosphere, calls it the 'capital of memory', a place where the past is almost palpably in the air, 'clinging to the minds of old men like traces of perfume upon a sleeve'. The great chronicler of *fin-de-siècle* Alexandria is the poet Constantin Cavafy, born here in 1863. He spent much of his childhood in England; it was not until 1879 that he returned, at the age of sixteen, to live here. There is a tantalizing possibility that the eccentric, homosexual Cavafy may have brushed past Rimbaud in some Alexandrian backstreet – down Tatwig Street perhaps, where he haunted the billiard halls and brothels. Rimbaud was in the city on at least three occasions between 1878 and 1880.

Alexandria must surely have touched the buried poet in him, but one is shooting in the dark, because he remains silent about this marvellous city of which he had dreamt so long. It is very characteristic: the destination is always further on. *'Au revoir ici, n'importe où'*. His only letter from there promises more – 'Next time I'll send you some descriptions and details of Alexandria and Egyptian life: today, no time' – but the promise was not kept, and one is left with this brief bulletin, datelined vaguely 'Alexandrie, 1878'. He has been looking for work. There is a 'big agricultural project some ten leagues from here' which he has visited, but there is no vacancy at present. He thinks he can get a post with the Anglo-Egyptian customs – a droll addition to the curriculum vitae: Rimbaud *douanier* – but this does not happen either. Nor does he get involved (as a tenacious legend has it) in shipwrecking and offshore piracy off the Cape Guardafui on the Horn of Africa. That was literally somebody else, as we shall see.

In fact he stays in Alexandria for only a fortnight. The work he finds takes him across to Cyprus. He is signed up by a French company working out of Larnaca: Ernest Jean & Thial fils. He describes his employer as a 'French engineer, an obliging and talented man'. He crosses to Larnaca and in mid-December begins his new work as the overseer [*surveillant*] of a gang of quarrymen.

The quarry, which Rimbaud describes as 'six leagues' from Larnaca, has been identified as Potamos, near Xylophagou, on the east coast of the island. There were about sixty Cypriot workers, hired daily from the surrounding villages, and a shifting workforce of 'Europeans' (the distinction is his). 'All the Europeans have been sick, except for me.' He is supposed to be paid 150 francs a month, but after two months has only had twenty francs.

The life is hot, harsh, isolated and dangerous; is a kind of rehearsal for the African years:

> The quarry is in desert land on the edge of the sea. We are also building a canal. We load the stones onto the five barges and the steamboat of the company. There is also a kiln and a brickyard. The nearest village is an hour's walk away. There is nothing here except a chaos of rocks, and the river, and the sea . . . [15 February 1879].

He is in charge of the hiring, of the food, of the money, and also of the explosives. His description of his quarrying work sounds like some lost line from the *Season in Hell* – '*Je charge et fais sauter et tailler la pierre*'. He simply means that he packs the rocks with dynamite and blows them up; but there is something elemental in it: 'I make the stone leap and split'.

After five months he is exhausted:

> The heat is oppressive. They are cutting the grain. The bugs torture us night and day. And then there are the mosquitoes. You have to sleep out in the open by the sea. I have had some quarrels with the workmen and I've had to request some weapons. [24 April 1879].

Another letter refers to 'the tent and the dagger' he has ordered from Paris. One glimpses the note of fear and isolation: a long way from anywhere, sleeping rough, listening to the muttering of his polyglot crew.

He lasts six months, but at the end of May 1879 he is very sick. He has typhoid. He returns hurriedly to France. He carries back a letter of recommendation from his employers; he is inordinately proud of it, Delahaye reports, with a hint of mockery in his voice.

This was in September. It is the first time Delahaye has seen him for two years; it is the last time they will ever meet. Delahaye leaves this description:

> His cheeks, once so round, were now hollowed, quarried, hardened. The interval of two years had changed the fresh, rosy, English child's complexion which he had had for so long into the dark hue of a Kabyle [i.e. a Berber Arab], and over his brown skin, a novelty which amused me, there curled a little dark-blonde beard . . . His voice had lost the shrill and rather childish timbre

84

which I had hitherto known, and had become grave, deep and suffused with a calm energy.

He would hardly have recognized him, he says, were it not for his 'extraordinarily beautiful' blue eyes, which were quite unchanged. The tenor of this reminiscence is of a new manliness: the beard and the deep voice are signs of his 'full physical virility'. All traces of the boy-poet are gone.

Other Charleville friends also noted the change, and saw in it a kind of isolation. 'His contact with his friends was broken,' said Louis Pierquin. 'Long before his final departure, his silence and detachment struck us'. And Ernest Millot would later sum up this impression with the following reverie:

> I imagine myself meeting him one day, somewhere in the middle of the Sahara, after several years of separation. We are alone, and going in opposite directions. He pauses for moment.
>
> 'Hello, how are you?'
>
> 'Fine. Good-bye.'
>
> And he continues on his way: not the slighest emotion, not a word more.

*　　*　　*

A few weeks after this Rimbaud tried to get back to Alexandria, but he was still weak in the aftermath of typhoid, and this proves another abortive venture. In Marseille he is too ill to go on, and he returns to Roche.

Then, in March 1880, he sets off once again for Alexandria. This is the final embarkation, the final desertion of family, of friends, of France. This time he was gone. He was going – in one of the most resonant phrases of his African letters – 'to traffick in the unknown'. It would be eleven years before he would see Europe again, and then he was coming back to die.

He finds work once more in Cyprus, as the foreman of a construction gang, high among the pines of Mount Troodos, building a new residence for the British Governor-General. It was a good job, 200 francs a month, though costs were high. For a while, before the crew arrived, he lived alone at the work camp with an English engineer whose name was Brown. (The captain of the

Wandering Chief was also named Brown: these veiled Brits who flit through the story.)

Having been scalded and fevered at Potamos he is now cold and exposed. Troodos stands at over 6,000 ft. 'There's rain and hail up there', he writes home, 'and a wind that can knock you over. I had to buy a mattress, blankets, a coat, boots' [23 May 1880].

He expected the job to last until September, but he left abruptly in mid-June. At Limassol he took ship for Alexandria. The books he had asked his mother to send – *Sawmills for Forest and Farm*, in English, and Merly's *Livre de Poche de Charpentier* – never reached him. He came down through the Suez Canal, which he had first seen on the voyage to Java four years previously. He tried to find work in the Red Sea ports along the way: at Djeddah, at Souakim, at Massaouah. There was nothing going.

Then Hodeidah, and the fever. And then the boat, through the fatidical Gate of Tears, to Aden.

The date of his arrival at Aden is sometimes given as 7 August. A French steamship, *Les Merveilles de Fes*, docked at Steamer Point on this day, having passed through the Canal and the Red Sea. Despite the attractively baroque name, it is mere supposition that Rimbaud was aboard it. What faint evidence there is suggests otherwise. According to one of his acquaintances in Africa, the Greek Ottoman Righas, 'Rimbaud arrived at Obock, on a native boat, having had to leave some Greek island or other' [Righas to Laminne, *c.* 1911: see Laminne's letter to Berrichon, 24 January 1912]. This is very vague testimony, but there are two bits of detail to consider. The first is that Rimbaud called in at Obock – a small French settlement on the coast of what is now Djibouti – during this wandering descent of the Red Sea: this is not mentioned elsewhere, but is certainly plausible. The second is that he was travelling on a 'native boat', rather than a French steamer. (Righas uses the French word *boutre* which in this context means an Arab dhow.) This is at the least Righas's supposition, which is worth a lot more than ours.

Exactly how and when he arrived is a minor historical detail. But there is another, more puzzling question about these last stages of the journey that brought him to Aden. It is this: what was the reason for his sudden departure from Cyprus? According to his own bland account [letter to his family, 17 August 1880] it was because of certain 'disagreements with the paymaster and the engineer' (the latter, presumably, the Englishman Brown). These disputes were, he implies, minor enough: he can go back there if he wants. To his new employers in Aden, however, he will make no reference at all to his period at Troodos. 'He has come from Cyprus', Alfred Bardey notes in his journal, 'where he was the foreman of a gang of quarrymen. He left because the company which employed him had ceased trading'. This is another of Rimbaud's falsehoods as he arrives in Aden; another rewriting of the record, like his claim to have been born in Dole. The company he is referring to is Ernest Jean & Thial fils, who had indeed employed him in quarry-work and who had indeed gone bust. But he had left their employ over a year ago, suffering from typhoid, and had returned to France. He appears at this point to be concealing his recent job on Troodos, writing it out of his curriculum vitae. This is understandable enough, given the sudden termination, but there is the frisson of another, clandestine story concerning his departure from Cyprus in 1880. This is recounted by an Italian trader, Ottorino Rosa, who was to be a close companion of Rimbaud's both in Aden and Harar. According to Rosa, Rimbaud left Cyprus because he had killed a man.

This is what Rosa writes:

> Disgusted with the Bohemian life he was leading, he left his homeland in 1880, and ended up in Cyprus as an employee of a construction company. But he had scarcely arrived there when an unfortunate accident at work, which cost the life of a native [*sic*, i.e. a Cypriot], obliged him to take flight as soon as possible on a sailing ship that was leaving for Egypt. From there he wandered on, and did not stop until he reached Aden.

In an Italian version of the same passage, Rosa is more explicit about this 'accident': 'He had the misfortune to throw a stone which hit a native worker on the temple, thereby causing his death. Terrified, he took refuge on board a ship that was leaving and that was how destiny led him to Aden.' Rosa does not say that Rimbaud threw the stone *at* the worker, merely that he threw a stone which unfortunately hit the worker, but the story is open to that imputation: the fierceness of Rimbaud's temper was well-known.

These reminiscences of Rosa's were written down in early 1930, shortly before his death. (They were first published in 1972.) Rosa certainly implies that Rimbaud himself told him about this during the time they spent together in Harar in the late 1880s. The story is loosely corroborated by the Greek Ottoman Righas, mentioned above, who affirmed that Rimbaud left the 'Greek island' where he was working 'having committed some offence [*quelque méfait*].'

A curious comment of Bardey's may perhaps refer to the same circumstance:

> If I speak of him having wasted his life, it is because he himself often complained of doing so, saying, as his excuse, that he had only taken up this empty and pointless work [i.e. for Bardey] in order to escape from a more pressing difficulty. As he saw it he was submitting to circumstances rather than controlling them.

This comes from a letter Bardey wrote to Rimbaud's biographer Paterne Berrichon in 1898; it is much later than his journal; it replaces that first evasive version of Rimbaud's recent employment with this idea of him on the run from a 'pressing difficulty'. The logic of this would be that Rimbaud later told Bardey – and also Rosa – what he had at first concealed; however, the equally Rimbaldien logic would be that he invented this colourful episode, retrospectively, and that the 'disagreements' over money were the true prosaic reason for his departure from Cyprus. We do not know the truth.

*   *   *

So now he is here, on the terrace of the Grand Hotel, on a day in August 1880, another stranger to be sized up by the canny Monsieur Suel and his louche clientèle of traders and travellers.

The former poet, Arthur Rimbaud . . .

This is where I began, struck by that piquant sense of anonymity: the great 'master of phantasmagoria' glimpsed at Steamer Point with his suitcase, and his grubby cotton suit, and his letter of introduction from a trader called Trébuchet.

What do they see, I wondered, as he walks up the flint-block steps of the misleadingly named Grand Hotel? Now that we have followed him all the way here – in a biographical sense, at least – one can perhaps understand more clearly what they see. They do not see a poet because the poet is long gone: dismantled, abandoned, quite forgotten – '*je ne m'occupe pas de ça!*'. They do not see a poet, also, because they are not the sort of men who *expect* to see poets. They see instead the former soldier, deserter, seaman, tout, circus manager, quarryman and building-site foreman Arthur Rimbaud.

They see a tall, young man with big hands and burning blue eyes, and that secretive air of a man on the run from something.

They see him, and they recognize him. He is one of them. What was once a kind of disguise is now his real face.

They doubtless think he is just passing through: *de passage*. He doubtless thinks so too. But events will prove otherwise. Aden will become, bizarrely, a kind of home for him. It will become, at any rate, his base. The great African adventure begins here, and will end here eleven years later, when he is carried aboard a ship bound for France.

But for now he is just a new face: the object of a casual interest. He tells them what he chooses. His past is his own affair. His past is no more than a few stories from back up the line.

'Unfortunately I had to leave Cyprus . . . I looked for work in all the Red Sea ports . . . I tried to find something.' And now Aden, in August, forty degrees in the shade. He makes light of it: 'I only wish it was sixty, like it was when I was at Massaouah!'

(His actual conversation on this occasion is of course unrecorded. I take these phrases from a letter he wrote shortly after this. The letters are from now on the primary source for Rimbaud's life. Their clipped, nonchalant tones, explanatory but somehow evasive, certainly approximate to his conversational style. He 'spoke little', says Bardey; his comments were 'brief'; this is amply confirmed by others.)

Soon the questioners drift away, their curiosity quickly sated. It is too hot for curiosity. He sits alone, stretches out his long skinny legs, his size 41 shoes. The quiet of Aden settles over him; the quiet of having arrived. He thinks of that afternoon long ago at the Cabaret-Vert, coming in tired and dusty like this. He remembers the ticking of the clock, the green of the table-cloth, the sunlight turning his beer to gold, and that waitress with the gorgeous tits, who served him bread and butter and Belgian ham, and wanted a little kiss in return.

She had leaned down to him, and touched a fingertip to her face. 'My cheek's caught a cold,' she said. 'Just there!'

It is just ten years since that first great escape, on the tramp through the blue summer evenings of 1870, and he sees her now, quite clearly, but as if from a great distance: another country, another lifetime.

PART TWO

THE TRADER

'Everything passes through my hands . . . '

—Letter to his family, 22 September 1880

8

KARANI

ROM STEAMER POINT the road ran west along the coast to the
old town of Aden, nearly five miles away. You went by
gharry.

The ride took you past the vast coal-depot, the 'Bunker', which
dispensed up to 100 tons of coal a day to refuelling steamers and
cargo ships. Manned by half-naked Somalis and Seedis, the Bunker
was an extraordinary scene. An earlier traveller, Major Cornwallis
Harris of the East India Company's Engineers, describes how the
coalmen labour 'to the dissonant tones of a rude tambourine,
thumped with the thigh-bone of a calf'; how they 'heave the
ponderous sacks like giants busied at pitch and toss'; how they 'roll
at intervals upon the blackened planks to staunch the streaming
perspiration'.

Further on there was a small fishing village, with Somali palm-
thatch roofs: this is Maala, now a residential district of Aden, and
the only part of the city which has anything resembling a 'night life'.
From there the road curved and rose inland to the Main Pass Gate,
guarded by sepoys, and thence into the main conurbation of Aden,
called Crater. This consisted of the old Arab town, built across the
floor of an extinct volcano (hence the name); and the sizeable British
garrison, complete with church and social amenities, known as Aden
Camp.

Here stood, on the edge of this British cantonment, with its back
to the souk and its balcony towards the sea, a handsome, three-
storey trading house. This is the house now known as Maison
Bardey, and which was then, more precisely, the Aden branch office
of Viannay, Bardey et Cie, coffee exporters and general traders,
whose head office was at Lyon.

At some point shortly after his arrival at Steamer Point,
Rimbaud made this journey, and arrived at this house, where he
would live and work, off and on, for many years.

Alfred Bardey himself was not there: he was on a reconnaissance trip in Africa, establishing links with the ancient market town of Harar. Rimbaud meets instead Bardey's associate, the branch manager in his absence: Monsieur Dubar. It was a small world here in Aden: Dubar was the brother-in-law of Suel of the Grand. He was a former soldier, though not quite the 'retired General' he liked to style himself. Rimbaud will later describe him, in his severe term of approval, as *'très sérieux'*, a man of substance. He will later thank Dubar for sending him, from France, the camera which he had so long wished for, and which provides us now with the three precious self-portraits, taken in Harar, our only visual knowledge of Rimbaud in Africa.

On 16 August 1880, Rimbaud began work here. The following day he wrote home, for the first time in nearly two months:

> I have got a job at a coffee trader's. At present I get only seven francs a day. When I've got a few hundred francs together, I will head down to Zanzibar, where they say there is work to do.
>
> Send me your news.
>
> RIMBAUD,
> Aden Camp

Zanzibar remained a dream: he never got there. Nor to Bombay or Peking or Panama, or all the other places he yearningly mentions in his letters. He is here now.

*   *   *

This is the new shape, the new smell, of Rimbaud's life: the coffee trader. He is, of course, only an apprentice, an underling, at this point. The pay is poor, but together with free board, lodging and laundry, and the use of a horse and carriage, he reckons it adds up to about twelve francs a day. He works from 7.00 in the morning until 5.00 in the evening.

He is quickly an expert – he has an immense facility for *métiers*, as for languages – and will write a few weeks later:

> The company is doing several hunded thousand francs of business per month. I am the only employee and everything passes through my hands. I am very well up on the coffee trade right now. I have the complete confidence of my boss.

Since the decline of Mokha, after the Turkish occupation of the Yemen, Aden had become a major trading centre for coffee. It was a protectorate and a free port. Coffee arrived from the highlands of the Yemen by camel, and from the coastal ports by trading vessel. During the year 1876 nearly 75,000 hundredweight of Arabian coffee (or Mocka coffee, as it was known in Europe) arrived in the Aden market-place. The price of Arabian coffee in Aden was between five and six thalers per *frasleh*. (The *frasleh* or *faraslah*, the traditional unit of measurement for coffee in Aden, was just over 36 lbs.)

The coffee usually arrived 'in the berry', i.e. unhusked, known in Arabic as *jafal*. The pericarp or shell was then removed by grinding in a stone hand-mill, or by mechanical grinders of the type developed in the coffee plantations of Ceylon and Malabar. The beans were then cleaned and graded. This was Rimbaud's first job in the Bardey warehouse: he was in charge of the *harim* – this is the correct technical term – of Indian women, who cleaned, graded and packed the coffee. These women were mostly wives and dependents of the Indian soldiers who formed a sizeable part of the British battalion quartered at Aden Camp.

He had the rank of *karani*: the foreman, or second-in-command. The word literally means 'the wicked one', though as Bardey notes, it is a friendly appellation 'given to all seconds-in-command whether or not they are in reality good people'.

After cleaning and grading, 10 lb of coffee yielded 5 lb of clean coffee (*bun safi*), $3\frac{1}{2}$ lb of shell (*kashar*), $1\frac{1}{4}$ lb of husk (*duka kashar*), and $\frac{1}{4}$ lb of refuse. Both the shell and husk could be sold on the local market. The cleaned coffee was packed for export in huge gunny sacks each weighing $1\frac{1}{2}$ cwt. The average price of cleaned coffee ready for export was around fifty rupees per cwt. This included the cost of cleaning, packing and carriage to the wharf.

It was not just Arabian or Mokka coffee that passed through Aden. There was also – and this was of particular interest to the Bardeys, and hence to Rimbaud – an increasing quantity of coffee imported from Africa. It was called Berbera coffee (after the Somali port of that name) and was considered the equal of Mokka. Most of it was grown in the neighbourhood of Harar, and was transported down to the Somali coast by camel, packed in goatskin bags called *daboulah*. It was still a minor part of the Aden coffee trade (3,261 cwt of African coffee arrived in Aden in 1876, as against nearly 75,000 cwt of Arabian coffee) but Bardey, at any rate, considered it a commercial proposition, and it was to this end that he had made the arduous journey up to Harar.

This was big business, the tangible profits of the 'scramble for Africa'. In the financial year 1875–6, more than three million rupees' worth of cleaned coffee was exported from Aden. Nearly half of this went to France, the caffeine capital of Europe.

Besides Bardey's company, there were three other European companies involved in the coffee trade in Aden: César Tian, for whom Rimbaud would later work; Morand, Fabre et Cie, the company for which Rimbaud's friend Trébuchet worked in Hodeidah; and the Bienenfeld brothers, Vittorio and Giuseppe, who were Italians from Trieste.

* * *

Sometime in late September or early October, Alfred Bardey himself returned from his reconnaissance of Somalia and Harar, and the two men met for the first time. I have already mentioned Bardey's first impressions of this taciturn but *sympathique* young man, with the big gesturing hands. Of Rimbaud's impression of Bardey we know nothing.

Bardey was an energetic, dark-bearded young Lyonnais. He was the same age as Rimbaud, twenty-five: they were born less than a month apart. His father was in the silk business. After a brief spell of soldiering – he joined the 8th battalion of the Garde Nationale in 1870, aged sixteen: once more parallel to Rimbaud, who ran off to Paris in this year – he settled into the family business, learning the art of silk-weaving. In early 1880 he was a co-founder of Viannay, Bardey et Cie, whose principal business was the importation of 'colonial merchandise' [*denrées coloniales*], and together with Dubar, also a Lyonnais, he had sailed for Aden in May 1880 to establish a branch there, and to organize shipments of coffee.

In his journal, written at the time and collated many years later under the title *Barr Adjam* – an Arabic phrase meaning 'the land beyond', and referring to that hinterland of Eastern Africa which both he and Rimbaud made their stamping-ground – Bardey gives a detailed description of Rimbaud's situation and duties in the Bardey warehouse. It has never been given in English, so I quote it at some length.

M. Dubar tells me of a young man he has working for him in the workshops where they do the grading [*triage*] of the coffee . . . The overseeing of these workshops, which are called *harim* because of their female personnel, requires a European employee. This has been, for some weeks now, the young man in question, whose name is Arthur Rimbaud . . .

Dubar has taken him on, temporarily, as the overseer of the workshop [*chef d'atelier*], a job which consists of taking delivery of the bales of coffee purchased by the two brokers attached to our agency . . . The coffee is brought to the warehouse by the *hammals* [porters], weighed out in the units of the region, *maunds, fraslehs, rotols*, and paid for in Indian rupees or in thalers. Having been graded by hand by the Hindu women of the *harim*, under the direction of a *mokadem*, a forewoman, of the same race, the coffee is passed *safi* (graded), weighed in English or French pounds, and placed in a double package, consisting of *attal* (palm matting) inside, and *garair* (coarse material of local weave) outside, ready for export.

M. Dubar is very satisfied with Rimbaud, who already knows enough Arabic to give orders in that language. This earns him the respect of the native people working for him. [BA, pp. 219–20]

A rather Rimbaldien incident, shortly after Bardey's return to Aden, is also related in *Barr Adjam*:

The great ostrich given to me by Abou Bekr has been brought to the agency, but on the very first night the ostrich died. In its agony it broke, with its strong feet, the thick solid door of the shed where it was kept. Its beautiful black and white feathers are all I will be able to bring back to France. [BA, p. 220]

A ghostly hammering in the Aden night; in the morning, a dead giant on the floor; Baudelaire's albatross (a symbol of the poetic imagination grounded by daily life) springs to mind.

* * *

The Maison Bardey – the house in Aden where Rimbaud lived and worked over the next few months of 1880, and at various other times over the next five years – is described with some succinctness by Alfred Bardey himself. (It was never *his* house, of course. He rented it: it was a business premises, owned by a rich Jewish merchant, Menahem Missa. It was first pointed out to Bardey by the ubiquitous Suel, Manager of the Grand, and one would not be surprised if Suel had a stake in it somewhere.)

Bardey described it as standing near the imposing, red-tiled British law courts ('*le tribunal*') and, more precisely, as standing opposite 'a tall white minaret which ended in a small cupola with a gold crescent on top'. It was a 'large house'. It had arcades on the ground floor, and a verandah above. It was 'surmounted by pediments in the shape of inverted arches, two over each arcade', which gave the façade a 'pleasingly symmetrical aspect'. [BA, p. 33]

Thanks largely to these precisions, the Maison Bardey was rediscovered, in early 1990, by the Rimbaud scholar Alain Borer and some local historians. It stands on what is now called Arta Street. I visited it the following year and was dismayed to find they were already turning it into a museum: a turn-of-the-century coffee-trading experience. The place was swept clean, was even more literally an 'empty inn' than the Grand, which was at least still populous. There was the smell of paint and new wood, and a litter of half-finished wiring for new strip-lights and ceiling fans.

They are *recreating* it, which first entails killing it stone dead.

The house is deep and spacious: colonnades, alcoves and cool grey flagstones on the ground floor. Coming in from the hot street and the car-horns one is immediately cooled. It is – this is the only detail about the house that Rimbaud bothers to give us – 'very well ventilated'. The light is beautiful in here. Bars of brilliant sun break in through the chinked shutters on the south side – the souk side – of the building.

But the silence, though also refreshing, is surely quite wrong. This arcaded lower floor is where the actual warehouse was: Rimbaud and his *harim* of Hindu soldiers' wives. This was a place of labour, a colonial sweat-shop. One imagines the squall of languages, the humping of gunny-sacks, the grumbling of *hammals*, and the coffee-dust rising thick in the air, giving that oddly bitter taste to the sunlight that breaks in through the shutters.

Upstairs, the remains of a finely tiled floor. The balcony looks onto a small garden of palm-trees, and the white minaret mentioned by Bardey, and then the shimmering brown crag of Seerah Island with its medieval fortress. Perhaps this view was before Rimbaud as he sat and wrote his first brief description of Aden: 'Aden is a frightful rock . . .'

This was only ten days after he had signed up. Already he is sick of the place: not a blade of grass, not a drop of good water, the heat excessive, everything very dear, and so on. Aden is 'far from everywhere' and he is almost homesick.

'How are things at the house? Is the harvest in? Send me your news.'

Leaning on the balcony now, the white minaret reminds me of a helter-skelter in an English fairground, and of holding my daughter's hand as we climbed with our mats up the wooden spiral stairs: thus also a moment of homesickness.

The second floor is occupied by the Aden Chamber of Commerce, which had the whole building previously. A handsome woman wearing a scarlet cardigan and a white Muslim headscarf comes out of a door marked 'Conference Section'. My guide Mustapha nudges me and whispers, 'The daughter of Rimbaud?' He is beginning to get the hang of this biography business.

This was where the personnel, Rimbaud among them, had their rooms. He refers in one letter [5 May 1884] to *l'immeuble de la Cie* – the company apartment – which presumably means these upstairs rooms.

A rickety wooden stairway leads up to the big flat roof, surrounded by an undulating balustrade of dirty white stone – the 'pediment in the form of inverted arches' described by Bardey. The city is laid out below us. Roofs and minarets and unfinished breeze-block buildings, the rocks and the sea, and the sound of the souk rising on the warm morning air. There is a scattering of old lumber on the roof, and a carton full of rusted cans of sardines.

Here, at least, they have not cleaned everything away. I hardly think there is any personal debris of Rimbaud up here, but this is where he slept most of his nights in Aden – 'For a year now I have been sleeping continually under the open sky.' [15 January 1883] – just like that teenage runaway on the roadside in France, when the stars seemed to 'rustle like silk' overhead.

*   *   *

I hesitate to call this place Rimbaud's 'home'. It was the place where he worked, and where he lodged while he had the work. (After his formal separation from the company in 1885, his postal address was the Grand Hôtel de l'Univers.)

Alain Borer computes that during the eleven years of Rimbaud's African adventure (1880–91) he lived in Aden for a total of just over four years. He lived longer continuous periods in Harar, but Harar was out in the wilds. He returned to Aden for rest though hardly, perhaps, for recreation.

Aden becomes Rimbaud's 'home', but only in a reduced, negative sense. In those long *années de pérégrinage* that precede the final disappearance into Africa, one saw that strange circling movement of Rimbaud's travels. He ranges around, further and further, but is always drawn back to a nominal centre, a despised but necessary bolt-hole: Charleville and, more particularly, Roche. In his new life Aden assumes that role, indeed in some of his letters he seems to equate his life in Aden with life back home in France:

> Let me reassure you: there's nothing extraordinary about my situation. I'm still working in the same old joint [*boîte*], and toiling away like a donkey . . . If I don't write to you any more it's because I'm very tired and also because with me, as with you, there is nothing new to write about. [10 May 1882]

More than once he calls Aden a 'hole' – *un trou* – the same word he had used of Roche. There it was 'La Mother' who had 'put me in this sad hole'; in Aden it was something even bigger than she. It was the 'miserable necessity' of having to work. It was fate itself:

> At the moment I am earning a living here, and since every man is slave to this miserable necessity, in Aden as elsewhere, it is better in Aden than elsewhere, where I would be unknown, and completely forgotten, and where I would have to start all over again . . . In the end, as the Muslims say: It is written! That's life, and it's no laughing matter! [10 September 1884]

His bulletins from Aden settle into a tedious, harrowing vein of heat, boredom and priciness:

> I am like a prisoner here . . . [25 August 1880]

> I am by now completely habituated to every form of boredom, and I suppose complaining is my way of singing . . . [10 July 1882]

> Forgive me for enumerating my boredoms to you . . . My life here

is a real nightmare. Don't imagine that I enjoying it at all. Far from it . . . [5 May 1884]

I feel that I am becoming very old very quickly, in this idiotic occupation, in the company of savages or imbeciles . . . [10 September 1884]

And so on and so on. A sense of imprisonments and hopelessness, of *abrutissement*, sears through these clipped colourless texts which are all that remain of his time in Aden, full of complaints and money matters, and a bitterness that just occasionally, despite himself, touches the buried poet inside him:

We are in the steam-ovens of springtime now. Our skins stream, our stomachs grow sour, our skulls are troubled, the business is down, the news is bad . . . [26 May 1885]

One must also take into account the misleading aspects of the letters. The mood of depression and cafard which they express may in itself be the occasion of the letters. In other words, when he is down he thinks of home and writes a letter. When he is busy, or even – dare one say? – contented, he does not write home. (Or sometimes he just writes a one-sentence letter which says nothing more than 'I'm doing fine'.) There is also that tortuous sense of his relationship with his mother being worked out through the mercantile concerns of the letters, and indeed through this very idea that he is definitely *not enjoying himself* and is therefore following duty rather than pleasure, a priority which would meet with her approval.

This is one of the many paradoxes of these maddening but indispensable texts, of which Albert Camus has written: 'To sustain the legend [of Rimbaud] one has to be unaware of these decisive letters. They are sacrilege, as the truth sometimes is.' [*L'Homme Révolté*, p. 117]

*   *   *

This is Rimbaud's little expat circle now – the Frenchmen Bardey, Dubar, Suel. He had not yet met Bardey's second-in-command, Pinchard, who had been left up in Harar, and who was to be Rimbaud's immediate boss up there in months to come. Nor did he get to meet Henri Lucereau, a 'tall, vigorous young man' who had been commissioned by the French government to search for the source of the Sobat (a tributary of the Blue Nile). He had left Aden shortly before Rimbaud's arrival, and was soon to die, at the hands of marauding Gallas, in the Itou hills west of Harar.

Rimbaud probably did meet a curious figure who haunted the Grand in 1880, as described by Bardey:

> In one of the back rooms of the hotel lodges a strange traveller who has returned from a long sojourn among the tribes of Africa. Having worn out his clothes, he has stitched together a complete costume out of the skins of animals he has killed. This get-up, which includes a little peaked cap, also of skin, as well as various other curios he has accumulated, gives off a disagreeable smell . . . He seems to have acquired all the customs of the savages with whom he has lived. At the insistence of our host [i.e. Suel] he wears an Arab *foutah* around his waist . . . His naked torso, partly tatooed, shows the scars of hunting trips in the bush. Contorting his body and brandishing a spear he does a war-dance. His face takes on expressions of cruelty, of terror. He mimes the stalking and killing of panthers. He never dines with the other guests, but eats alone in his room, a habit he picked up among the tribes where, it seems, he is treated as a brother. I cannot remember the name of this crazed hunter. He originally came, if my memory serves, from the highlands of Italy or Southern Austria. [BA, pp. 25–6]

Rimbaud never became quite such a curio, but after nearly ten years in Africa he will humorously suggest that he looks 'baroque' enough to go on show at the Paris Exhibition. In this *'chasseur enragé'* one gets an authentic cameo of the explorer gone native, the traveller on a one-way ticket.

There were other Europeans Rimbaud would meet here in Aden, men who become companions, colleagues, perhaps even friends: the Marseillais explorer Jules Borelli; the traders César Tian and Maurice Riès; the Italians Ottorino Rosa and Ugo Ferrandi. We will meet them in due course, and hear their brief recollections and glimpses of Rimbaud. All of them express this definitive idea of Rimbaud's severance from his past –

> I first knew Rimbaud in Aden . . . He never spoke of his previous life, and I had better things to do than to question him . . . He had

certainly given up all his old ideas (if he ever really held them, except in words) . . . [Jules Borelli to Enid Starkie, 1936]

Neither my father [César Tian], nor his manager Maurice Riès, nor their friend Jules Borelli, whom I knew very well, suspected at the time that Rimbaud was a poet . . . Nothing in his papers of that time drew their attention to what he had been before 1880 . . . Poetry was dead for him . . . [André Tian, *Les Nouvelles Littéraires*, 1947]

Far be it from me to judge his past as a poet, but I can state with absolute conviction that he was a passionate trader . . . In conversation [he] always expressed satisfaction that he had turned his back on what he called the pranks [*frasques*] of youth, on a past which he abhorred . . . [Maurice Riès to Émile Deschamps, 1929]

Entirely devoted to commerce, he never spoke of his past, and behind that extravagant and somewhat spiky shell of his [*son écorce un peu hargneuse*] there was no reason to suspect his genius as a poet and man of letters. Of Verlaine he never spoke a word. Only once did he tell me that, disgusted by the Bohemian life to which his restless and adventurous spirit had led him, and the milieu to which he devoted himself very young, he had suddenly and definitively decided to abandon France . . . [Ottorino Rosa, MS notes *c.* 1930]

It was easy to find traders in the cafés [of Djibouti] who remembered the poet. But when I told them about the young genius, they were astonished. They had never considered him anything but a good merchant, somewhat adventurous in business, even having 'ideas' (which in their minds was not altogether a compliment). They added that they could never have known about the poetic career of their former colleague: Rimbaud never spoke to them about his previous existence, nor about literature. [Pierre Mille, conversations in Djibouti, 1896]

Some of this is moulded by hindsight, by a loosely shared 'idea' of Rimbaud, but the consistent impression is of a man who has hardened his heart and 'turned his back' on 'a past which he abhorred'.

*   *   *

Some of these men – Borelli and Rosa, in particular – came to know Rimbaud quite well, but of all of them it was probably Alfred Bardey who knew him best. He was Rimbaud's employer for about five years, with a brief hiccup when the company went into liquidation in 1883. He worked with him and quite frequently lived with him. Rimbaud's severance from the company in 1885 was marked with angry recriminations on both sides – Rimbaud rails at these 'peasants' [*pignoufs*] who are trying to 'enslave' him, while Bardey feels justifiably let down by someone he had trusted – but they remained in touch, and continued to do business together in a small way. Bardey later shrugged off this *rupture* with his famous comment: I could no longer hold onto him, any more than I could hold onto a shooting star.'

Bardey comes across as an easy-going, warm-hearted man. He achieves that status, once enjoyed by Delahaye and Izambard and indeed Verlaine: the fascinated but exasperated companion, the 'brother'. Writing to Rimbaud from France, thanking him for some photographs, Bardey says: 'I would like to be able to return the favour, but you are a bit strange [*bizarre*] and I don't know what to send that might please you' [24 July 1883]. He found Rimbaud puzzling, annoying and at times alarming:

> Habitually taciturn and tranquil, Rimbaud became exaggeratedly surly [*bourru*] in moments of difficulty, spraying out such epithets as 'that filthy place X', 'that idiot Z' or 'that imbecile Z', not with the idea of making himself seem superior – something that all sorts of people do without fooling anyone – but out of pure mania . . . [BA, p. 352]

> His mordant and caustic spirit made him many enemies. He never knew how to drop that unfortunate and mischievous satirical mask which concealed the real qualities of his heart. He needled [*égratigna*] people a lot but never did any great harm, or only to himself, as a repercussion of his own cruel mockeries, of which certain travellers in Shoa and Harar still seem to retain a bad memory. [letter to Berrichon, 10 July 1897]

When asked by Berrichon to write a preface for an edition of Rimbaud's African letters, Bardey declined the honour. He said: 'I don't want Rimbaud coming to tweak my toes during the night. He was annoying [*ennuyeux*] enough during his lifetime.' [9 December

1897] He first wrote *'désagréable'*, then changed it to *'ennuyeux'*. In fact the comment betrays a touch of fear.

But Bardey was certainly alive to Rimbaud's good qualities, chief among which was his tremendous charity and generosity:

> His charity was very discreet and very generous. It was probably one of the few things he did without a sneer or a cry of disgust . . .

> I'm sure you know that Rimbaud was often utopian and that he didn't pay for the damages [*ne paya pas la casse*] . . .

> He was good, naturally and without show, to the *meskines* [beggars] and sometimes also to travellers who had lost everything in some venture and were in need of repatriation. In our office and warehouses I saw some unexpected instances of this, which were not in themselves extraordinary but which nonetheless surprised me because they did not seem to accord with his cold and rather closed-up manner.

When Rimbaud died in 1891 Bardey was among the first to pay tribute to him. Writing to the Société de Géographie, he says:

> I have learned of the death of M. Arthur Rimbaud. He is better known in France as a decadent poet than as a traveller, but under this latter title he also deserves to be remembered . . . Because of his love of the unknown, and because of his personality, he avidly absorbed the essential qualities [*choses intellectuelles*] of the regions in which he travelled. He learned languages to the point where he could freely converse in each region; and he assimilated himself, as much as possible, to the manners and customs of the native people . . . All who have known him over the last eleven years will tell you that he was an honest, capable and courageous man.

A prickly, bitter sort of character, clearly, but in these reminiscences Bardey acknowledges the qualities on which all Rimbaud's African friends are agreed – his charity; his honesty; and his profound immersion in the life and culture of the 'natives', both Arab and African.

As this last comment reminds us, Rimbaud's circle in Aden was not just the French, but also this very cosmopolitan world which is still a feature of the Red Sea area. Among his acquaintances are Greeks, Armenians, Indians, Arabs and Somalis. He certainly knew at this time the young Greek, Constantin Righas, who would soon be accompanying him to Harar; and perhaps also his brothers, Dimitri, Athanase and Ottoman, though these appear on the record some-what later. He also dealt daily with the two local 'brokers' who were Bardey's agents in the Aden coffee souk. There was Megjee Chapsee, 'a Hindu *banian*' (trader), who dealt with the market-traders, and especially with other Indians. And there was Almass ('diamond'), of whom Bardey writes:

> Almass [is] a former negro slave, who performed so well in service that his master freed him and made him his heir. Dressed like an Arab of quality, he purchases coffee from the Arabs who bring their caravans from the Yemen.

Rimbaud undoubtedly also knew at this time Ali Shamok (or Chemmek), whom Bardey described in 1883 as 'our longest-serving warehouseman and foreman'. Whatever their relations to begin with, there came the day when something snapped. On the morning of 28 January 1883, they came to blows. A fracas ensued, and – the situation of foreigners being always parlous in these countries – a swift letter of explanation from Rimbaud to the French vice-consul, Monsieur de Gaspary.

*　　*　　*

But these angers and scuffles belong to later years in Aden. At this early stage Rimbaud was indeed just passing through, as he himself believed ('I will definitely have to stay here at least three months before getting back on my feet a bit, and finding a better job', he wrote on 25 August 1880).

Aden is for him, as it was for Bardey and the others, a staging-post for Africa. In his memoirs, Bardey fixes a vertiginous moment of Rimbaud's destiny with the following company-style entry:

> Rimbaud is present at certain discussions I have with M. Dubar, concerning Harar and the prospects afforded by establishing ourselves in that region. He instantly asks me to send him there . . . On M. Dubar's recommendation, I accept Rimbaud's proposal. He it is who will carry up to Harar the funds and the cotton fabrics necessary to support the agency and begin a new commercial

operation. A young Greek who is part of the personnel at Aden, Constantin Righas, will accompany him.

There is no doubting Rimbaud's enthusiasm: his request to be sent to Harar is made *'instamment'*. There is no doubting his status, either. It is, instinctively, *Monsieur* Dubar (the partner), but just plain Rimbaud (the employee).

In fact his status is about to be formalized. The 'discussions' referred to by Bardey took place in October 1880. On 1 November, some ten weeks after his arrival at Aden, Rimbaud agreed a three-year contract with Viannay, Bardey et Cie. This was confirmed in writing by Dubar on 10 November. Rimbaud agreed to join the company 'as an employee at their office [*agence*] in Harar, East Africa, or at any other branch [*comptoir*] or office on the coasts of Africa or Arabia'. His salary was fixed at 150 rupees per month, together with a one per cent share in profits (though he had hoped for two per cent: see letter of 2 November 1880) and all board and lodging.

In his letters home he had spoken grandly of trips he planned to India, and to Zanzibar. 'I will probably go to Zanzibar, where there are things to do' – *'où il y a à faire'*: a favourite loose phrase at this time. But now his talk is of Harar.

> The company has set up a branch in Harar, a region you can find on the map to the south-east of Abyssinia. Coffee, skins, gum, etc. are exported from there, purchased in exchange for cotton fabrics and other merchandise. The country is very healthy and cool, thanks to its altitude. There are no roads at all, and hardly any communications.

He orders, in this month, via the company head office in Lyon, 'two suits of wool' for those cool upland nights. Ten months later, up in Harar, he will still be waiting for them, shivering in the thin cotton clothes he wore in Aden.

9

CARAVAN NO. 3

Thus, in the middle of November 1880, with the profound relief of movement after three months sweating in the 'ovens' of Aden, Rimbaud embarked for Africa in the company of Constantin Righas.

He crossed the Red Sea, probably by dhow, to the small but ancient port of Zeilah, on the Somali coast. This was a journey of some ninety miles, and took anything between twelve and eighteen hours. The boat passed the island of Masha, much visited by harvesters of gull's eggs, and entered the Zeilah creek, at the bottom of which lay 'a strip of sulphur yellow sand' and some 'whitewashed houses and minarets peering above a long low line of brown wall'. (The description is by the English explorer Richard Burton, arriving here in 1854, also en route for Harar; he was 'pleasantly disappointed' by the sight of Zeilah.)

Here Rimbaud set about equipping and organizing a small *gaflah*, or caravan, for Harar, presumably following the instructions given by Bardey:

> I instruct them both [i.e. Rimbaud and Righas] to embark immediately for Zeilah, with the purpose of recovering and if possible using some of the camels which I left, in very bad shape, at the wells and pastures of Tocochah, being looked after by the *sepianes* [porters]. However, at the time of my departure [i.e from Zeilah to Aden in September], many of the *sepianes* were sick with smallpox which they had caught on the journey, and which is still rife throughout the Somal. With or without these camels, but certainly under the protection of Abou Bekr [Sultan of Tadjourah], who is well-disposed to us at present, they will form a small caravan, no 3, destination Harar. [BA, p.221]

These instructions were issued sometime before Bardey's departure from Aden in November aboard the P & O steamboat *Sumatra*, bound for Marseille. Rimbaud must have left Aden very shortly after the signing of his contract on 10 November, for his caravan was ready to leave Zeilah by 16 November. This was Bardey's third caravan of 1880: numbers 1 and 2 he had led himself, the first up to Harar in July, the second down from Harar in September.

*　*　*

Zeilah in 1880 was a straggling little port of about 1500 people: a shallow harbour, a new jetty built from the ruins of the old town-wall, a few hundred native huts of woven straw, a dozen large whitewashed houses, and a small mosque, all shimmering quietly under the torrid sun of the Somal. The population was a cosmopolitan mix: Somalis, mainly of the Issah and Gadiborsi clans; an administrative and commercial class of Arabs; a smattering of Indians and Greeks; and an underclass of slaves from the interior. Though the Somalis were part of the settled community of Zeilah, they were essentially a shifting, nomadic presence of herders and traders. They were referred to by the Arabs, and then the Europeans, as *bedouin*.

Zeilah had been a significant port for centuries: it appears on a Roman map of the 1st century AD. The Somalis are a trading people at this East African crossroads. Burton was surprised to meet Somalis who had travelled throughout Arabia, India and Egypt, and were fluent in three or four languages. The boats in the harbour traded to Arabia and Western India, often navigated by Hindu pilots or *rajput*. There was even, Burton learned, an overland trade route to the Atlantic:

> I repeatedly heard, at Zayla and at Harar, that traders had visited the far West [of Africa], traversing for seven months a country of pagans wearing golden bracelets, till they reached the Salt Sea, upon which Franks sail in ships. [*Footsteps in East Africa*, p. 189]

The French and British were beginning to establish themselves here, but the town was still under the rigid control of Abou Bekr Pasha, the Sultan of Tadjourah. This powerful figure held sway over the whole Somali territory. All commerce with the interior depended on his good will (and that of his eleven sons). It is very likely that Rimbaud now met, for the first time, this slave-trading sultan whose son he would later describe as 'the most incorrigible bandit in all Africa'.

Abou Bekr was a Danakil. This fearsome, fervently Muslim tribe, now known as the Afar, controlled the trade routes across the Danakil deserts to the north. They were a byword for savagery and aggression; their customary trophy was an enemy's testicles. Bardey describes him as a skinny, elderly man of medium height, with dark black skin, thin lips and a wispy grey beard. His face 'had almost always an evasive look'.

You are ushered into his courtyard. He lounges on a couch of animal skins. He is wearing a dirty white Arab *gandourah*, and an enormous gourd-shaped turban of white muslin. He has prayer beads in his left hand which he sifts and turns and flicks with a sound like miniature billiard balls. In his right hand he holds a tooth-cleaning stick, and all the while you converse he is working away at his teeth, which are still good despite his age. After each polishing, with a soft hiss, he ejects a gob of saliva, without much caring where it lands.

Coffee is brought, in minuscule cups with a copper surround like an egg-cup to keep you from burning your fingers.

To every statement of intent concerning the caravan he replies '*Insh Allah*': if God pleases. This is the habitual reply of any good Muslim, but in the mouth of Abou Bekr you know it means: 'if I please'.

His underlings – also Danakil but wearing Egyptian tarbouches – bring a series of small documents for his attention. They recite the contents; he listens scarcely at all. With that air of weariness which small-town potentates affect, he detaches from a chain around his neck a signet-ring, engraved with Arabic characters. Dunking his finger in a wooden ink-well, he covers the flat of the ring with black ink, and applies it to the document.

'This is,' Bardey notes, 'the entirety of the paperwork here.'

Years later, in Harar, Rimbaud would have a seal like this, engraved with Arabic characters. This has since disappeared, but it was among Rimbaud's effects when he died, and an impression of it is found on a letter written by Madame Rimbaud to Ernest Delahaye in 1897. Some of the words are illegible, but the name can be read: 'ABDOH RINBO', and beneath it a phrase which seems to translate as 'Transporter of Incense'. Abdoh is a contraction of Abdullah, so the name translates as 'Rimbaud the servant of Allah'. This is his Muslim cachet: something like his business card as a Harar trader.

*   *   *

Though there will be rancour in the future between Rimbaud and the Abou Bekr clan, for now the sultan was (as Bardey puts it) 'well-disposed' to the caravan. Rimbaud would also have to obtain permission to travel through Somali territory at a *hourour*, or assembly of local elders, held in the town square in front of the mosque.

Swiftly, it seems, Rimbaud and Righas prepare Caravan No. 3 to Harar. It will carry up 'cotton stuffs' and other tradeable items, as well as the 'large sum of money' Rimbaud mentions in a letter of 2 November. They hire or rehire the guides (*abbans*), porters (*sepianes*) and camel-drivers, those whom the smallpox has not killed. Among these might be the head camel-driver and the head porter mentioned by Bardey, both called Abd'Allah, and distinguished respectively as 'Long-haired Abd'Allah' and 'Squint-eyed Abd'Allah'. They purchase the provisions necessary (a daily ration of a pound of rice and two ounces of *ghee* per man). The camel-drivers are generally the owners of one or more camels in the caravan: 'Their backs are yours to put on them what you wish, but the beasts themselves are ours,' they say. (This adage of the camel-drivers is recorded by Henri d'Orléans in 1897.) A mature camel was expected to carry 12 *frasleh* (200 kilos). The going rate for camel hire in Zeilah in 1880 was five thalers per beast, but they could also be bartered for cloth at the rate of one cotton *tobe* (the Somali robe or blanket) or one roll of *guinea* (an indigo-dyed cotton, so-called from a gold stamp on it like a British guinea) per camel [BA, p. 38].

Bardey describes Caravan No. 3 as 'small'. His own Caravan No. 1, formed in Zeilah six months previously, comprised six Yemenis brought from Aden, a little over thirty camel-drivers, and about fifteen porters.

The majority of the personnel would be Issah (or Eesa), the principal Somali tribe of the region. The Issah are still numerous in northern Somalia, and are the predominant ethnic group in Djibouti, the small republic that was formerly French Somaliland. (Zeilah itself stands just south of the Djibouti-Somalia border.) The Issah are a tall, handsome, aquiline race, with that high-browed look

III

often accentuated by a receding hairline. Burton describes them as fickle, irascible and warm-hearted, and observes that 'traitorous as an Eesa' is a proverb in Zeilah, 'where the people tell you that these bedouin with the left hand offer a bowl of milk and stab with the right'.

The Issah women's generous curves were the target of a Yemeni joke: 'Your hips swell like boiled rice.' The retort was to compare the slimmer haunches of the Arab women to tadpoles.

The men looked very wild, with their hair worn in long plaits and smeared with butter. This was a habit of the Ancient Gauls, of whom Rimbaud says: *'My clothes are as barbaric as theirs, but I do not butter my hair'* ['Bad Blood']. Thus the pagan past and the African present mingle in the market-place at Zeilah.

The Issah carried traditional weapons – javelins and assegai spears, swords and shields – and Rimbaud and Righas doubtless carried guns: Remingtons, typically. In his letter of 2 November, Rimbaud wrote nonchalantly of the dangers of the journey, at once scaring and reassuring his mother: 'It goes without saying that you cannot travel there unarmed, and that there is some danger of leaving your skin in the hands of the Gallas – although the danger there is no longer very great.'

Despite this last reassurance, the dangers were great enough, and just about the time that Rimbaud's caravan was leaving Zeilah, on 16 November, the news arrived that Henri Lucereau's caravan had been attacked and 'torn to pieces' by Gallas in the Itou region north-west of Harar. A Galla song says:

> 'A spear without blood is not a spear,
> Love without kisses is not love.'

It is probable that Rimbaud set off for Harar with this grim reminder of the dangers ahead of him.

Back in Aden the two events became known simultaneously, in the form of a telegram to Colonel Dubar from the French company Tramier-Lafargue at Zeilah. It read:

CARAVANE PARTIE 16. LUCEREAU ASSASSINÉ ITOUS.

On 1 December, Dubar wrote to Lucereau's brother in Chartres, sending a few sparse details of this 'unhappy event', and promising:

The first courier I receive from Harar will contain further details

Arthur Rimbaud aged seventeen. Photograph by Étienne Carjat.

Manuscript of 'Première Soirée',
Rimbaud's first published poem.

Première Soirée.

I.— Elle était fort déshabillée
Et de grands arbres indiscrets
Aux vitres jetaient leur feuillée
Malinement, tout près, tout près.

Assise sur ma grande chaise,
Mi-nue, elle joignait les mains
Sur le plancher frissonnaient d'aise
Ses petits pieds si fins, si fins.

— Je regardai, couleur de cire
Un petit rayon buissonnier
Papillonner dans son sourire
Et sur son sein, — mouche au rosier

— Je baisai ses fines chevilles.
Elle eut un doux rire brutal
Qui s'égrenait en claires trilles,
Un joli rire de cristal

Les petits pieds sous la chemise
Se sauvèrent : « Veux-tu finir ! »
La première audace permise,
Le rire feignait de punir !

— Pauvrets palpitants sous ma lèvre,
Je baisai doucement ses yeux :
Elle jeta sa tête mièvre
En arrière : « Oh ! c'est encor mieux !..

Georges Izambard.

Rimbaud in Paris, June 1872.
Sketch by Verlaine.

14 Rue Nicolet, Montmartre, scene of the first meeting with Verlaine.

Paul Verlaine.

Un Coin de Table by Henri Fantin-Latour, 1872.

Verlaine and Rimbaud in London.
Sketch by Félix Regamey.

Communard exiles in London.
Drawing by Félix Regamey.

(*Left*) First London lodgings: 34 Howland
Street. (*Above*) 8 Great College Street.

Vitalie Rimbaud.

Small ads, 1873-4.

The family farmhouse at Roche.

HUDRÉAUX EPICIER.

FICELLE.
Miel Rosat.

MELASSE.
ARTICHAUTS.

E.D.   A.R.

Rencontre.

LA MUSIQUE ADOUCIT LES MŒURS.

1ᵉ étage.

Rez de chaussée
chez le propriétaire

LES VOYAGES FORMENT LA JÜNESSE.

Grand Hôtel de l'Univers, Aden, *c.* 1905

Remains of the Grand, 1991.

(*Facing page*) Sketches of Rimbaud by
Delahaye and Verlaine, 1875-77.Clockwise
from top left: at Vitalie's funeral; in
Scandanavia; in Java; the pianist; en route to
Vienna; in Charleville, back from his travels.

The 'Maison Bardey', Arta Street, Aden, 1991.

Rimbaud's contract with Viannay, Bardey & Co, 10 November 1880.

Aden office of César Tian, Rimbaud's employer from 1888.

about this latest atrocity, but I do not expect to have any news for a month. Our last caravan [i.e. No. 3] left Zeilah on 16 November, and the return caravan will not be back on the coast before the end of December.

In his journal Bardey transcribes this letter, then tetchily adds: 'in fact our employees' – in other words, Rimbaud and Righas – 'wrote nothing at all.' This is, he adds, 'a malady peculiar to the land of Africa: it is important to cure this.'

The 'malady' he means is silence, or anyway the *ennui* and lassitude which makes people not bother to write: a prescient diagnosis of his employee's condition in Africa.

*   *   *

The precise circumstances of Rimbaud's trek from Zeilah to Harar in 1880 – his first African journey – are unrecorded. The only information Rimbaud furnishes is that it took him twenty days and that he did it on horseback. Voluble in complaints, and in the bland details of his employment, he is silent about his first experiences of the African interior, his first taste of bedouin life.

He is not entirely silent about the route itself, however. There is a brief, scrawled log-book in his hand, describing (in reverse order) the stages and the distances of the trek. This is, ironically, an account of his *last* African journey, back down from Harar to Zeilah, in 1891. A few brusque descriptions appear in this tragic document.

Fortunately, other sources help to re-create the scene. Alfred Bardey had done the same journey – up in July, down in September – and would do it again early the following year. He has left extensive descriptions of it in his journal. There is another contemporary account by Jules Borelli [*Éthiopie Méridionale*, Paris 1890], who would later travel with Rimbaud in Abyssinia; and another, nearly contemporary, by Prince Henri d'Orléans, who trekked from Djibouti to Harar in 1897, and published his 'notes and impressions of the route' [*Une Visite à l'Empereur Ménélick*, 1898]. However, his was a commodious entourage compared to Rimbaud's *gaflah*.

From these sources one can trace the precise itinerary and capture something of the flavour of Rimbaud's first trek to Harar.

The route he took can be traced on available modern maps, such as the Tactical Pilotage Chart (TPC) series, though many of the names have vanished. It runs south-west from Zeilah, across the coastal plains and into the foothills of the Harar mountains, then turns due south towards Harar itself. The trail rises from sea-level to a high-point of about 7,000 feet. It is a distance of roughly 200 miles. The journey took, in this instance, twenty days: an overall average of ten miles per day, though the early stages would be longer than the later, steeper ones. The caravan moves slowly and stops frequently; there are unforeseen delays and accidents and wrangles. In the years to come Rimbaud would do this route many times: once, on horseback and unencumbered by a caravan, he made it from Zeilah to Harar in six days. There is throughout these African years a sense of drastic physical exertion, of testing himself to the limit: a sense of extremity.

On 16 November, with the preparations complete and the permissions granted, Rimbaud's unwieldy circus – '*I alone hold the key to this savage parade*' – pulls out of Zeilah. The first stop is at the wells of Tococha, about four miles from the town. Here water is taken aboard, carried in the huge goat-skin canteens called *gherbes*, which give it a brackish, animal taste. The journey properly begins at Warumbot (Warabad on the modern map), three miles further inland. This is the trail-head: the last supplies loaded, the last straggle of vendors, the last news of what might lie ahead – and in this case, quite possibly, the first news of Lucereau's fate – and then the caravan is leaving, into the parched plains of Mandao. This name, according to Bardey, signifies '*Fou qui s'y arrête*' – only a madman stops here.

Across the far side of this desert is Dadap, the end of the first stage (or second if one includes Warumbot). The rhythm of the bedouin: travel in the cool of the evening, travel all night till dawn if necessary, but never travel in the middle of the day.

The next stage is from Dadap, via Doudouhasa (four hours) to Ensa (or Hensa). Here there are wells to refill the rancid *gherbes*. This about forty miles from Zeilah. From here they move south-west, through rocky country, via Kombavoren, to Las Mane or Lasman: a five-hour stage. This was then a Somali tax-point ('*droits de passage*'), and is probably the little border-town today called Abdul Khader, which stands at the conjunction of two roads coming out of Ethiopia.

*   *   *

These first few days cover about 100 miles of scorched, inhospitable terrain across the very northern tip of Somalia. Officially, at least, it is still part of Somalia. Actually, it is part of Somaliland, which has seceded from Somalia, but which has not yet achieved recognition as an independent state. In physical reality it is a long way from anywhere.

It was dangerous then and it was still dangerous in 1991 when I first visited the area. Literally to 'lose' your skin or your testicles was no longer very likely, but in the immediate aftermath of Somalia's ruinous, six-year civil war, you were certainly likely to lose your vehicle, your belongings, your clothes, and perhaps – in the casual, facilitating manner of these scenarios – your life. Outside the fortified compounds of the UN and the aid agencies, Northern Somalia was a badlands, the few usable roads patrolled by roaming bandits in the home-made assault cars they called 'technicals' – typically a commandeered UN land-cruiser with the roof sawn off and a rocket-launcher poking out.

The fear of the savage 'raid' is replaced by the fear of the road-block, which may be soldiers or may be *shifta* – bandits – and which either way would feature jumpy Somali teenagers loosely cradling the Kalashnikovs which at that time seemed cheaper and easier to acquire than a pound of *dourah* wheat.

The route Rimbaud travelled is no longer used because Zeilah is no longer a port of any consequence. It was marginalized by the construction of the Addis–Djibouti railroad early this century. From 3,000 ft up in a United Nations Cessna – as near as I was able to get, or anyway as near as I was prepared to get in the interests of literature – one sees the occasional straight line of a track which may or may not be the remains of the old camel-trail. The landscape is, of course, quite unchanged: an unremitting vista of sand and rock and thorn-trees and dried-up watercourses. November, when Rimbaud travelled, is deep in the dry season.

The land is salt-stained towards the sea, then a dull tawny brown like cured camel-hide, and then the first ridging and bumping of the mountains.

Now the trail begins to rise. The route enters the region known as Samadou, the 'black country', with its dark volcanic soil. The caravan trudges on, passing through Arrouina, which Bardey describes as 'the territory of the Ouardik', and then arrives at the long-awaited oasis of Biokobobo.

Biokobobo is considered the halfway stage of the journey, with 'excellent water' and an *oued* or wadi to swim in: a full rest-stop for two or three days. The mountains around Harar are now visible to the south: twin peaks. The city lies between them, but is still invisible. Biokobobo is the point marked on the Tactical Pilotage Chart as the Kobe Crossing, altitude 3,200 ft, just below the northern dog-leg of the Ethiopia-Somaliland border. It is now just across the Ethiopian side of the border, though the borderline is an arbitrary one, and the people are predominantly Somali.

From Biokobobo the route follows down along the line of the present road from Aysha to Dire Dawa (this is the longer and less-used road which lies to the south of the main road: the latter follows the railway line.) This was a difficult stretch for the *caravanier*. Water supplies were very uncertain. The caravan passes through Ali Bini (three hours), crosses the plain of Dahelimale to the village of Cotto. The countryside here, Rimbaud noted in 1891, is 'covered with scrub'. At Cotto they rest a couple of days, then press on. The caravan skirts a hill of about 3,600 ft called Ouordji (or Wordji), passes a mosquito-infested river near Boussa, and arrives at Gueldessah.

The transition from the desiccated lowlands of the Somal to the relative cool and fertility of the hills is – as transitions in altitude so often are – an exciting one. The uplands are now mostly inside the Ethiopian border, and can be travelled by jeep. You pass through a wide, spacious, high-plains landscape. It is brown and arid in December but magically sprinkled with green after the first rains of April or May. The road is long and straight; outcrops of rock in the distance, and round, humpy mountains further off: the Harar massif.

Figures in the landscape, intermittently: farmers turning up the dark soil. They work long, thin strips of land with a medieval-looking plough pulled by an ox (or, once, an ox and a donkey). The tall, thin walkers, striding easily, carry their walking-staff horizontal across their shoulders and their arms crooked loosely over it. The women are wrapped in light, flowing, gauze-like robes: vivid yellows and blues and reds.

Scattered across the plains are the typical dwelling of the Somali herdsmen, the *akal*. This is basically a bender, a rounded hump of skins and rugs layered over a makeshift wooden frame, and nowadays typically topped off with a UN-issue blue polythene sheet. It is a movable house, its materials easily transportable on the back of a camel: these are nomads, or as Rimbaud would say, *bedouin*.

There are a few villages, and some isolated farms with an air of permanence – a dry-stone wall topped off with a palissade of branches; a spiky boundary hedge of *holcus* – but mostly there is just this light scattering of *akal*, in groups that seem to have just landed, to have dropped down noiselessly into the low furze of thorn-trees. The herds browse – goats and the curious black-faced Somali sheep with scruffy, platypus-shaped tails. The bright clothes are spread to dry on the bushes.

There is a profound sense of the pastoral here: a medieval world of strip-farmers and wayfarers. In the Save the Children jeep a voluble man called Lucio – half-Italian, half-Amharic – discusses the local economy. The price of a camel has virtually doubled in the last three years. A mature camel sells now for 3,000 birr, and a youngster for up to 1,500.

And then there comes the true tribal border. 'I am here in the country of the Gallas', writes Rimbaud on his arrival in Harar, and there is indeed a definable point where the 'country of the Gallas' – or, as they are now called, the Oromo – begins. The humped forms of the *akal* give way to the very different houses of the settled Oromo. These are circular in shape, built of wood and mud adobe, with a graceful, conical cupola of woven straw above, coming to a point where the high-angled rafters come through and, typically, a brightly coloured pot or two hang there, crowning the apex like a star on a Christmas tree.

*   *   *

On the old camel-trail from Zeilah in 1880 you passed this tribal frontier around Gueldessah (or Jeldesa), at the foot of the Harar massif. The western direction of the road would carry them on towards Dire Dawa (then a tiny speck of a village, now Ethiopia's second city) and thence across the Awash river to Abyssinia. For Harar they now turn due south and begin the arduous climb into the mountains.

Now the trail rises steeply to Ballouah and Egon. From here, at 7,500 ft – 'Haut Egon' as Rimbaud calls it – you look back over the vast Somali plain. In the rains there are marshes around Egon, but on this first journey, in December, the land would be drier.

The summit is reached at Kombolcha, and now at last the destination becomes visible: the great lake at Alem Maya to the west, and due south below them, secretively cupped in a wide, fertile valley, the city of Harar: the brown rind of the town-walls around it, built of mud and packed rubble; the dusty huddle of roofs and minarets; the valley dropping away the other side, with neat plots of coffee and *dourah*; and high above, the ever-present kites, wheeling over the city like scraps of charred paper over a bonfire.

The trail winds down gently, and the weary *caravanier* reaches the northern wall of the city, and the Zeilah Gate.

One thinks of the closing sequence of the *Season in Hell* – 'armed with an ardent patience we will enter splendid cities' – and one listens instead to the clipped bulletin of his first letter from Harar, 13 December 1880:

> I have arrived here after twenty days on horseback across the Somali desert. Harar is a town colonized by the Egyptians, and under control of their government. The garrison is several thousand strong. Here is our branch-office and our warehouse. The trading produce of the region is coffee, ivory, perfumes, gold, etc. The land is elevated but not infertile. The climate is cool, and not unhealthy. All the merchandise from Europe is brought up here by camel.

He concludes this brief description with a laconic foretaste of his long years in Harar: 'Anyway, there's plenty to do here.'

10

HARAR

THE ZEILAH GATE is not so much a gate as a massive door set into the town wall, approximately flush with its rubbled surface. It is reminiscent of a medieval college gate in Cambridge, or a cathedral door, or a fortified manor-house. It has the same thickness and darkness of wood, the same misshapen nail-heads, the same comfortable sag away from the perpendicular. It suggests a certain kind of enclosing; monastic as much as strategic. The huddle of dwellings around the gate also has – despite the tin roofs – a medieval look.

The Zeilah Gate is known more grandly as Bab El F'touh, the Gate of Conquest. This commemorates the Islamic *jihad* waged by a sixteenth-century emir of Harar, Ahmed Gragne (Ahmed the left-handed), who marched out through this gate to attack the Christian highlands of Abyssinia. The Harari name of the gate is Asum Beri: 'Asum' is Axum, the old capital of Abyssinia.

Outside the gate are knots of people, some in transit around the walls, some entering the gate, and some lounging and gossiping around the key figures of the scene: a barber, plying his cut-throat trade in a yellow corduroy cap; and a grinder turning his noisy wheel with a pedal. The barber's mirror reflects black faces and feathery vivid foliage, and women with their faces half-hidden by saffron-yellow saris.

The man being shaved is a Harari tailor called Hussein, a gentle, grizzled man in his fifties. He used to live in the village of Kombolcha, he tells me. This village, above Harar on the Egon plateau, was the final stage of the journey from Zeilah: the place where Rimbaud first looked down on Harar. He had a small sewing-shop there, but had to abandon it during the Ethiopia–Somalia war of the late 1970s. He lost everything. 'Everything was taken out from my shop – sewing machines, everything, taken out by the soldiers.' He came to Harar. He arrived here, at this gate, on foot.

'I came with empty pockets,' he says. 'Without anything.'

Through the gate a narrow, curving, upward-sloping street leads to the main square, now called Makonnen Square. There are goats, and horse-carts with car tyres that hiss over the cobbles, and undulating balconies, and the sudden smell of peppery cooking, and two men examining a rooster who has the unmistakable demeanour of a cockpit veteran.

It was up this street that Rimbaud came, on or about 6 December 1880. So, at any rate, one assumes from the parallel of Bardey, who states that he entered Harar by the Bab el F'touh, or Zeilah Gate, and thence passed into the 'wide upper square' of the town.

*　　*　　*

Harar – pronounced 'Harra', with the stress on the first syllable and a thin Arabic trill on the 'r' – is not quite a 'splendid' city, but it is certainly a very special one. It retains a strangely secretive aura: a sense of isolation. It is easier to get there now than it was in 1880, but still not very easy.

Founded in the twelfth century by Arabs from across the Red Sea, Harar was from the first a Muslim enclave: part fortress, part market-town. Politically it was an independent emirate, or city-state. The emirs of Harar held sway over a large and fertile province, Hararghe, and its peaceable agricultural inhabitants, the Galla or Oromo. The emir also controlled the caravan route between the coast and the Abyssinian interior. The city prospered on a rich trade in coffee and slaves. Medieval Harar, wrote Evelyn Waugh,

> . . . differed little from the other Moslem Sultanates which once covered the African coast and trade-routes . . . [It] had its shrine which formed a centre of pilgrimage; its market where goods of exotic value were displayed; a place of riches and security which easily became a splendid legend among the surrounding barbarians. Even in 1935, after a generation of Abyssinian misrule and Indian and Levantine immigration, it retained something of the gracious fragrance of Fez or Meknes [*Waugh in Abyssinia*, pp. 85–6].

The city is fiercely Islamic: an outpost of the faith in Africa. It is considered the fourth most holy city in Islam (after Mecca, Medina and Cairo) and has a disproportionate number of mosques within its compact ground-area – ninety-nine traditionally, cognate with the ninety-nine names of Allah; eighty or so according to those who have tried to count them. The Grand Mosque, with twin towers and slender minaret, dates from the sixteenth century, the time of Ahmed Gragne.

For centuries Harar was closed to outsiders, particularly to Christians. Richard Burton claims to be the first European to have entered its gates: he did so in 1855. His first description of the city:

> Harar is about one mile long by half that breadth. An irregular wall, lately repaired but ignorant of cannon, is pierced with five large gates, and supported by oval towers of artless construction. The material of the houses and defences is rough stones, the granites and sandstones of the hills, cemented, like the ancient Galla cities, with clay. . . . The streets are narrow lanes, up hill and down dale, strewed with gigantic rubbish heaps, upon which repose packs of mangy one-eyed dogs; and even the best are encumbered with rocks and stones. The habitations are mostly long, flat-roofed sheds, double-storeyed, with doors composed of a single plank, and holes for windows pierced high above the ground, and decorated with miserable woodwork.

Much has changed since then – two new gates; a scattering of ornate, turn-of-the-century, Indian-influenced villas; the Ras's palace; the Christian church erected by King Menelik; the sprawl of extramural tin-roof suburbs – but the heart of the city is unchanged, with its steep, rocky little alleys twisting between secretive courtyards and ramshackle sheds. (Burton's disparaging tone, Waugh points out, was partly expedient. The poor condition of the place enhanced the case for a British takeover.)

The town today has a population of about 65,000. It is the third largest town in Ethiopia, and the capital of Hararghe, the largest of the seven administrative regions into which modern Ethiopia is split. But Harar is a capital that feels like a large, cramped village. It has an inward and secluded feel. News moves around fast, and foreigners – or *ferenji* – are still to some extent news.

Ferenji! Ferenji! You hear this word spoken as you pass: not unkindly. Rimbaud doubtless heard it often enough. He uses the word himself – '*Frangui*' – of another French trader.

Harar has spilled out of its walls, but they are still the defining structure of the place: entering and leaving, intramural and extramural, the sense of enclosure within and immensities without. There are seven gates now, two more than in Burton's and Rimbaud's day. In this higgledy-piggledy town they are vital for your orientation; it is not entirely helpful that each of them has several names. The most impressive of the old gates is the west-facing Shoa Gate, the entry-point for produce from the Abyssinian highlands. It is also called Bab el Nasri, the Gate of the Christians. It has a fine arch with Arabic designs and some later Turkish alterations, and a large market outside it which used to be the extra-mural 'Christian market'.

The southerly gate is, confusingly, called Bab el Salaam (the Gate of Health) in Arabic but Buda Ber (the Gate of the Evil Eye) in Amharic. The former name refers to its strategic position: 'health' meaning the safety of the citizens. The 'evil eye' (Hussein explained) refers to a former market for pots and tools and ornaments that was here. The tinker's arts of smelting and fireworking were traditionally associated with magic, hence the gate's name. The sun beats down on this southerly gate, and can also seem to be an evil eye.

To the south-east is Suktat Beri, in the Somali quarter of the town. This gate leads up from the cattle-plains of the Ogaden, and is also called Senga Beri, the Gate of Bulls. The eastern gate is the Erar Beri, the Erar Gate, referring to the Erar river; or the Argo Beri, referring to the Argobba whose mountain villages lie to the east. To the north is the Zeilah Gate.

Rimbaud knew every one of these gates, and the trails and lands and peoples onto which they opened.

*   *   *

The people of Harar are the Harari or – their own name – the Adari (the stress is again on the first syllable). They claim descent from Arab and Persian settlers and consider themselves a more ancient lineage than the Galla or Oromo, whose origin is Bantu.

The Adari are reserved, independent, oblique. Their skin is dark coffee, their hair tightly curled. They have a rounder face than the Amhara, whom they resemble more than they do the Oromo. They have their own language, originally spoken only in and around Harar. Adari is a Semitic language derived from Ge'ez. (Ge'ez or Ghiz is the ancient literary and ecclesiastic language of Axum, which is also the basis of Amharic.) It contains a strong mix of Galla and Somali, both in vocabulary and structure, and is also said to have affinities with Armenian.

It was once true to say that Adari was spoken only within the walls of Harar, I was told, but now it is spoken in parts of Addis Ababa, and in Chicago and California and Australia as well.

There is a small corpus of printed literature in Adari. It uses the Arabic alphabet, and consists mostly of Muslim law-texts, and some religious poetry and prose. Among the traditional Adari skills – now almost extinct – was bookbinding. It may have been a work of Adari scholarship which Rimbaud and Bardey were discussing in 1883:

> I am going to get *The Famous Abyssinian Campaign of Ahmed Guirane* [i.e. Gragne] translated, as well as the *Calendar*, which is definitely Persian though written in Arabic ... [Bardey to Rimbaud, 24 July 1883]

> Would you like some other Harar curiosities? *The History of Ahmed Guirane* has a second volume, I'm told, more interesting than the first, geographically speaking. [Rimbaud to Bardey, 26 August 1883]

The 'Ethiopianization' of Harar – or more specifically the 'Amharization' of Harar: the Amhara being the dominant ethnic group of Ethiopia, and Amharic the official language – began with the conquest of the city by King Menelik II in 1887, but has only really taken root in the last few decades. One who has observed it at first hand is the redoubtable Richard Pankhurst, the son of Sylvia and the great-nephew of Emily Pankhurst. This frail-seeming figure, professorial in an old-style, gentleman-scholar mould, has lived in Ethiopia for thirty years, through the decline and fall of Haile Selassie, through the grim era of General Mengistu's regime – the 'Derg' – and through the long, famine-struck years of war that finally ousted him in 1990. He is a leading authority on the history of Harar. Despite the Amharization, he told me, the traditional ethnic distinctions of the city remain much the same:

> The Adari were coffee-planters, land-owners, the growers of *chat*; or they were urban people, traders. The Oromo were tenant farmers, not owning their land. At first they were serfs, then tenants. They had to give in their spears at the gate before

entering the city. This relationship remains broadly true, though now there are some Oromo landlords with Amhara tenants.

Harar also had its own coinage. The old Harari currency was the mahalek. The earliest surviving coins have the date AD 1240. This was a time when the rest of Ethiopia functioned on a primitive barter-system involving cloth, iron and bars of Danakil salt. The mahalek was minted well into the seventeenth century. 'This is a measure of Harar as a great trading community,' says Dr Pankhurst. 'They are producing their own coins. This is not found anywhere else in Ethiopia.'

Bardey mentions these 'little white coins' – 'minuscule roundels of metal stamped with the seal of the last emir of Harar'. They are 'hardly bigger than sequins [*paillettes*]'. He notes the exchange rate of 1880: sixteen to the Egyptian piastre and three hundred to the thaler [BA, p. 143].

At the time of Rimbaud's arrival the chief trading coin throughout the Horn of Africa was the *talari*, in other words the Maria Theresa thaler or dollar. First struck in 1760, these Austro-Hungarian dollars swiftly became the currency of the region. They were used for buying mules and slaves, and for weighing gold and medicines. They were still legal tender when Evelyn Waugh was here in the 1930s.

Today you may buy Maria Theresa dollars from street-hawkers and curio-shops throughout the Horn. They are large, robust silver coins, with the dumpy, ringleted features of the Holy Roman Empress Maria Theresa on one side, and the imperial double-eagle crest on the other. She was the daughter of Emperor Charles VI and the mother of Marie-Antoinette. The rubrics

Obverse, R.IMP.HU.BO.REG.M.THERESIA.D.G;
Reverse, ARCHD.AUST.DUX.BURG.CO.TYR.1780.X

allude to her as Empress of Rome, Queen of Hungary and Bohemia, Archduchess of Austria, Duchess of Burgundy and Countess of Tyrol. The street sellers hurl the coins to the sidewalk to show that they are genuine massy silver rather than fakes, though what particular timbre is meant to show this I don't know. It's another language one doesn't understand.

There is a sense of solidity and tactility in this new métier that Rimbaud has taken: silver thalers and sequin-sized mahaleks;

fraslehs of ivory, *okietes* of musk, *daboulahs* of coffee; gold and salt and cloth: 'everything passes through my hands.'

*   *   *

The conquest of Harar by the Egyptians under Raouf Pasha, in 1874, opened the city up to European trade. Bardey and his assistant Pinchard were probably the first Frenchmen to set foot in the city, in August 1880, closely followed by Rimbaud at the end of the year. There was already a sizeable contingent of Greeks and Armenians. Bardey mentions various Greek traders who own little stores around the market place: they came in with the Egyptian troops, he says, and remained as the suppliers of the Egyptian garrison, about 4,000 strong. He names the three Moussaya brothers, and also the Caralambo, the Manoli and the Sotiro families. One of the Sotiros became a close associate of Rimbaud: a man he liked, a man he travelled with, one of his enduring friendships during the African years. Dr Pankhurst told me that in Harar in the 1960s he had lived next door to an elderly Greek called Magdalenos, whose father had come to Harar when Rimbaud was here.

Politically annexed by Menelik in the mid-1880s, Harar also lost much of its strategic importance as a trading post with the opening of the trans-Ethiopian railway in 1924. This established a direct link between the Abyssinian highlands and the Red Sea which by-passed Harar. It became a tangent rather than a transit-point.

The twentieth century has brought a trickle of diluting foreign influences – the Indian military academy set up by Haile Selassie, the French-run *leprosarium*, the Italian quarter built outside the walls during Mussolini's occupation of Ethiopia; and then the modern influx of aid agencies, contract teachers and UN wallahs.

In the early 1960s Harar had a population of about 35,000. Thirty years later it is nearly twice that, but this is a slow, semi-stagnant growth compared to other East African towns. The outside world is still that: something outside. The twentieth century leaves its amenities and preoccupations at the town gates, as the Galla once left their spears. Harar is one of those places where the foreigner feels even more foreign than usual – even people from Addis Ababa feel like foreigners here.

Perversely, the perpetual foreigner Arthur Rimbaud made the place his home.

11

BET RIMBO

THE SIGHTSEER IN Harar has a limited itinerary. There are the mosques and a couple of museums; the ugly monument to Ras Makonnen with its panoramic view. There is the Hyena Man, of whom more later. And there is the house which is called 'Bet Rimbo', the 'Rimbaud House'.

It is a large, handsome, picturesquely dilapidated house surrounded by a walled courtyard. It has a long verandah in front of the ground floor, and the remains of a finely decorated wooden façade above. The design of the frontage shows a mélange of styles – Gothic-shaped windows, two tall gables, latticed shuttering. The latter is reminiscent of the Grand Hotel in Aden, and suggests an Indian influence, perhaps Gujarati, though there are also elements of Turkish and Egyptian styles. (I am reminded of the summer-houses or *kosk* one sees on the islands off Istanbul: a style one might describe as 'Ottoman Gingerbread'.) A smaller second storey sits on top of the house: a kind of solarium. This has a single gable which rises up between the other two. The overall effect is of a complex sort of chalet.

Inside, the rooms are tall and airy. On the upper floor there are naïve murals suggestive of Indian life, and panes of coloured glass which give a curious filtered light – I think of that evening light like a 'burning aquarium' in the *Illuminations*.

It is a house steeped in atmosphere, a forlorn mansion absolutely fit for the pacings and mutterings of the exiled poet, and as one enters its crudely patched-up portals it is easy to forget – or anyway to suspend – the inconvenient fact of the matter, which is that Rimbaud almost certainly never lived here.

The first problem is the date of the house. There is some evidence that the house dates from the early 1900s: in other words, that it was built after Rimbaud's death. This is not based on any documentation, but on the observation that the beams on the ground floor seem to be made from railway sleepers. These, it is said, would be surplus sleepers left over from the construction of the Addis–Djibouti railway line. The railroad did not reach Dire Dawa (the nearest point to Harar) until 1902, eleven years after Rimbaud left Africa.

This is not, perhaps, as conclusive as the sceptics make out. The beams do look like sleepers, but even if they are, they might have arrived in Harar earlier than 1902. The main problem with the Bet Rimbo is that it is at odds with all the written evidence about Rimbaud's domiciles in Harar.

*   *   *

Between 1880 and 1891 Rimbaud lived in Harar over three distinct periods, lasting altogether about five years. The biographers are generally rather confused about exactly where he lived. Most of them have never been to Harar, though coming here does not exactly dispel the confusion. Some of it, at least, can be clarified by a careful reading of the available sources: principally the Bardey memoirs, and also some other reminiscences. There are at least three identifiable houses that Rimbaud lived in – textually identifiable, that is – and none of them is the Bet Rimbo.

The first house is for some reason entirely ignored by his biographers, though it is clearly described by Bardey in his journal of his first visit to Harar in 1880.

Bardey arrived, together with his assistant Pinchard, on 22 August 1880. They entered by the Bab el F'touh or Zeilah Gate; they paid their respects to the Egyptian governor-general, Nadi Pasha; and later that evening they were conducted to a house that had been 'reserved' for them. From the 'large upper square' or *'maidan'* (parade ground) which they had first entered – these are Bardey's descriptions of Makonnen Square – they take the south-running street which 'descends steeply towards the lower town', and arrive at the chief market-place of Harar, the Faras Maghala (literally 'horse market'). Down the first street to the right off Faras Maghala, they are shown into a courtyard with a low, mud-walled house at the end of it. This is the house 'reserved' for them. Bardey describes it as follows:

It has only two rooms, each lit by a window barred with pieces of

127

wood. Its walls are a rough clay [*pise*] of rubble packed with mud. The ceiling is formed of unseasoned and ill-fitting posts, like beams, supporting a thatch of reed-stalks covered with earth . . .

In each of the rooms is a single *angareb*, a simple bed consisting of a wooden frame over which is stretched, in Bardey's punctilious description, 'a trellis formed of strips of uncured leather'. This is the only furniture.

Bardey sums the place up, stoically enough, as '*sommaire mais satisfaisant*' – basic but satisfactory.

They dine that night with a jovial trio of Greeks, the Moussaya brothers, who tell them something else about their new residence:

They warn us that our house is very close to the meat-market, which is also the slaughterhouse, and it is therefore prudent to keep our doors shut, otherwise the hyenas, who are the town's sanitation service, might pay us a visit.

It was at this house that Bardey and Pinchard first set up their *installation* or depot. It was at this house that Bardey left Pinchard, in September 1880, when he returned to Aden and to his first rendezvous with Rimbaud. And it was almost certainly at this house that Rimbaud arrived, in December 1880, 'after twenty days on horseback'.

The house, a primitive local construction, has disappeared, or been modified out of recognition. One can find the street, or at least the most likely street in the tangle of alleys leading off the Faras Maghala, but there is no clue to the exact whereabouts of the house, nor of the erstwhile abattoir. It was certainly not the Bet Rimbo. It is an entirely different kind of house; and it was located, judging from Bardey's directions, on the south side of the Faras Maghala, the opposite side from the alleged Rimbaud House.

*　　*　　*

Sometime after Rimbaud's arrival, probably early in 1881, the company took over a much grander residence. The earliest mention of it in Bardey's journal is at the end of March 1881. On 31 March he was at Zeilah, about to travel back up to Harar with one of his partners, Pierre Mazaran. There he met the governor, Nadi Pasha, on his way down from Harar, en route for Egypt. At this meeting [BA, p. 262], the pasha told him that permission had been granted for the company to occupy 'the building provisionally occupied by Pinchard'.

Thus Pinchard – and with him, Rimbaud – had 'provisionally occupied' these new premises sometime in or before March 1881, but judging from this first mention of it, not that long before.

This house had been built in the 1870s by the first Egyptian governor of Harar, Raouf Pasha, as his residence. It was the most modern and impressive building in town. Bardey says:

> Raouf Pasha's house, the only one with an upper storey, faces the large upper square of the town. A high enclosing wall runs along the road which goes up from the Bab El F'touh. A single entrance gives access to a large courtyard.

This pinpoints its location precisely. It stood on the north side of Makonnen Square, next to the street leading to the Zeilah Gate. Other passages in Bardey's journal confirm this. When he first arrived in Harar in 1880, entering the square from the Zeilah Gate, he had on his left a 'great mosque', and 'on the right a square house with an upper storey'. By 'square' [*carré*] he means in the European style, rather than the conical structures of the natives Galla *guimbi* or *tukal*. This is clearly the Roauf Pasha house, though Bardey does not name it, or indeed know it, at this point. A later entry, in mid-1883, speaks of 'passing the *medine* i.e. *maidan* or parade ground) on the large square, where our offices occupy one side and the barracks another' [BA, p. 286].

This house, in which Rimbaud lived and worked in 1881, and again during his second spell in Harar in 1883–84, is no longer there. It was demolished early this century by the Ras (or Duke) of Harar, Lij Yassou, a grandson of King Menelik. He intended to build a hotel in its place, though the project was abandoned. Another, unremarkable building was subsequently built on the site. In the early 1970s, when the British traveller Duncan Forbes was here, it was a cinema. It is now a bar or saloon, blue-painted, where the people gather to play dominoes and drink Bedele beer and watch the perpetual *passagiato* of the square.

The 'great mosque' mentioned by Bardey is also gone. It is now the chief Christian church of Harar: the Medhane Aleme. This was built by King Menelik after his conquest of Harar in 1887. The chronicles recount his entry into the city:

> After exchanges of civility with the Emir, such as 'You are a son of a bitch' and 'You are the son of twelve fathers', Menelik II climbed upon the minaret of the Great Mosque in order to piss over it, in the presence of a shocked crowd. He thus accomplished a promise he had made, but he also knew the importance of such an action.

The shape of the church mimics that of the demolished mosque.

The house is gone but one can take a ghostly tour of the premises with the aid of Bardey's journal. You go in through the 'single entrance' in the outer wall. This opens into a large courtyard. In the left-hand corner of the courtyard is a rough staircase running up to the first-floor terrace. To enter the house itself you must go through another, smaller gate. This leads into the garden, in which there are two citron trees and 'some herbs and vegetables of the region'. 'All the doors open onto the garden,' Bardey notes. 'The house has been constructed in such a way as to give its inhabitants no communication with the exterior.' The windows are small and without panes. They are furnished with strong wooden bars, and with shutters made from old packing cases.

You enter the house via a 'square room entirely open at the front' which serves as 'a kind of porch'. Its ceiling is of mud and wattle. Among the beams 'numerous red birds flutter around hardly noticed by the people'.

A flight of scarlet pigeons thunders around my thoughts . . .

Three doors lead off this porch, one to the left and two to the right. The ground floor was the warehouse, the office: *le magasin*. Upstairs was where they lived. Bardey is most precise: 'Arthur Rimbaud and Constantin Righas live on the first floor, lit by two windows, the only ones with a view of the square. The room is furnished in the native style, which is how they like it.'

In a later letter to Berrichon [16 July 1897] Bardey adds that Rimbaud sometimes 'slept in the midst of the merchandise' that he bought: this included animal skins, which were 'not always very healthy'. He had, it seems, an actual preference for sleeping rough.

There are two surviving photographs of the house, not entirely reconcilable with one another. One shows only a part of the frontage. The lower floor is of packed rubble, the upper covered with rough plaster. To the right, a pair of stone steps. The photo is obviously later than Rimbaud's time – the windows do have panes, though most of them are broken; and the awning-like roof over the doorway shows through a magnifying glass the familiar undulations of corrugated tin.

There are four upper windows shown. The middle two are close together. Is this the room 'lit by two windows' where Rimbaud and Righas slept?

Another photograph, of mysterious provenance, shows the whole house, clearly taken from the garden. This has different features from the photograph described above – a covered first-floor balcony, dissimilar windows, etc. – but it is possible they show the same house at different times. (It is also possible that neither shows the house, as one doesn't know the circumstances of the attribution.)

One of Rimbaud's self-portraits shows him leaning on a balcony: he describes it as a picture of 'me standing on a terrace of the house'. Nothing other than the rickety balcony is visible, however.

*   *   *

The third house associated with Rimbaud is as elusive as the others, but it is possible it is still there. This is the house he lived in during his last and longest sojourn in Harar, from 1888 to 1891. (He definitely did not live in the Raouf Pasha mansion during this period; the Bardeys were no longer trading in Harar, and the house had returned to official use.)

The descriptions of this house are vague. In 1930 the French missionary André Jarosseau, Bishop of Harar, recalled that Rimbaud had lived his last days here in 'a little house in the square'. The trader Armand Savouré, who spent a month as Rimbaud's guest in 1888, left this piquant description:

> quite a nice [*assez bonne*] house, but no furniture. I had nothing to sleep on but my camp-bed from the journey, and during the whole month I never found out where he slept, only seeing him writing, day and night, at a makeshift table. [letter to Georges Maurevert, 1930]

This is wonderful, but unhelpful as to the house itself. Rimbaud's Italian friend Ottorino Rosa published what purports to be a photograph of the house – or part of it – in his book about Ethiopia,

L'Impero del Leone di Giuda, published in 1913. The photo's principal subject is an ostrich, but in a later manuscript Rosa states that the house in the background, 'with the wide roof', is the one Rimbaud lived in during his last years in Harar. Nothing in the photograph serves to identify it, however. It is just a part of an unnamed street, and is only in the shot at all because an ostrich happened to be standing in front of it.

Rosa says the house was later demolished. Against this one places the indefatigable researches of a French Capuchin missionary, Père Émile Foucher, who devoted more than thirty years of study to the subject of Rimbaud in Harar. He died in 1993 with little of his work published; it is my great regret that I arrived in Harar too late to meet him. Father Émile believed he had found Rimbaud's last house in Harar. 'People say' – he told the British writer Philip Marsden-Smedley – that in about 1888 Rimbaud purchased a house from a local land-owner named Garad Mohammad Nagaya. The house lay to the south of the upper square, close to the *guebi* of Ras Makonnen. Makonnen was the Abyssinian governor of the city, installed by King Menelik: Rimbaud dealt closely and amicably with him.

The Ras's palace was rebuilt in the 1930s – it is acidly described by Evelyn Waugh as a 'white, bow-fronted, castellated European thing like a south coast hotel'. It now houses the local Ministry of Culture, and a lugubrious museum. (Among the exhibits I was shown here was a pair of Afar sandals. They were cunningly shaped so that any tracks they left in the desert sands might be going in either direction. I thought Rimbaud would appreciate these shoes designed to baffle the follower of footsteps.)

With the help of the museum staff I found the house which Father Émile had pinpointed as Rimbaud's. It is a low L-shaped building between the palace and the Shoa Gate: a rough courtyard, a few dogs, goats, chickens. It is just about close enough to Makonnen Square to tally with Mgr Jarosseau's description, 'a little house in the square' (though it cannot, of course, tally with Rosa's statement that the house was demolished sometime before 1930). Two families live here now, at either extreme of the 'L'. The rooms in the middle are disused; the doors open onto scrub and rubble; the land slopes down steeply behind the house.

The utter simplicity of the place is moving, as an *idea* of Rimbaud's total severance from European norms of style and comfort, but the identification of the house as his is still tenuous. If Rimbaud had bought the house, he would have dealt with the local Sharia court, which oversaw all land transactions. The court records – available on microfilm at the Institute of Ethiopian Studies in Addis Ababa – contain no trace of any purchase by him, though it is true the records for these years (1888–1891, or 1303–06 in the Hejira calendar) are extremely patchy due to the Abyssinian occupation and also the famine at this time.

* * *

These houses are ghostly edifices, only faintly recoverable from fragments of evidence, much of it contradictory. But one thing at least is certain, which is that none of them is the Bet Rimbo or Rimbaud House to which the tourist is now led. Nothing corresponds in size, design or location except in this very general sense: that Raouf Pasha's house was a large fancy house on the northern side of the 'upper square'; and the Bet Rimbo is a large fancy house on the northern side of the market square or Faras Maghala. A process of transposition has taken place. The Bet Rimbo approximates to the 'real' Rimbaud House – or one of them – and has the signal advantage of still standing.

The Bet Rimbo is a substitute. It is the kind of house a famous European *ought* to have lived in during his time in Harar. It is an accommodation between the local guide and the credulous visitor, a deft short-changing, but it is also an accommodation between the historical opacity of Rimbaud and one's desire to see and touch something of his presence here, and somehow one feels profoundly grateful, as well as sceptical, as one stumbles up the steps beneath the twisty scaffolding that covers the frontage. This is Harar's version of Rimbaud, which is certainly worth something.

In the rooms on the right-hand side of the building lives a woman called Sunait. She is Amhara, a Christian, a single mother. She moves heavily: a slight disability that gives her a rolling gait. She is familiar with the name of Rimbaud, and with the *ferenji* who appear from time to time enunciating it. She invites us in.

In the tall central room, the *salon*, with its faded vaguely olive-green walls, there is a group of people seated on the floor, studiously chewing leaves of the stimulant *khat* (or *chat*, as it is pronounced here in Ethiopia).

Her family has lived here for forty years, she says. Now there is talk of turning the house into a museum. She is worried about eviction, but does not think it will happen. She gives us *gulban*, a kind of wheat mash made for Easter; she makes us coffee – the elaborate Amharic ritual, fragrant with frankincense – and toasts popcorn.

She shows me an old chest which I gather she's saying was 'made by Rimbaud'.

'*Oreegeenal.*'

She gestures to me to open it. I scuffle pointlessly through musty clothes in a drawer lined with yellowing Amharic newsprint.

The house may not be 'genuine' – as we like to put it – but one feels here a rapport that is not history so much as a kind of quotidian recurrence: the roasting coffee, the somnolent vigil of the *khat* chewers, the washing strung on the verandah, the children out in the rubbled courtyard, and the old Faras Maghala down below, where beautiful Galla women with faces smeared with ochre paste walk bent beneath fardels of firewood.

From those festive-coloured upstairs windows the sounds of the town come floating up – shouts from the market, a radio playing, the sound of hoofs on the stones of the street – and looking out over the roofs and minarets, across the green-striped valley floor to the distant ring of brown hills, you have as always in Harar that sense of immense and pitiless spaces surrounding this close-packed, drought-ridden city: that sense of being imprisoned by so much space.

As darkness falls, a straggle of people assembles on some waste-ground below the Zeilah Gate, where the 'hyena man' prepares his nightly ministrations. The hyenas of Harar no longer gorge on human corpses dumped outside the city walls, but there are still plenty around, and they are fed nightly by a wild-eyed, half-drunken man called Girma. (There have been other hyena men before him, though the post is not the hereditary dignity that some imply.) The scene is lit by headlights – aid workers' land-cruisers, tourist jeeps. Girma begins to call, a long, hoarse, wailing shout, vaguely reminiscent of the hollers in an early Rhythm & Blues record, and soon one sees them mustering furtively in the shadow of the town-walls.

He calls their names: 'Whisky! Mimi!'

There are perhaps a dozen: scruffy-looking creatures, Skid Row curs. They lurk on the edge of the light, whining and sniggering, inching closer to the heavy hanks of half-rotten meat which he whirls and tosses towards them. He calls again: 'Mola! Sherimot! Jayla!' (The latter two names, I later learned, translate as 'Tart' and 'Penis'.) Eventually one of them, Mimi, whom he cajoles in a tone of raucous tenderness, is there up close, and one is invited to step into the dusty spotlight, and to grip the proffered carcass, and to brace oneself against the unexpected force of the creature's thickly muscled shoulders and flesh-tearing teeth.

It is just a show for the tourists, like the Bet Rimbo itself, but the air is for a moment filled with the strange menacing music of the hyenas which Rimbaud heard, so often, lying awake through the long curfewed nights.

12

DOGS & BANDITS

INSTALLED AT HARAR in December 1880, in that first 'basic but
satisfactory' house between the market-place and the slaughterhouse, Rimbaud is immersed in the harsh pungencies of African
life. His first letters tell us nothing of what he saw and smelt. The
stench is reduced and refined into a bitter epitome of life's miseries:
'The main trade here is in skins: the animals are worked all their
lives then flayed afterwards' [15 February 1881].

His chief acquaintances at this time are the two Europeans
working with him at the Bardey depot: the manager Pinchard, under
whose orders he is; and his Greek colleague Constantin Righas, with
whom he travelled up from Zeilah.

Pinchard is not mentioned once in Rimbaud's correspondence
from Harar. He emerges in some colour from Bardey's journals,
though we do not learn his forename, only his initial, D. Bardey
describes him as a 'former junior officer in the colonial forces
[tirailleurs]'. He had served for some while in Algeria – like
Rimbaud's father – and spoke Arabic 'sufficiently'. Bardey first met
him in Aden, at the Grand Hotel: he was then working as a
coastguard at Cape Guardafui, on the tip of the Horn of Africa,
rescuing ships that had come to grief on the rocks, often lured there
by Somali wreckers, who ransomed the sailors in return for rights of
salvage. It is undoubtedly a garbled version of Pinchard's employment that lies behind the legend that Rimbaud was a wrecker and
pirate at Cape Guardafui in 1879 (when he was actually working in
the quarries of Cyprus). One surrenders the colourful bit of
Rimbaldien folklore, but retains something authentic: the way
Rimbaud's African life merges and blurs with that of his fellow
expats in the Horn of Africa.

Pinchard was Bardey's first locally hired employee: his knowledge of Arabic was invaluable. He is the first in Bardey's list, in

order of seniority, of the 'brilliant team' he assembled in Aden and Africa: Rimbaud is second.

He was a tough, experienced character, and Bardey was glad to have him along when he went up to Harar in 1880. The Somalis of the caravan nicknamed him Abou Kirch, the man with a big belly. Bardey concurs: a 'slight portliness, especially compared to the thinness of the Somalis'. Despite this 'he was very agile'. Bardey describes him hunting: 'he moved among the bushes as if he were playing hide-and-seek with someone we couldn't see. Then we heard the rifle shot and saw him picking up a gazelle.'

A snatch of conversation on one such foray. Bardey asks him: 'What would you do if we met a lion?'

'I'd stick the barrel of my gun in its face.'

And this is what you see when you finally climb down off your horse after a long day in the saddle: 'Pinchard is already installed in a folding chair at the door of our tent'.

And here he is translating for Bardey. A local man explains to them that on the tribal frontiers there are markets where the trading is done without speaking. Pinchard translates: 'Market of Silence'. Rimbaud would like that phrase, I think.

Little is known of Constantin Righas. Bardey simply describes him as 'a young Greek'. He was still up at Harar in January 1882, when both Bardey and Rimbaud were back in Aden. He was at that point 'very ill' and had gone to recuperate at the hot springs of Grasleh. It is then, in early 1882, that we first hear of his brother, Dimitri Righas, who is recommended to Bardey as a man 'who won't shirk at the job' [bouder à la besogne]. It is he, rather than Constantin, who remains on record after this. He will still be at Harar in 1891, when Rimbaud returns to France; he will be one of Rimbaud's last correspondents; he will die on 12 November 1891, just two days after Rimbaud.

Two other brothers, Ottoman and Athanase, were probably younger. Both were still in the area in about 1911, furnishing cloudy reminiscences of Rimbaud.

Another Greek whom he met at this time was Constantin Sotiro. He was to be one of Rimbaud's closest acquaintances in Harar, a man he genuinely liked. He was already here in 1880: Bardey mentions him as one of the small community of Greek traders who had come with the Egyptian army and who owned some 'primitive little shops' around the Faras Maghala.

His full name was Sotiros Konstantinu Chryseos. He came from 'the island of Hagiostratu' [i.e. Agios Evstratios], a small island south of Lemnos in the upper Aegean, at that time still under Turkish rule. He was thus a Turkish subject, though Greek by birth.

He was soon associated with the Bardey enterprise, and in mid-1881 he accompanied Bardey on a journey to Boubassa, south of Harar, following a route first opened up by Rimbaud. Pierre Bardey (Alfred's brother, who ran the Harar branch in 1882) calls him a 'rich employee'. This indicates a certain independence: he is a merchant-trader on his own account, well-established, and his status *chez* Bardey would have reflected that. Another visitor to Harar, the German traveller Philip Paulitschke, found him a 'splendid fellow', and spent most of his evenings in his company.

Rimbaud has left us a wonderful portrait of him, taken with his new camera in 1883: the dark, weather-beaten face, copiously moustached; the tarbouche and the woollen riding jacket; the cartridge belt slung crosswise; the rifle on which he leans; the riding boots and the spurs.

He is not a young man, one sees from the photo; in the wrinkles of his brow and the thin mouth there is mingled humour and regret. The banana trees flourish rampantly behind him.

Bardey adds a brief verbal sketch which is almost a gloss on this photo: 'Sotiro has his shoulder-belt strapped on, bristling with cartridges. He carries a Winchester repeating rifle, but this is mostly for show, as he is actually very short-sighted.' Another vignette catches him in his element, surrounded by curious tribesmen in the Ogaden:

> With his rifle slung over his shoulder, Sotiro holds an unlit cigarette in his left hand. With his right he takes a match out of his pocket, and strikes it on his trousers, at the back of his thigh. The .natives gathered round follow his actions with intense curiosity. When the little flame flares up, and he holds it up to his lips, the women and children give a cry, and start back . . .

We are in the world of the frontiersman; as a Frenchman in Djibouti once said to me, '*C'est très Far West.*'

Another man Rimbaud knew well enough to photograph (the picture has disappeared but Bardey speaks of it) was the Egyptian colonel, Ahmed Ouady. He was Nadi Pasha's Chief of Staff, and he spoke excellent French. And among the locals there was Hadj Afi, their chief *abban* or guide: a 'svelte, muscular man' of about thirty, with a handsome face marked with smallpox, and a little white *calotte* tipped back on his head, giving him 'an air of gallantry'. He is a man, says Bardey, *'qui n'est pas embarrassé'*, which may mean he was at ease, or that he was, in a more Rimbaldien sense, 'unencumbered'.

* * *

Rimbaud is soon full of plans and projects, is energized by novelty. They are going to have a camera sent out, he writes home, and also 'some equipment for preserving flora and fauna'. He will send them 'birds and animals never before seen in Europe'. He has already got some *curiosités*, which he will send 'when the opportunity arises'. The camera would be a long time coming, but the preserving equipment is perhaps the *'boîte de fer blanc'* mentioned in a letter from Pierre to Alfred Bardey:

> I am sending you a bird's head in a steel box filled with alcohol. I believe this bird is unique to the Harar area; it is known here as *koumou*. Perhaps you saw it when you were here. It is the size of a large turkey, and is completely black, [30 November 1882; BA, p. 324]

Into the vacuum of his life Rimbaud pours these new practicalities, this concern with 'precise things' which is a way of replacing, of forgetting, the dangerous imprecisions of the spirit. He asks his mother to send him a book. the *Guide du Voyageur*, translated from the German: 'A Theoretical and Practical Manual for the Explorer'. This is, he hears, 'a very intelligent compendium of all the sciences required by the explorer, in topography, mineralogy, hydrography, natural history, etc.' He also writes to a Monsieur Bautin, manufacturer of precision instruments in Paris. The letter is a bizarre glimpse into the churning ambitions which are rising in him in his cramped little house in Harar:

> Dear Sir,
>
> I am interested in developing the market for precision instruments of all kinds in the East, and I am therefore writing to request of you the following service: I wish to receive a full report on the best manufacturers, in France or elsewhere, of mathematical, optical,

astronomical, electrical, meteorological, pneumatic, mechanical, hydraulic and mineralogical instruments. I am not interested in surgical instruments. . . . I would also like catalogues of sports equipment, fireworks, conjuring gear, mechanical models, miniature constructions, etc . . .

Please also send me a *Complete Manual of Precision Instrument Making*, if there is one which is sensible, up-to-date and practical.
[15 January 1881]

This now is the literary criterion of the man who once called himself the shaman of poetry, the fixer of vertigos. He wishes it to be 'sensible, up-to-date and practical'.

One talks of Rimbaud's desertion of literature, but this was not at all a desertion of reading and writing *per se*. His frequent requests for books show an almost touching belief in the value of printed information. Over the years he requests a total of nearly sixty titles from his mother and others, including works on carpentry and candle-making, railway-building and tunnelling, tanning and trigonometry. After one particularly long list [2 December 1882] he adds: 'I beg you, don't just ignore my request . . . Without these books I'd be lacking a whole pile of information which is indispensable to me. I'd be like a blind man.' *Une foule de renseignements* – this is somehow expressive of the chaotic multiplicity of his interests, the polymath gone haywire.

But Rimbaud is a man of dangerous mood-shifts, of sudden disappointments and depressions. Notes of loneliness and bitterness creep in. At first they are held in check, with effort – 'I am really going to try and make this work interesting and lucrative' [15 January 1881] – but soon he caves in to the old devil of ennui and restlessness. On 15 February he writes gloomily:

I do not expect to remain here for long; I will soon know when I am leaving. I have not found what I expected; I am living in dreadful conditions and making no money. As soon as I have 1500 or 2000 francs I will be gone, and very glad of it. I expect to find something better a bit further on. Send me news of the Panama project: as soon as the work starts there I will go. I would really like to leave here right now . . . If you think I'm living like a prince, let me tell you for sure that my life here is really stupid, and is really stupefying . . .

There is a sapping of the mental powers: 'I have received your letter of 8 December, and I even think I've written you a letter since. If so, I have lost all memory of it, here in this country.' There is, above all, a deadening sense of familiarity: even here, 'far from everywhere', he is still the same person and it is still the same world:

> You shouldn't go thinking that this place is completely savage. There's the Egyptian army, artillery and cavalry, and their administration. Everything's really much the same as it is in Europe; except that here it's another pack of dogs and bandits.

The horror of stasis: to arrive at the empty inn, at the end of the adventure, and find your old self waiting for you. It is the familiar cafard of the traveller, as in Horace's *'Cœlum non animum mutant qui trans mare currunt'* – Those who chase across the sea change their skies but not their souls.

But he cannot go back. Soon he will write:

> Every day I lose my taste for the climate, and the way of life, and even the language of Europe . . . You send me the latest political news. If only you knew how little I care: for over two years now I haven't touched a newspaper. All those debates are incomprehensible to me now. [6 May 1883]

The impossibility of returning to France is a frequent theme – it is too cold, he has no status there, and worst of all he will be conscripted for military service. And Europe, in turn, seems to forget about him. He is beyond the pale of the known world, and there is only the vaguest sense of where he is. Verlaine confuses Harar with Herat and thinks he is in Afghanistan. He is variously said to be in 'Hazar', in 'Harar or Horor', in 'Ouganda', and so on. As far as they are concerned, he really *has* disappeared.

*   *   *

April in Harar. The jacaranda are in flower, leaving a carpet of lilac-coloured confetti on the roadside. There is bougainvillaea in sunny corners, and sudden rainstorms which sometimes turn to hail, and which fill the gutters with a rush of rust-coloured water.

And now he is, ill. He first mentions this in the letter of 15 February quoted above, which may account for its gloominess: 'I have picked up [*pincé*] an illness, nothing serious in itself, but this climate here is a devil for any kind of illness. Cuts never get better, the tinest nick on your finger suppurates for months and goes gangrenous very easily.' He makes light of it – an infection, perhaps something gastric. He grumbles about the lack of doctors and medicines, about the humidity of the summer and the chill of the winter.

Alfred Bardey, however, who joined Rimbaud at Harar in April, is more specific. In a letter to the early biographer Berrichon [7 July 1897] Bardey states that when he arrived in Harar he found Rimbaud sick with syphilis. Rimbaud 'had recently contracted syphilis' and 'had the unmistakable marks of it in his mouth'. He was considered infectious, and was careful not to let his colleagues use his *couvert* or drink from his glass.

Bardey's journal and Rimbaud's letters trace the course of his illness. In May, according to Bardey, he took to his bed 'for ten or fifteen days'. The following month, after a two-week expedition upcountry, he was 'forced to return to bed'. For several days he was dangerously ill: 'there were times when he thought his last hour had come' [BA, pp. 273–4]. On 22 July Rimbaud writes: 'For a fortnight now I have had the fever as bad as I had it two years ago at Roche' – in other words, as bad as the bout of typhoid which forced him home from Cyprus. On 5 August, it is 'beginning to abate a little'.

These are not necessarily continuous – there are recoveries and relapses – but it seems the illness he had 'picked up' in February was still not shaken off six months later. Bardey's statement that it was syphilis is plausible. Harar was a garrison-town packed with soldiers; prostitution was endemic. A bit of Harari folklore, still current, is that the women of the town took to wearing trousers at this time, not just to follow the Turco-Egyptian fashion, but to protect themselves from the lubricities of the Egyptian soldiers.

It seems that Rimbaud took some comfort from a Harar streetgirl and suffered the consequences. (At least one assumes that it was a woman he caught it off. There is no evidence of Rimbaud's homosexuality in Africa; the few liaisons one hears of are all with women; Bardey, aware of Rimbaud's earlier reputation, is adamant that he practised no 'perversions' in Ethiopia.)

The beauty of the Adari women is proverbial. Rimbaud does not tell us so, but anyone else who has travelled there will. 'The beauty of the women was dazzling,' Waugh reported in 1930. He commends their slender grace and narrow hips, their broad straight shoulders and high, pointed breasts, their golden-brown skin and brilliant silk shawls, their slim calves in tight trousers with spiral stripes 'like sugar sticks in a village post-office', and much else besides.

An unanswered question. Was it this dose of syphilis which eventually led to the degenerative condition that killed him ten years later? Some have claimed this, but the medical evidence is inconclusive.

*　　*　　*

Before Bardey's arrival in mid-April Rimbaud was briefly in charge of the Harar depot – Pinchard had left for the coast, suffering from malaria. Now the house fills up again, for with Bardey comes a fresh-faced business associate Pierre Mazaran; and five Franciscan priests under the leadership of Mgr Taurin-Cahagne, who has been named Bishop of Harar and 'Apostolic Vicar of the Gallas'. (Rimbaud was expecting them: 'We are getting a Catholic bishop,' he wrote in January. 'He will probably be the only Catholic in the country.')

Rimbaud rides down to Gueldessah to meet them. The three young Frenchmen journey up to Harar together, while the missionaries recoup at Gueldessah.

Bardey and Mazaran are installed in the ground floor of the Raouf Pasha mansion (this is the occasion of Bardey's description of the house quoted in the previous chapter). A few days later the five clerics arrive in Harar, and having nowhere else to lodge, are also put up *chez* Bardey.

On 16 April Rimbaud writes home. He hopes to be making an expedition upcountry. 'A troupe of French missionaries has arrived; it is possible I'll accompany them into the surrounding country, hitherto inaccessible to whites.' This seems an ironic coda to the diabolic poet of the *Season in Hell*.

The missionary Christian presence in Harar is continuous to this day. Père (later Monsignor) André Jarosseau arrived the following year. A black-browed, shaggy-bearded man with a mingled look of pugnacity and saintliness, he was twenty-five years old, three years younger than Rimbaud. He was from the Vendée. He was elevated to the bishopric of Harar in 1900, becoming the 'Third Apostolic Vicar of the Gallas'. Rimbaud is probably referring to him in his letter from Harar of 4 August 1888: 'There is a Catholic mission with three fathers, one of them a Frenchman like me, who educate the little negroes [*négrillons*].' There are photographs of him in his ministrations, wearing a small skull-cap, rough robes and a large cross. After some discouragement and persecution, he attained a position of influence at the Ethiopian court, and was tutor and adviser to the young Haile Selassie, born in Harar in 1892.

He is wonderfully depicted by Waugh, who met him – 'a very old man' – in 1930. (Waugh calls him 'Monsignor Jerome', which is either a monastic sobriquet or local corruption of Jarosseau.)

> He was tall and emaciated, like an El Greco saint, with very long white hair and beard, great roving eyes, and a nervous, almost ecstatic smile; he advanced at a kind of shuffling jogtrot, fluttering his hands and uttering little moans.

After showing Waugh round the church – 'shabby and unremarkable' – he invited him into his *divan* to talk. Here Waugh 'steered the conversation as delicately as I could from church expenses to Arthur Rimbaud'. At first they were at cross-purposes, because the bishop, being a little deaf, mistook the word *poète* for *prêtre*, 'and inflexibly maintained that no Father Rimbaud had ever, to his knowledge, ministered in Abyssinia'.

> Later this difficulty was cleared up, and the bishop, turning the name over in his mind, remembered that he had, in fact, known Rimbaud quite well; a young man with a beard, who was in some trouble with his leg; a very serious man who did not go out much; he was always worried about business; not a good Catholic, though he had died at peace with the Church, the bishop understood, at Marseille. He used to live with a native woman in a little house, now demolished, in the square; he had no children; probably the woman was still alive; she was not a native of Harar, and after Rimbaud's death she had gone back to her own people in Tigre . . . A very, very serious young man, the bishop repeated. He seemed to find this epithet the most satisfactory – very serious and sad [*Remote People*, pp. 78–9].

This is a wonderful, misty snapshot of Rimbaud's career in Harar, though it is spread over some years, and most of it concerns his last sojourn in 1888–91. It was then that he had the 'trouble with his leg', and then – it appears from this account – that he was living with a

Tigrayan woman in a 'little house in the square'. (We will return to her later.)

Mgr Jarosseau was still alive and lucid six years later, and on 22 September 1936 he wrote a long letter to Rimbaud's English biographer, Enid Starkie. He writes in a rather ornate style, but his recollections are once again priceless:

In Harar, where I was acquainted with Monsieur Rimbaud in 1882 and also in 1888, his life was no longer that of the poet who had, while still young, offered up to the French Muses certain inspirations which announced the birth of a superior talent. Many have wondered why Arthur Rimbaud had deserted Parnassus to come to Harar, and spend his life in obscurity as a simple man of commerce. Some have thought that in entering the world of commerce he was obeying a secret ambition to become a disciple of Crœsus; others have believed that this brilliant innovator of French literature recognized that he had ruined his life by devoting himself to those swervings [écarts] of the imagination which propelled him towards a glorification of evil, and had exiled himself into Africa to put an end to the torments of his soul. This latter opinion seems to answer better to the nature of M. Arthur Rimbaud, who certainly, both in his commercial work and in his travels along the rocky paths of the Harar region, held his luminous spirit high above the servile preoccupations of the trading world. The carelessness of his dress, the sobriety of his life, his charity towards the impoverished natives, showed clearly enough that M. Arthur Rimbaud was not chasing the allures [célébrités] of wealth. If he had adopted this life as a commission-agent it was doubtless because in Africa, it brought him into contact with the great contrasts of Nature.

Another of his recollections. One day Rimbaud came in search of him, asking for something to read. 'I had nothing except my New Testament,' Jarosseau recalls. 'I lent it to him. He was glad of it too, the poor child.' [Max Guineheuf, Mercure de France, April 1948.]

Bardey sometimes went to Mass in the room in the Catholic mission that served as a chapel: it helped him to 'think of his homeland' on a Sunday morning. He adds that Rimbaud never went to any services: '[He was] indifferent to all things religious, without being ostentatious about it. But he had extremely cordial relations with the missionaries. He enjoyed himself in their company, though he generally avoided the company of Europeans' [letter to Berri-chon, 10 July 1897].

Jarosseau eventually left Harar in 1940, and died in Toulouse the following year, at the age of eighty-four. His memorial tablet in the little Catholic church in Harar, placed there by the Free French forces of East Africa in 1942, says:

> He lived for 58 years in Harar, where he would have wished to die.
> By his charitable actions, by his indefatigable and tender zeal, he
> has cemented the friendship of Ethiopia and France.

A later missionary was Père Émile Foucher, whom I have mentioned as the leading local expert on Rimbaud in Harar. He died in 1993: I arrived in Harar a few months too late to meet him. In the neat, weirdly provincial little kitchen of the Catholic mission I was hospitably received by two of his colleages – a Frenchman, Frère Constant; and a Maltese, Frère Thaddeus. They are small, amiable men, monkish Rumpelstiltskins. They express their regrets. They do not know what has happened to Père Émile's papers. The current bishop – an Ethiopian, Mgr Weldetensae – is in Rome. I leave empty handed, with a sense of precious knowledge running like dust through my fingers.

Down below the Erar Gate, where Somali women sit amid the flies selling gourds of camel's milk, we find the grave of Father Émile, a simple stone cross and a metal plaque, crudely incised:

> ABBA EMILE FOUCHER
> FRENCH CAPUCHIN
> PARISH PRIEST OF HARRAR
> BORN 1.10.1919
> DIED 14.06.1993
> IN INDIA 12 YEARS
> IN ETHIOPIA 33 YEARS

The epitaph is in English; the letterer has carved 'prish' instead of 'parish'.

*   *   *

On 4 May 1881, Rimbaud writes home, as restless as ever:

> I am definitely leaving this place very soon, to go trafficking in the

unknown. There is a great lake a few days' journey from here. It's in ivory country. I'm going to try and get there. The people of the region are probably hostile. I'm going to buy a horse and get out of here. If things turn out bad and I don't come back, you should know that there's a thousand rupees due to me, back at head office in Aden: you could claim it if you thought it was worth the trouble.

This 'great lake' is sometimes said to be Alem Maya (or Haramaya), but this was scarcely a day's ride from Harar, and is not especially big. Duncan Forbes suggests it was Lake Hertale. This lies on the Awash River, in the Great Rift Valley which separates the Harar massif from the Abyssinian highlands. There are no elephants there today, but there were then, before the ivory-slaughter had begun and before the acacia forest had been stripped.

It is anyway not certain that Rimbaud made this trip. Bardey makes no mention of it. On the contrary, he says that Rimbaud was ill in May, for about a fortnight, and that when he felt better he set off on an expedition to Boubassa, about thirty miles south of Harar. This was not in search of ivory, but to buy skins.

The Boubassa expedition lasted two weeks. He returned some time before 10 June, when he writes home: 'I'm back from an expedition upcountry.' Other than this, Bardey's journal is our only source of information about this venture:

> Rimbaud requests permission to go to Boubassa in the south. This is the furthest point reached by the Egyptian colonizers in the time of Raouf Pasha . . . We are advised that the natives have brought quantities of cow and goat skins to the Boubassa region in the hope of selling them to us, as they do not have the means to bring them to Harar.

Bardey is sceptical about the value of the skins, but agrees to the expedition, 'hoping at least that Rimbaud will bring back useful information'.

Camels are made ready, loaded with 'cotton stuffs' to trade. The caravan assembles at the southerly gate of Harar, Bab el Salaam, sometime during the last week of May. And there, courtesy of Bardey, we have this vivid glimpse:

> At the moment of his departure, at the head of his little convoy, Rimbaud winds a cloth [*serviette*] around his head, in the guise of

a turban, and drapes a red blanket [*couverture*] over the top of his usual clothes. His intention is to pass as a Muslim . . .

Everyone laughs at his 'new costume' and – a rare sight – 'Rimbaud laughs along with us.' He is taking a risk, he admits, with this 'orientalizing' of his costume. (This is Bardey's word: perhaps verbatim from Rimbaud.) His 'red cloak' will attract robbers, but 'for the prestige of the company, he wishes to be taken for a rich Mohammedan merchant' [BA, p. 273–4].

This is marvellous: a sudden vignette layered with revelations. The upbeat tone is, one guesses, intimately connected to the fact of departure. He is at the town gate, on the move, heading into 'the unknown'. He is for a moment, happy. And beneath the badinage is something deeper: this 'orientalizing' of himself, this theatrical costuming, is a classic moment of Rimbaldien effacement. I have spoken of Rimbaud 'disappearing' into Africa, of his desire to lose himself: we witness it here, in a snatched moment of historical clarity outside the Bab el Salaam.

It is sometimes said that Rimbaud 'became' a Muslim out in East Africa. This is an exaggeration, but it is certainly true that he was conversant with the Koran (a copy of which he was urging his mother to send as early as 1881); that he came to know and appreciate the Muslim way of life; and that he was glad to be thought of as a Muslim by those he traded with. He finds in Islam a trait which goes with his own resignation, which turns his black pessimism into a shrug of fatalism. This is a mood one might trace back to earlier days: a poem like 'The Drunken Boat' with its sense of helpless psychological drifting. In the text of the African letters this surfaces as a kind of deadpan version of Muslim fatalism: 'It is more than probable that I will never find peace of mind; that I will neither live nor die at peace. In the end, as the Muslims say: It is written! That's life: it's no laughing matter' [10 September 1884]. 'It is written' is the Muslim adage *mektoub*.

His voracious intellectual interest in the subject is attested by contemporary witnesses. The Italian explorer Ugo Ferrandi, who spent time with him in Tadjourah in 1886, says:

He was an Arabist of the first order, and at his house there he would have learned discussions about the Koran with the local elders . . . The natives considered him to be something of a

Muslim. He advised me to imitate this course, seeing that I had some knowledge of Islamic customs.

Another acquaintance, Armand Savouré, writes: 'He was one of the best Arabists that ever lived, and around 1886, went off preaching the Koran as a way of penetrating those regions of Africa that were still unknown.' This probably gets it about right – a genuine fascination with the intellectual rigours of Islam mingled with a more expedient idea of its usefulness to him as a trader and traveller. It is part of Rimbaud's great gift: this immersion in the East African life that is a concomitant of his flight from his routine, European identity. 'He avidly absorbed the essential qualities of the regions in which he travelled,' said Bardey, 'and assimilated himself as much as possible to the manners and customs of the native people.'

The seal he had made for him – exactly when is not known – styled him 'Abdoh Rinbo': Rimbaud the Servant of Allah. If so, it was very much on his own terms.

* * *

In mid-December 1881, a year after his arrival in Harar, Rimbaud left to return to Aden. A sense of disappointment and defeat, of the entropic dwindling of the unknown into familiarity, trails down with him:

> I grow accustomed to this life of fatigue . . . I feed on my angers, so violent and so pointless . . . [25 May 1881]

> What do you want me to tell you about my work here, which I already find so repugnant, or about this country, which is horrific, and so on? I can only tell you of the struggles I've had, and the dreadful fatigues, and all they have earned me is this fever . . . [22 July 1881]

The isolation of Harar, so intrinsic to his desire for escape and anonymity, has become a burden:

> My orders and letters go round in crazy circles in this joint. Just imagine, I ordered two woollen suits from Lyon last November, and they haven't come yet. I needed a medicine six months ago; I ordered it from Aden, and I haven't received it yet. Everything is on its way – on its way to the devil! [2 September 1881]

He is also angered and frustrated by what he feels to be the underhand dealing of his employers. He has had some 'disagreeable disputes [*démêlés*] with the management' [2 September 1881]. The particular complaint is that money-orders drawn on his accumulated earnings (a total of 1,165 rupees, worth over 2,500 francs) have not reached his mother. This saga rumbles on for months. The money is not for himself, he adds, rather poignantly: 'If you have need of it, take it: what is mine is yours. For my part, I have no one to think of except myself, who asks for nothing' [7 November 1881].

And so he takes the trail back down to Zeilah. His last communiqués are dated 9 December. One is a curt memo, or perhaps a telegram, to Alfred Bardey: 'I would be glad to see you personally in Aden.' The other is to his family: 'Don't write to me at Harar: I am leaving very shortly, and it is very unlikely I shall ever come back here.'

But he is wrong. He will remain in Bardey's employ, and he will come back to Harar.

13

THE CAMERA

1882: A YEAR of stasis. He frets in Aden, 'toiling like a donkey', uncertain of his future, dreaming of far-flung journeys – to Zanzibar, to Panama, to Shoa – but going nowhere. There is, throughout this year, one idea which grips him and sustains him: to become a photographer.

He and Pinchard had already talked of this, during the long evenings at Raouf Pasha's house in Harar. Now an opportunity presents itself. In the summer of 1882, Colonel Dubar returned on leave to France. In late September Rimbaud wrote to him, in Lyon, asking him to purchase a camera for him. He informs his mother: 'this Monsieur Dubar is very dependable [*sérieux*] and will send me what I need.' He is sending her 1000 francs, via the company office in Lyon, to pay for it. He intends to take the camera to Shoa, where 'they have never seen one before, and where it will earn me a small fortune in next to no time' [28 September 1882].

As this shows, Rimbaud's intentions were in part commercial. Photography was still a rarity outside Europe. He will make a 'small fortune', both from selling portraits *in situ*, and from sending photographs back to France to feed the avid European interest in the exotica and *curiosités* of Africa. 'Reproductions of these unknown countries, and the extraordinary people they contain, must surely sell in France', he later announces confidently [6 January 1883].

Photography had been an interest of Rimbaud's for years. It tends to be forgotten that the title of his great collection of prose-poems, *Illuminations*, carries a specific meaning as much as a metaphoric one. This is stated by both Delahaye and Verlaine. Delahaye glosses *illuminations* as 'an English word meaning "coloured plates" or "aquatints"'. It is 'quite sufficient', he continues, to take it in this sense, though Rimbaud also intended the metaphoric meaning of *illuminations*, 'that is: intuitions or visions'.

According to Verlaine, Rimbaud himself actually wrote the words 'Painted Plates', in English, as an explanatory subtitle. (This cannot be verified, as there is no surviving authorial MS of the collection; indeed how far it ever was a collection by Rimbaud is uncertain.)

The literary inference would be that he thought of the prose-poems as verbal photographs, or as we might put it today, 'snapshots'. A number of them fit into that category. I would relate this to another comment of Delahaye's about Rimbaud as a poet:

> Rimbaud hardly ever needs to 'invent' things. A passionate believer in observation, he prefers to make use of the real, of things he has experienced, but then displacing them from their true context, splitting them into parts that can be used in a new way, joining and mingling things which were in fact quite separate, stripping every subject of its actual nature to give it another, etc. [*Rimbaud*, p. 37]

Those Victorian 'painted plates' are just that: reality observed by the camera and altered by the paintbrush.

In October, the trusty Dubar wrote from Lyon, saying he had purchased the *'bagage photographique'*. On 3 November Rimbaud writes to his mother, hoping the cheque for 1000 francs has reached her, so Dubar can be reimbursed. 'I look forward to news of this, and trust all will proceed without any hitches [*accrocs*].' In mid-November he receives another letter from his mother. She has the 1000 francs, but the camera and its *'bagage'* come altogether to 1,850 francs! This is a big sum of money, equivalent to nearly six months of Rimbaud's salary. This shows how badly he wanted it.

His mother thought it wasn't worth it, as we might guess, and as we learn from his irritated letter to her:

> You say I've been fleeced. I know perfectly well what a camera on its own costs – a few hundred francs. But there are also a lot of very expensive chemicals, some of them compounds of gold and silver, worth up to 250 francs a kilo, and there are the plates [*glaces*], paper [*cartes*], basins [*cuvettes*], flasks [*flacons*], and the packaging – all very expensive, which increase the cost. I've ordered enough materials for a two-year expedition. As far as I'm concerned I've got a good deal. My only fear is that the equipment will be damaged at sea. If it arrives intact, I will make a big profit out of it, and I'll send you some curiosities . . . I know the price of

money, and if I gamble on something, I do it advisedly [8 December 1882]

*　　*　　*

Meanwhile, tormented by impatience and delays, living always 'in a state of expectation', the tensions mount inside him, and one day something snaps.

On the morning of 28 January 1883 Rimbaud came to blows with one of the workers at the Bardey warehouse, Ali Shamok (or Chemmek). They must have known one another fairly well, since Bardey describes Ali as 'our longest-serving warehouseman and foreman'. The fight developed into a more general fracas, and – the situation of foreigners being always parlous in these countries – Rimbaud wrote a swift letter of explanation to the French vice-consul, Monsieur de Gaspary.

It was at eleven o'clock in the morning that the scuffle occurred: the end of a long morning's work. As Rimbaud puts it, in a florid, semi-legalistic phraseology full of righteous innocence:

> the said Ali Chemmek behaving himself extremely insolently towards me, I permitted myself to give him a light slap [*un soufflet sans violence*]. The coolies of the company, together with certain Arabs who were present, grabbed hold of me, to give him the opportunity to riposte. He struck me in the face, and ripped my clothes, and then grabbed a stick and threatened me with it.

This immediate response of the 'coolies' and 'Arabs' is suggestive of the simmering colonial tensions at the Bardey warehouse.

Ali Chemmek then left the warehouse, to lodge a complaint against Rimbaud at the municipal police station. There, Rimbaud says, 'he made several false claims, for instance that I had threatened him with a knife, etc, etc.'. These lies were 'intended to poison the case against me, and incite a hatred of me among the natives'.

In a later letter to Berrichon, Bardey recalled the incident and its sequel:

> There exists at the Aden law-courts a document in which I stand surety for the future good behaviour of Rimbaud, who was in danger of expulsion or conviction after a rather nasty scuffle [*rixe*]

with the Arab, Ali Shamok. I made show of solidarity by dismissing the latter.

This is the end of the affair. A moment of heat and anger, and then the dust settles, the Frenchmen rally round, and Ali Shamok, 'who had been so useful to us', is sent on his way. Rimbaud has enemies in Aden, as he did in Paris and London.

Bardey concludes his reminiscence with a huffy comment: 'It does no good to have these people turning against you: commercially speaking, you understand.' This perhaps reflects what he said to Rimbaud that night.

*   *   *

At the end of this trying month, Dubar wrote announcing the departure of the camera. The cost had risen by another 600 francs. The package went astray, to Mauritius, and took nearly six weeks to reach Aden. At last, on 14 March, it is unloaded at Steamer Point: 'I've received the gear which has given you so much trouble . . . The camera and all the rest is in excellent condition, although it has been on a little trip to Mauritius.' It arrived just in time – or was he indeed actually waiting for it? – because a week later he is off once more to Harar.

He has now renewed his contract with Bardey's company and will be in sole charge of the Harar branch. He has a three-year contract, until the end of December 1885, at a salary of 160 rupees (330 francs) per month, plus a 'certain percentage' of the profits. The whole thing is worth 5,000 francs *per annum*, he reckons (i.e. the percentage bonus would be worth about 1,000 francs over the year), plus free 'lodging and expenses'. Despite this there is much uncertainty, both because of the political situation at Harar, where Egyptian control is weakening; and because of the financial situation of the company. 'I fear the company will soon close down, and the profits won't cover the costs.' He is promised three months' salary 'as indemnity', if the company fails.

20 March 1883: 'I leave the day after tomorrow for Zeilah.'

Assuming the usual caravan route via Biokobobo and Gueldessah, he would have arrived in Harar around the middle of April. His first letter home is not until 6 May, but as he often reminds his family, his letters are dictated by the departure of couriers and caravans for the coast.

He is in unusually buoyant mood – 'I am always better up here than in Aden. There's less work, and much more air, more greenery' – though he is conscious of time moving too quickly: 'At the end of the year I will have spent three whole years in this joint.'

And he has been busy with his new camera:

> This venture is working out well, and if I want I can quickly recoup the 2,000 francs it has cost me. Everyone wants to be photographed here; people are offering as much as a guinea per picture. I am not yet properly set up, or very skilful, but I soon will be, and I will send you some curious things.

(Always this idea of the 'curious', a word that hovers between a scientific idea of rarity, and a more commercial idea of the saleably bizarre.)

*   *   *

It is in this letter of 6 May 1883 that Rimbaud sends home his first photographic fruits, the three precious self-portraits. Halfway through the letter he says: 'I enclose two photographs of myself by myself', but by the end the two have become three. (He had developed another one? He had decided to send it after all though technically imperfect?)

> The first shows me standing on a terrace of the house; the next one standing in a coffee plantation; the third one with arms folded in a banana plantation. All of them have come out too white because of the bad water I have to use to wash them. But I'm going to do better work very soon. This is just so that you can remember my face and to give you an idea of the surroundings here.

The three photos thus curtly described remain our only visual knowledge of Rimbaud in Africa: a vivid counterpart to the verbal descriptions of him, though also – as he says – tantalizingly illegible. They have come out too white. *Tout cela est devenu blanc*: it has all become blank.

A Rimbaldien irony: he sends them these photos so they can 'remember his face' – *rappeler ma figure* – but his face is precisely what is veiled.

You can make out the clothes; at least, the costume. On the terrace he wears a dark blazer, not impossibly the woollen *drap* he ordered from Lyon for the Harar nights, still chilly in late April. One notes in this picture the faintly comic pose – the right hand grasping his lapel, the left resting on the makeshift wooden balcony, the jaunty angle of the feet. He is almost the company man.

In the other two photos he is out and about – in a coffee plantation, in a banana grove. He wears in both a light-coloured jacket with big practical pockets; loose white trousers; white cotton T-shirt or singlet; and slightly clog-like leather shoes. This accords exactly with a description by the Italian traveller Ugo Ferrandi, when he encountered Rimbaud at Tadjourah in 1886: 'He was dressed very simply, in European clothes: a pair of rather baggy trousers, a vest [*tricot*], and a loose-fitting grey-khaki jacket.' Ferrandi also describes him as wearing a *calotte* – in other words the small pill-box Arab hat, the tarbouche or fez – 'also grey'. I have looked for a long time at these photos. In two of them (on the terrace and in the banana grove) he seems to be wearing a hat, but one cannot be sure: they might be blotches or shadows. Later drawings by his sister Isabelle also show him in this characteristic fez. It is as expressive of his African years as the London topper is of his Bohemian years.

The roughness and shabbiness of his clothing is often mentioned. Augustin Bernard said: 'he looked more like some poor Armenian or Greek fellow than a Frenchman'. And Ottorino Rosa describes his 'bizarre' manner of dress – bizarre for a European, he means – as follows:

> He lived like a native, very carelessly dressed . . . I remember that the English Resident at Zeilah, Lieutenant Harrington, seeing him dressed so oddly, took him for a simple building-worker [*ouvrier maçon*] . . . He used to make his own clothes, out of white American cotton, and to simplify things he had ingenious ways of avoiding the tiresome need for buttons.

This adds a subsidiary glimpse of Rimbaud with needle and thread, and a length, perhaps, of the 'American Sheeting No. 2' which he mentions often in his ledgers.

Paul Claudel, one of the first French writers to see Rimbaud's African years as something other than a regrettable aberration, saw in the shabby suits of these photographs 'a hint of the convict'.

Of the man himself, out of the blankness, a few details emerge in poignant clarity: the big sun-darkened hands; the rucks and folds on his trousers; the right leg bent and the hand resting on the thigh, just about at the point where the surgeon's saw would take it off. And in the face itself, though blurred, is a haggardness, a hollowed-out look, a leatheriness – *'lost climates will tan me'* – and a deep but defiant loneliness.

Comparing these photos with those of the handsome young 'hooligan poet' of Paris, one gets a measure of just how far Rimbaud has come on this journey to become 'somebody else'.

*   *   *

It is perhaps revealing that Rimbaud's earliest photos are self-portraits. It is natural enough for the beginner, though it suggests also a note of theatricality, the African years as Rimbaud's *œuvre vie*: the life as work of art. One remembers those lines from the *Illuminations* in which an old traveller says: *'Exiled here, I had a stage on which to perform dramatic masterpieces.'*

There are four other photographs known to be by Rimbaud. At least one other – a portrait of the Egyptian courtier and soldier, Ahmed Ouadi – is now lost. What survive are two superb portraits, and two general views of Harar which are less successful. The portrait of Sotiro I have already discussed. The other portrait is generally described as of a local 'coffee merchant'. It shows a lean, skull-capped man, probably Adari, sitting cross-legged on a pile of sacking. The face is slightly blurred – he has moved a little during the longish exposure – but the clutter of wares around him and the pillared courtyard in which he sits are caught with great clarity. One's eye travels among these objects: a pair of sandals, the long-necked jugs, the woven bowl, the two little coffee-cups, the banana-leaves serving as trays or wrapping, the rawhide mat, the wooden pestle, the heavy weighing-scales suspended from the ceiling, the padlocked door, the rubble walls, the steep camber of the stairway, and, in a little pile of stuff under the stairs, the unmistakable shape of a skull. Partly out of frame is a bowl of something which may be unroasted coffee-beans. The debris in front of the man seems to be fragments of wood, perhaps an aromatic bark for the roasting process. On his lap a cloth is spread, and from the action of his hands it looks as if the cloth contains *khat*. Bardey describes the

Hararis as 'immoderate users' of *khat*, which 'induces a beatific drunkenness and brings in the long term the nervous disorders [*maladies de peur*] which are very common in Harar' [BA, p. 176]. According to his Italian friend Ottorino Rosa, Rimbaud himself 'experimented with' *khat*. This picture is like a marvellous inventory: a caressing of the rough nap of Harar life.

The general views are hard to identify. One shows a crowded area of people and stalls. It is very likely the Faras Maghala. The other shows a small Muslim shrine, or *khoubba*. These have a certain associative interest, but on the evidence that remains Rimbaud's forte as a photographer was for portraits: figures in a landscape, people captured or indeed captive in a moment of time.

These studies are broadly contemporary with the self-portraits, though the earliest mention of them is in July, when Alfred Bardey writes from France to thank him for sending them:

> I felt a great pleasure at seeing something of Harar once more. Ahmed Ouady hasn't changed. Send him my compliments and congratulations. And Sotiro is splendid, and looks just the part in the midst of that jungle which you call the gardens of Raouf Pasha . . . [Vichy, 24 July 1883]

The latter phrase preserves an authentic Rimbalderie: the craggy surroundings of Harar as his 'garden'.

The enthusiasm soon waned: fiercely brief as always. In Aden, in early 1885, perhaps in response to a request from his family, he writes: 'I'm not sending you my photograph. I am careful to avoid all unnecessary expenses, and anyway I'm much too badly dressed.' And then, a couple of months later, comes the curt announcement: 'I've sold the camera, to my great regret, but not at a loss' [14 April 1885].

14

EXPLORING

U P IN HARAR in 1883 Rimbaud has two objectives in mind: photography and exploration. These are a combined objective, to describe these unknown regions in images and words. Here is the first glimmer of a literary intent in Africa: the reporter, the travel writer, the man of science documenting the 'unknown'.

This idea has been taking shape during the year in Aden, in conjunction with the idea of photography. He announces in a letter to his family:

> I am going to compile a work for the Société de Géographie, with maps and engravings, on Harar and the Galla regions . . . I will take the camera up to Harar, and bring back views of these unknown regions. This is a very interesting idea. I also need instruments to make topographical surveys and take latitudes. When this work is completed, and accepted by the Société de Géographie, they will perhaps furnish me with funds for other journeys. [18 January 1882]

At the same time he wrote to his old friend Ernest Delahaye, now living in Paris, asking him to send him the following list of map-making equipment, to be paid for by Mme Rimbaud from the moneys he was sending her:

> 1. A small traveller's theodolyte. (If this costs more than 1,500–1,800 francs, forget the theodolyte and buy the following two instruments: a good sextant; a Cravet compass.'
> 2. A mineral collection with 300 specimens.
> 3. A pocket-sized aneroid barometer.
> 4. A surveyor's line made of hemp.
> 5. A mathematics set, containing ruler, set-square, protractor, compass, decimetre, drawing-pens, etc.
> 6. Drawing paper.

Another request at this time was for a telescope, or a 'field officer's eye-glass'.

He also asks Delahaye to track down some books for him, including Kaltbrünner's *Manuel du Voyageur* (which he had already requested, several times, from his mother), Salneuve's *Topographie et Géodesie*, Davy's *Météorologie*, Wagner's *Chimie Industrielle*, and Guillemin's *Le Ciel*, together with the 'best works available' on trigonometry, mineralogy and hydrography, and, finally, the latest *annuaire* of the Bureau des Longitudes.

Not the least remarkable thing about this letter is that Rimbaud addresses it not to Ernest, but to 'Alfred' Delahaye: a slip of the pen, of course, but one suggestive of Rimbaud's profound jettisoning of the past. His best friend, and all that he represents, recedes into oblivion.

A few days later another letter is despatched, this time to a Paris gunsmith, M. Devisme. Rimbaud announces that he is 'currently forming a party of elephant hunters', and issues the following queries:

Is there a special gun for elephant hunting?
Its description?
Its specifications?
Where can it be purchased? Its cost?
The type of ammunition: poisoned, explosive?

He wishes to buy two such guns, on trial, and if they prove successful, a further half-dozen.

All this hovers on the brink of ridiculousness: Rimbaud with telescope and elephant gun: '*O white hunter running barefoot through the panic fields . . .*'

*   *   *

A sequel of sorts to these plans or daydreams is a five-page document, written by Rimbaud in early December 1883, entitled 'Rapport sur l'Ogadine'. This is, in his own dry phrase, 'a commercial and geographical report' [letter to head office, 23 September 1883], but Alfred Bardey considered it interesting enough to send to the Société de Géographie, of which he was a member. The report was read out at a meeting of the Society, in Paris, on

1 February 1884. It was published later that year [*Comptes-rendus des Séances de la Société de Géographie*, Paris 1884, pp. 99–103].

It is hardly a masterpiece, but this is the first piece of writing (other than the letters) of Rimbaud's African years: a breaking of the silence. It is brusque, lucid and accurate. Bardey commends it as 'precise'. It did not go completely unnoticed. The Austrian explorer Philip Paulitschke, who travelled the region in 1885, declared it to be 'very important and extremely useful, despite a certain dryness'.

Though written by Rimbaud, the report was almost entirely based on an expedition by his Greek colleague Constantin Sotiro. The pronoun used in the report is 'we', but Alfred Bardey states quite clearly that Rimbaud remained in Harar. In his journal for 1883 Bardey writes:

> At Harar operations continue as before, with Sotiro more and more active in exploring the surrounding areas, under the orders of Rimbaud, whose position as head of the agency prevents him from venturing too far from the town. Certain important expeditions take place, the main one being Sotiro's journey into the Ogaden . . .

The report, he says, was 'compiled' by Rimbaud from the 'information and notes brought back by Sotiro'.

Rimbaud had certainly traced some of the area himself, but this is essentially an editorial job. He has debriefed Sotiro; he has taken his 'information' and his 'notes' (Sotiro's French, we know from his letters, was extremely patchy; certain surviving MS notes of his are in Italian), and he has knocked them into shape.

This is a fulfilment of his confident announcement the previous year that he was going to 'compile a work for the Société de Géographie', but the exploring has been done by somebody else, and his role in it is uncongenially clerical.

*   *   *

The 'explorer', like the photographer, is an imagined version of himself, and like all such versions it will prove unsatisfactory. This is already implicit in some letters he wrote at this time about the French explorer Pierre Sacconi.

Sotiro set off into the Ogaden in June or early July 1883. At the same time another expedition, 'parallel to ours', went into the area, led by Sacconi. Sacconi and three of his servants were murdered by Hammaden tribesmen, 150 miles, from Harar. The news reached Harar on 23 August.

Rimbaud's reaction is unsympathetic, and shows his deep scepticism about the European explorer who lumbers ignorantly into these 'exceptionally dangerous' regions. He blames the inadequacy of the guides, but most of all he blames the 'appearance' [*tenue*] of Sacconi himself,

> who (through ignorance) did everything contrary to the manners, religious customs and rights of the natives ... He went in European costume, and even dressed his camel-drivers as *hostranis* (Christians); he ate ham, and knocked back little glasses [i.e. of liquor] in the sheiks' councils, and tried to make them do the same; and he conducted his suspicious-looking geodesic surveys and twiddled his sextants, at every stage of the journey.

With this poor performance – and it is very much considered as a performance: again that theatrical note – Rimbaud contrasts the *savoir-faire* of his colleague Sotiro:

> M. Sacconi bought nothing, and had no other goal than reaching the Webi and winning some glory as an explorer. M. Sotiro ... followed a good route, very different from M. Sacconi's, and found a good *abban* [guide], and camped in a good spot. He travels, moreover, dressed as a Muslim, using the name Adji [i.e. Haji] Abdallah, and he observes all the political and religious formalities of the natives. At the place where he camped he became an object of pilgrimage, as a *wodad* (scholar) and *scherif* (descendant of the disciples of the Prophet) ... [23 August 1883]

> M. Sotiro should really be congratulated for the know-how and diplomacy he has shown in this situation. While our competitors have been hunted, reviled, robbed and murdered, and through their own misfortunes have been the cause of terrible conflicts between the tribes, we have established ourselves on friendly terms with the Oughaz [chief] and are known throughout all the Rere Hersi region. [10 December 1883]

This is Rimbaud's championing of the trader over the rather showier explorer, who really understands little of the land he is travelling in. The explorer holds aloof, speciously confident in his European identity, in his superior sciences. It is the trader who enters into the nature of the place, who becomes a part of it. Sotiro's winning of respect as a *wodad*, or itinerant Muslim scholar, seems to sum this up.

This distinction between the trader and the explorer is one Rimbaud would hold to. It is implicit in his prickly relationship with Jules Borelli, very much the explorer, and in Borelli's generous comment after Rimbaud's death: 'Rimbaud was travelling for business purposes and I for scientific ones. How much better would science have been served had our positions only been reversed.'

The success of Sotiro's mission is further elaborated in the last paragraphs of Rimbaud's report. (These were not included in the report as printed by the Société de Géographie; Bardey probably considered them confidential.) The area is commercially pristine: 'in living memory no one had seen in the Ogaden a quantity of goods as considerable as the few hundred dollars' [i.e. thalers] worth we sent there.' He notes the profits of the native traders, who 'go down with a few *sodas* or *tobes* [i.e. cloths] on their shoulders, and bring back hundreds of dollars' worth of ostrich feathers'. Or again: 'A few donkeys loaded with no more than a dozen lengths of sheeting have brought back 15 *fraslehs* of ivory.'

This is the new alchemy – not the *alchimie du verbe*, but the mercantile transformation of cotton stuffs into ostrich-plumes and ivory.

*   *   *

The literary qualities of Rimbaud's *Rapport* are almost audibly absent, held in check, pared away – it is a piece of crisp, factual reportage – but it seems that the circumstances of the report are not entirely divorced from his growing literary status back in France.

In about August 1883, Alfred Bardey was on a Messageries Maritimes steamship bound for Aden, returning after a spell of convalescence at Vichy. There he met a young French journalist named Paul Bourde. Bourde was en route for China, to cover the latest events in Tonkin for *Le Temps*. By coincidence, he was a native of Charleville, and had known Rimbaud at college. He was also a follower of literary fashions and knew of Rimbaud's growing reputation, *in absentia*, as a pioneer of the modern French poets variously known as the Symbolists, the Decadents or – the phrase which has stuck, the phrase dreamed up by Verlaine – 'Les Poètes

Maudits' (literally the 'cursed' poets; more specifically the 'outcast' or 'outlaw' poets). Rimbaud's poem 'Vowels' had recently been published and hailed as a seminal text; Verlaine was writing an article about him for the Left Bank review *Lutèce*; he was a name to be conjured with once more.

At some point on this journey, it appears, Rimbaud's cover was blown, and Bardey learned from Bourde the truth about his enigmatic, buttoned-up, 'bizarre' young branch-manager in Harar. That he was a poet of repute; that he was something of a legend; that he had lived the life of a Bohemian; that he had known the great Verlaine and called him *tu*!

When Bardey next saw Rimbaud in Aden, he recounts, he presented him with Bourde's *carte de visite*, and told him – not without a smirk of success, perhaps – that his secret was out. Rimbaud was visibly shaken, angry. He spat the words: 'absurd, ridiculous, disgusting'. It is not quite clear from Bardey's wording whether this is Rimbaud's comment about his poems, or about his former lifestyle in general, or about the fact that Bardey had found out about it. It is probably the former, in the same vein as his retort to Maurice Riès some years later: that his poems were just *rinçures*, dregs.

Yes, Rimbaud admits, he had known some writers and painters in the Latin quarter, 'but no musicians' (he had apparently forgotten his friend Cabaner). Then, with an almost visible gesture of dismissal: '*assez connu ces oiseaux-là*!' Enough of these types.

Of his friendship with Verlaine he will say nothing. Bardey presses. But you lived together in England? Rimbaud shrugs it off. '*Une ivrognerie.*' This is all he will say of it. It was drunkenness; it was just a binge.

Bardey also says that Rimbaud received a letter or letters from Verlaine around this time, and that he wrote back, just once, with a 'curt and laconic' message that Bardey synopsizes as '*Fous-moi la paix*', in other words: 'Fuck off and leave me alone'.

No trace of these letters survives, and some of Bardey's chronology is confused – he is writing many years after the event – but there is no reason to doubt the essence of his reminiscence: the meeting with Bourde, the revelation of Rimbaud's past, Rimbaud's horror at the revelation.

He has lasted for three years in this strange zone of silence, but the past is close behind and now it has caught him up. And though the fact-mongering compiler of the 'Report on the Ogaden' is a million miles from the *poète maudit* of old, it may well have been Bardey's new awareness of Rimbaud's literary reputation that led him to send the report to the Société de Géographie.

On 1 February 1884, the day on which his report was read out, at the Society's august premises on the Boulevard Saint-Germain, the Secretary General, Monsieur Maunoir, addressed him a courteous letter, requesting a photograph and a brief curriculum vitae. They wish to include in their 'albums' the portraits of those men 'who have made a name in the geographic sciences and in exploration'. This accolade, it appears, did not interest Rimbaud. He did not reply to the letter. This may be a modesty, because he considered the report to be Sotiro's work rather than his own. Or it may be this sense of being jinxed by his own past, trapped by his own fame.

15

FAITHFUL SERVANT

A shadowy figure is at Rimbaud's side during these African years. His name was Djami Wadai, and he was Rimbaud's 'faithful servant' in Harar.

That simple description of him comes from Rimbaud's sister Isabelle: almost all we know about Djami comes from her, via her accounts of Rimbaud's last days. She states that he worked for Rimbaud for eight years. He was first hired, therefore, in about 1883, during Rimbaud's second spell in Harar.

The Aden trader César Tian refers to Djami as Rimbaud's '*domestique*', and to Rimbaud as Djami's '*maître*'. The Greek Sotiro, in a letter to Rimbaud, speaks of 'your Djami'. The possessive perhaps conveys a sense of affection, but more probably an idea of ownership. Ottorino Rosa also mentions him – Italianizing the name as 'Giama' – and refers to him as having a house in Harar. This probably means his family's house, rather than his own, but shows he had a certain status.

Rimbaud tells us nothing about him directly, but seems to have spoken about him often to Isabelle. In her memoir, *Mon Frère Arthur*, written in 1892, she describes Djami – or anyway her idea of him – as 'this native boy who attends to the various tasks of the house, the courtyard, the warehouses'; and as 'your faithful servant who for the last eight years has venerated and cherished you with his obedience' [*Reliques*, p. 83].

This seems somewhat filtered through Isabelle's sentimentalizing imagination. A more authentic glimpse of him comes from a letter she wrote to her mother on 28 October 1891 – a fortnight before Rimbaud's death – in which she gives an extraordinary description of Rimbaud's delirium as he lies on his hospital bed in Marseille:

> Sometimes he calls me Djami, but I know that this is because he misses him, and so he keeps coming into his dreams. For the rest,

he mixes everything up – but somehow artfully. We are in Harar, we are always leaving for Aden. We must find camels, organize the caravan. He walks very easily with his new artificial leg, we ride out together on fine mules with rich harnesses. Then he must work, do the accounts, write his letters. Quick, quick, they are waiting for us. We must pack up our bags and go. Why has he been left to sleep so long? Why don't I help him to get dressed? What will people say if we don't arrive on the appointed day? No one will trust his word any more. No one will have faith in him any more. And he starts to weep and to complain at my clumsiness and negligence, because I am always there with him, and it is my duty to make all the preparations.

Thus we learn from Rimbaud's delirious ramblings something of the nature of Djami's duties – to wake Rimbaud up and help him to dress, to pack up the bags, and indeed to ride out alongside him on those long, punishing rides which (so Rimbaud believed) were one of the causes of the damage to his leg.

The hallucinated likeness between Djami and Isabelle hinges on that idea of presence, of being by his side: Djami was 'always there with him' in Harar, as Isabelle was in Marseille.

*   *   *

Rimbaud's affection for Djami can be gauged from his desire to provide a legacy for him after his death. This was, as far as we know, Rimbaud's only bequest. Isabelle was his executor in this. On 19 February 1892 she wrote to the French consul in Aden:

For eight years he [Rimbaud] had as his servant a native of Harar named Djami. Having always had the benefit of this man's fidelity and service, and wanting to give him a token of satisfaction, he charged me with sending him, in a way that was *sure and certain*, a sizeable sum of money . . .

(The italicized words are underlined in the letter, and are perhaps verbatim: the dying man's urgent repetitions.) She asks the consul to get in touch with Djami, and to inform him that she has the sum of 750 thalers [3,000 francs] for him,

with the recommendation of his master and benefactor to make good and sensible use of the money, whether employing it in some commercial transaction, or reserving it for some other honest and prudent enterprise which is sure to return him some reasonable profit; but that this money should never be the pretext for idleness or intemperance.

This has a touchingly paternal note to it.

She adds the following description of him: 'He is a young man of twenty-two to twenty-three years old, completely illiterate. He only understands a few words of French.'

After Rimbaud's departure for France, Djami had returned to Harar. On 13 July 1891, the Swiss trader Felter, the Harar representative of the Italian company Bienenfeld, wrote to Rimbaud: 'Your servant Djami is in my employ, and I will send him down to you with the mules for my wife.' (Felter was at this point expecting Rimbaud's return to Africa, and was hoping he would escort his wife up from the coast to Harar.) This is confirmed by Isabelle: 'After the departure of my brother from Harar, Djami entered the service of M. Felter, the Harar agent of Beinenfeld & Co, and I presume he is still there' [letter to the French Consul in Aden, 19 February 1892].

The long saga of the inheritance can be followed in the correspondence between Isabelle and César Tian, who was charged with overseeing it. It concludes with the receipt, signed and affirmed by Mgr Taurin Cahagne, 'Vicaire Apostolique des Gallas', in Harar on 7 June 1893. It states that 750 thalers – 'a legacy made by M. Raimbaud [sic] to his servant Djammi Wadai' – has been delivered, by order of the Ras.

It has come too late, however, for the recipients of the money are described as the 'heirs of Djami'.

*   *   *

A very brief biography of Rimbaud's 'faithful servant' emerges from these posthumous papers.

Djami Wadai was born in or near Harar in about 1870. He entered Rimbaud's service in about 1883, when he was thirteen or fourteen years old. We do not know if he accompanied Rimbaud when the latter left Harar in mid-1884; we can certainly assume he was Rimbaud's *domestique* throughout the last years at Harar. He accompanied Rimbaud on the last dreadful journey to Aden. After Rimbaud's departure for France he returned to Harar, and was immediately employed there by the Swiss trader Felter. He died, in his early twenties, sometime between July 1891 (when he is mentioned by Felter) and June 1893 (when Rimbaud's legacy was delivered to his 'heirs').

The famine in Harar in these years probably killed him. Had the legacy reached him sooner it would probably have saved him.

* * *

Certain attenuated questions of sexuality surround the name of Djami, and probably cannot be resolved.

That Rimbaud was at certain points in his youth a practising homosexual is not in doubt. But whatever his inclinations in his teenage years, there is no evidence of his homosexuality in Africa. Alfred Bardey fiercely repudiated accusations (or anyway assumptions) of that nature: 'Though it is practised elsewhere, in Turkey for instance, sexual inversion [*sic*] does not occur in Abyssinia at all. Rimbaud was neither debauched nor perverted' [interview with Jean-Paul Vaillant, *c*. 1929]. However, there is a tantalizing snippet in one of Alfred Ilg's letters. Ilg was a close friend during Rimbaud's later years in Africa: we shall meet him in due course. In a letter to their mutual friend Léon Chefneux, Ilg writes: 'Rimbaud tells me he is going to Harar to . . . do some business, but he doesn't tell me what kind of business: probably in coffee, incense and skins. (Menahins!?)' [Zurich, 31 May 1888]. Jean Voellmy, who first published this letter in 1978 [*Rimbaud Vivant* No. 15, p. 22] glosses the Arabic word at the end:

> *Menahins* means in Arabic 'foretellers of the future', which can hardly be the sense in this context. It is possible that the word was badly written, and that it was actually meant to be *melahin*, which means [. . .] itinerant boy prostitutes [*enfants vagabonds et pervers*]. This explanation seems the more acceptable not only in the light of Rimbaud's previous history, but also with regard to the punctuation marks which appear after the word in this letter.

Voellmy's explanation is ingenious, but even if this is what Ilg intended to write, it cannot – given the bantering tone of Ilg's letters – be taken as a serious assertion.

The most one can say is that the idea of Rimbaud purchasing boys for pleasure in Harar is aired, humorously, among his friends.

(Cf. Ilg to Rimbaud, 16 June 1889, where the word *toucher*, meaning to draw on funds, is quibbled over in a sexual sense: 'and don't forget we're always very-very-very happy to have something touching us somewhere, if you'll forgive the pun'.) This is not enough to support any theories about a sexual relationship between Rimbaud and Djami.

It must have been hell to work for Rimbaud: one notes the anger and impatience in that imagined rant recorded by Isabelle. Yet what survives of Rimbaud and Djami is a sense of unexpected affection, of an intimacy in the midst of solitude. This is the true text of the legacy: that when the end came there was no one who meant more to him than this illiterate African boy.

16

THE ABYSSINIAN WOMAN

I
T WAS SOMETIME in 1883 or early 1884 that Rimbaud met, or hired, or quite simply *bought* – one does not know what verb to use; one does not know what actions and feelings were involved – the unnamed 'Abyssinian woman' who lived with him in Aden; who is described by Bardey and by Bardey's housekeeper Françoise Grisard; whom he taught to read and speak French; and whom he finally rejected, sending her back across the Red Sea, to Obock, with a bit of money to see her back home.

Another intimacy, quite certainly sexual: a 'masquerade', as he summed it up when it was all over.

Rimbaud left Harar in early March 1884, the office closed down due to the wars, and arrived in Aden after 'six weeks of travel in the deserts' on or shortly before 24 April, the date of his first letter home. It is generally said that he brought the Abyssinian woman back with him from Harar. It is also said, by Enid Starkie among others, that she was herself from Harar. This is unlikely: the evidence points to her being from Shoa, in the Abyssinian highlands. Rimbaud had not at this point been to Shoa, so must have acquired her elsewhere. He may have done so in Harar, at the 'Christian market' outside the Shoa Gate, which undoubtedly included slave transactions. It is also possible that during that mysterious 'six weeks of travel' in March–April 1884 he went up to Obock on the Red Sea, which he writes of a few months later as if he has been there, and that he acquired her at the slave market in nearby Tadjourah.

The witnesses of her in Aden – mainly Bardey and Grisard – supply the following portrait. She was 'an Abyssinian woman' and a 'Catholic' – i.e. she was a Christian Amhara. She was tall and slender [*élancée*] and '*assez jolie*'. She was '*pas très noire*', i.e. coffee-coloured rather than black. When living with him in Aden (the only time she was seen by the witnesses) she dressed in European style, and she smoked cigarettes.

Bardey says:

> It was in Aden that the liaison with the Abyssinian woman took
> place, from 1884 to 1886. The relationship was intimate, and
> Rimbaud, who to begin with lodged and ate with us, rented a
> separate house so that he could live there, with his companion,
> outside the hours he worked in our offices. [letter to Berrichon, 16
> July 1897]

Bardey states that they had no children. This was a disappointment
for the first generation of Rimbaud searchers, still hopeful of
tracking down his offspring – if not his lost manuscripts – in some
picturesque Red Sea dive. The statement seems now more positive
than negative: the liaison, in Bardey's mind, was of the kind of that
might have produced children but did not.

Bardey concludes by saying that this woman was 'conveniently
[*convenablement*] repatriated' by Rimbaud. (It is not quite clear
what he means – 'convenient' to whom? – but see the letter to
Franzoj below.)

Bardey's housekeeper, Françoise Grisard, came every Sunday
afternoon to Rimbaud's house to do the cleaning ('I was the only
person he received', i.e. permitted to visit him there), and she knew
'l'Abyssine' quite well. She says that Rimbaud took great care to
teach her French, which she hardly spoke at all; and that she
(Grisard) taught her how to sew, etc. He went out with her in the
evenings. She was very shy and sweet [*très douce*]. She would not go
out unless he accompanied her. They walked together through the
souk.

He treated her with great respect and kindness, Grisard says. '*Il
me paraissait très bon pour cette femme.*' He intended eventually to
marry her. '*Il voulait l'instruire . . . et se marier.*'

Given the talk of marriage and children which surrounds her, it
might be thought that his intimacy with l'Abyssine ties in with
certain wistful comments found in his letter from Harar of 6 May
1883:

> The solitude's a bad thing down here. I'm beginning to regret not
> having married and had a family . . . What is the point of all these
> comings and goings, these exhaustions and adventures among
> strange people, these languages crammed into one's memory,
> these nameless sufferings, if I cannot one day, a few years on,

settle down in some more or less agreeable spot, and start a family
of my own, and have at least one son whom I can spend the rest of
my days teaching according to my principles [*élever a mon idée*],
whom I can embellish and arm with the most complete and up-to-
date teaching one can give, and whom I will one day see becoming
a celebrated engineer, a man made powerful and wealthy through
science? But who knows how long my days will last up here in the
mountains? I could disappear among these people, and the news
would never get out . . .

Intimations of mortality; the desire for perpetuity through children –
is this expressed in his love for l'Abyssine?

The Italian trader, Ottorino Rosa, who knew Rimbaud in Aden,
published what he claims to be her photograph in his book,
L'Impero del Leone di Giuda. Subtitled *'Note sull' Abissinia'*, this
book was privately printed at Brescia in 1913. The photograph, no.
142, is captioned 'Donna Abissina', and in his note on it Rosa says
that this woman 'lived with the genial [i.e. genius] poet Arthur
Rimbaud in Aden'. However, he says that they were living together
in 1882, whereas Bardey and Grisard date the liaison to 1884.

In a later manuscript, Rosa adds that he himself 'kept' this
woman's sister, but 'got rid' of her after a few weeks. The verbs he
uses suggest the norms of this kind of relationship – the woman is a
menial and no doubt sexual servant, to be hired and fired at will –
and suggest also how far the relationship of Rimbaud and l'Abyssine
went beyond those norms.

The photograph is – like the self-portraits of Rimbaud – as much
a concealment as a portrait. She is wrapped in the long white shawl
[*natala*] traditionally worn by the Amhara; her hair is covered in a
white scarf [*shash*]; her eyes gaze off into the distance. She is
beautiful, though one does not get the impression of slenderness
remarked on by Françoise Grisard.

There is no certainty this photo is genuine. Alain Borer estimates
that Rosa's 'honesty cannot be open to doubt', and that 'although he
mixes up the dates, as do all those returning from East Africa', he
should be trusted. At the very least this photograph is deemed by
Rosa to be a likeness, actual or approximate, of Rimbaud's
Abyssinian mistress.

* * *

From Rimbaud himself there are only some brief remarks, made rather bitterly at the end of the affair. They are found in his letter to Agosto Franzoj, dated *c.* September 1885. This was discovered among the papers of Ugo Ferrandi, who worked for the Bienenfeld Brothers in Aden and later in Harar, and knew Rimbaud quite well. The letter was first published in 1949, by Enrico Emanuelli, in the Italian literary magazine, *Inventario*. It reads as follows:

Dear Monsieur Franzoj,

I'm sorry, but I have hardened my heart and sent the woman back.

I will give her some thalers and she will take the dhow for Obock, which is now at Rasali. From there she will go where she pleases.

I've had this masquerade in front of me for long enough.

I should not have been so stupid as to bring her from Shoa, and I will not be so stupid as to be responsible for [i.e. bear the cost of] transporting her back there.

All the best,

Rimbaud

(I have translated the opening sentence loosely. The phrase Rimbaud uses is *renvoyé sans remission*. This seems to mean he has sent her back 'relentlessly' or 'without fail', but it could be meant literally, i.e. 'without forgiveness', implying some fault in her which Franzoj knows of.)

I see no reason to doubt – as Steinmetz and others do – that this is the woman described by Bardey, Grisard and Rosa. It seems the affair ended in about September 1885 – the date of this letter – and not in 1886 as Bardey says.

The letter is unequivocal about her origins. She had originally come from Shoa and he is giving her a few thalers to get herself back there, if 'she pleases'. This accords with Bardey and Grisard's description: an 'Abyssinian' woman who was 'repatriated' by Rimbaud.

There is also a tradition that Rimbaud lived with an Argobba woman. This is based on gossip collected in Obock and Djibouti in the early years of this century [Dufaud, *et al*], which spoke of Rimbaud's sexual fondness for the 'native element', and of 'an

Argobba woman by whom he had several children, though these have all disappeared without trace'. The children seem to be a fantasy, but the precision of the comment is interesting. The Argobba or Argouba was a small tribe speaking a Semitic-based language related to Amharic. They claimed descent from the Portuguese who came to Ethiopia in the sixteenth century. The woman were renowned for their beauty, and wore a characteristic robe of black and scarlet emblazoned with a cross. Though most lived in the Shoa highlands, there were also Muslim Argobba living close to Harar (the south-eastern gate of Harar is called among other names, Argo Beri, i.e. the Argobba Gate). Bardey refers to this Argobba area in his memoirs, saying 'the people there have their own language and claim that their origin is not the same as the Hararis' [BA, p. 276]. Interestingly, this area lay on the trail to Boubassa, the very place that Rimbaud came to buy skins in mid-1883.

The *'femme Argoba'* is a mere rumour. As we have it she is distinct from the *'femme Abyssine'*, who is briefly mentioned in the same source. It is just possible they are one and the same, however. Abyssinia is an area rather than a tribe: the Argobba of Shoa were certainly 'Abyssinian', though much less numerous than the dominant Amhara. The Portuguese connection might tie in with Grisard's description of her – 'to my eyes her face looked very European' – and perhaps also with the woman in the Rosa photograph. The presence of Argobba near Boubassa may provide the link to Rimbaud, who had not himself yet been to Shoa.

'L'Abyssine' is certainly different from the native woman who was Rimbaud's servant and perhaps mistress during his last years in Harar. The latter is described by Mgr Jarosseau, Bishop of Harar, in the reminiscence elicited by Evelyn Waugh in 1930. Rimbaud, he told Waugh,

> ... used to live with a native woman in a little house, now demolished, in the square; he had no children; probably the woman was still alive; she was not a native of Harar, and after Rimbaud's death she had gone back to her own people in Tigré. [*Remote People*, pp. 78–9]

This woman is indistinct: virtually all one can infer about her from Jarosseau's remarks is that she must have been quite young. (He thinks she is 'probably' alive forty years later; he would not be assuming great longevity.) Waugh is put out by the fact that she is Tigrayan: how, he wonders, 'in Harar, surrounded by so many radiant women, he should have chosen a mate from the stolid people of Tigré – a gross and perverse preference'.

Ottorino Rosa also speaks of this woman, but describes her as a Galla. He also says, repudiating an idea that Rimbaud led a 'life of debauchery' in Harar: 'she did not even lodge with him, but at the house of his servant Giama [i.e. Djami].' Both of these statements contradict Mgr Jarosseau. Which of them was right about her origins is hard to say.

Thus on the contemporary evidence, sketchy as it is, Rimbaud lived with at least two African women. He was with the first in Aden in c. 1884–5, and with the second in Harar in c. 1888–91. There may well have been others, though certainly not enough of them to justify the picturesque local gossip recorded by Pierre Mille, who after some research in Djibouti in 1896, put together a story under the heading of 'Flesh-covered Dictionaries'. According to this Rimbaud kept a whole harim of women speaking different languages.

This is pure folklore. The hidden source of it may be that '*harim*' of female workers he oversaw at Aden. Also folklorique, one suspects, is a scurrilous anecdote retailed by Ottoman Righas in about 1911:

> one day, when Rimbaud was at home in Harar, an infibulated girl came into the house. Rimbaud wanted to get up her straightaway, and coming up against the obstacle, wanted to operate on the unfortunate girl with his pocket-knife. She screamed her head off, and a crowd gathered, and things nearly turned out badly.

This story of casual violation probably says more about Ottoman Righas than it does about Rimbaud. It is at odds with all other reports of him in Harar, and with the notes of tenderness running through the reminiscences about the Abyssinian woman: 'he seemed to me very good to her'.

*   *   *

One sees 'l'Abyssine' again and again in the bars of Harar and Dire Dawa and most of all in Djibouti, where the French presence begun by men like Rimbaud a hundred years ago is still a fact of life. This port city, nominally the capital of the independent Republic of

Djibouti, is run by French 'advisers' and 'technicians' and indeed traders, and supports a permanent garrison of about 4,000 French troops, including one of the last African detachments of the Foreign Legion.

What was once an actual traffic in slaves and concubines is now a process of economic migration drawing young girls from the poverty of Ethiopia to a life of prostitution in the bars and clubs of Djibouti. A huge proportion of the bar girls there are Ethiopians: it is said there are 20,000 in the city. *Les filles. Les nanas.* They come on the train from Addis and Dire Dawa, drawn to this tinseltown of big-spending soldiers and air-conditioned night-clubs. They put on tight dresses and lipstick and a big smile, and click their chewing-gum, and learn the catchphrases of the great lingua franca of prostitution.

Gina is twenty-three, an Amhara from the pleasant lowland town of Dire Dawa. She has been in Djibouti fifteen months now. She came on the train. She ran away from home, where she was engaged to a young man she didn't really like, an arranged marriage. She was a virgin when she came to Djibouti: *moi n'étais pas cassée.* Her first man was a young French soldier whom she picked up at a club called the Mick Mack.

The girls have a tough time in Djibouti. They get hassled by the grossly underpaid police for backhanders: I saw a policeman spit in the face of an Ethiopian girl and take off his leather belt as if to whip her. They get sneered at by the upstanding Muslim Djiboutiens. In the bars and *boîtes* and disco-cellars of the city where they work, the Immigration Police make regular raids. Those without papers are hauled off to jail, more baksheesh is extracted. They live in a hostile world, a world that insults them.

They make their rooms, or the backrooms of the bars, or even the steps on the street, a little corner of Ethiopia. The smell of frankincense burning in the brazier; the brewing of the coffee; the chewing of *khat*; and beside their beds a Coptic bible.

In this harsh world Gina found someone who was good to her. For several months they lived together. He was a Belgian. He was a cook, working at one of the military bases. He had a wife and children back in Belgium. He looked very old, she said. He had lots of lines on his face, though he was only in his mid-thirties. He sounds like Rimbaud, whose hair was grey when he died at thirty-seven.

They lived in a room above the Historil café just off Menelik

Square. He came home late after work. He bought a suite of furniture which could hardly fit in there: a wardrobe, a dresser, and a huge bed, ornate and Italian-looking, Art Deco, with a bakelite radio inset into the headboard.

He didn't call me Gina, she said.

Gina is just her working name, her *nom de nuit*. He called her Ainalam. This is her real name, which means in Amharic the 'Eyes of Africa'. Here in Djibouti, she too is somebody else.

He lies in the hot room with the shutters half-closed and the sounds coming up off the bleached streets. He listens to her broken, improvised French – *marci* for *merci, ristoree* for *restaurant, bizoo* for *baiser*. He chews the little purse-shaped parcels of *khat* which she feeds into his mouth. He looks into the large, limpid eyes of Africa.

PART THREE

THE GUN-
RUNNER

'I dream of a war, just or brutal, unexpectedly
logical. It is as simple as a musical phrase.'

– Illuminations: 'War'

17

THE LABATUT AFFAIR

Sick of this 'masquerade' of his African mistress, beset by angers and uncertainties concerning his employment with Bardey, 'stupefied' and 'brutalized' by life in Aden, Rimbaud begins to consider new opportunities. On 20 October 1884 he celebrates – if that is the word – his thirtieth birthday:

'I see a third of my life is passed,' he writes, naively.

His thoughts are reaching out now towards Abyssinia, for commercial reasons, but also as somewhere he had always dreamed of. Abyssinia, and especially Shoa, was part of that gazetteer of unreached places which included Zanzibar, Bombay and Panama. It may be that his affair with 'l'Abyssine' had quickened his curiosity. At any rate, his letters now warm to this theme of beautiful, mysterious Abyssinia, especially when dreamed of from the heat and inanition of Aden:

> In Abyssinia the climate is sweet, neither too hot nor too cold; the people are Christian and very hospitable; one lives a life of ease; it is a very agreeable place of repose for those who have sweated for years along the incandescent shores of the Red Sea. [18 November 1885]

> Abyssinia . . . is the Switzerland of Africa, without winters or summers: perpetual verdant springtime and a life that costs nothing and is free. [28 February 1886]

Les rivages incandescents de la Mer Rouge . . . Une existence gratuite et libre. These thoughts of Abyssinia quicken the language, awaken its buried drama.

He is also newly interested in the little Red Sea port of Obock, north of the Bay of Tadjourah, four hours by steamship from Aden. The French had gained a commercial foothold here, thanks largely to the efforts of a pioneering French trader named Paul Soleillet. His comments about the place are very sardonic:

> There is a French warship at Obock: out of a crew of 70 men, 65 are sick with tropical fever. The captain died yesterday . . . [10 September 1884]

> Not far from here is the sad French colony of Obock. We are trying to set up an enterprise there, but I don't think much is going to come of it. It's a deserted, scorched beach, with nothing to live off, and no trade. Its only use is as a coal dump, for refuelling warships on their way to China or Madagascar . . . [7 October 1884]

> At Obock the tiny French administration is busy gobbling up government funds. The government won't get a single sou back from this dreadful colony, which so far consists of just a dozen freebooters [*filibustiers*]. [14 April 1885]

He is not interested in Obock as a place to visit, but for its commercial potential. The French presence there opens up a new channel of trade and communication to Abyssinia, one not subject – as both Aden and Zeilah were – to British control.

*　　*　　*

In late September 1885 these interests begin to acquire a particular focus – a new associate, Pierre Labatut; and a new merchandise, guns. So begins Rimbaud's career as a gun-runner, and the enterprise that he will refer to, on and on, with mounting bitterness and frustration, as '*l'affaire Labatut*'.

Pierre Labatut was one of the old hands of Shoa. At this time, according to Rimbaud, there were only 'ten or so' Europeans in Shoa, and all were 'engaged in arms traffic'. Of these Labatut was the foremost. A native of Gascony, a former sea-captain, he had already lived for about fifteen years in Shoa. He had married an Abyssinian woman, and lived *à l'Africain*. He was on good terms with the powerful Shoan warlord, King Menelik II. The latter had given him land at Ankober, the capital of Shoa. There he lived in a household consisting of a dozen servants and several camels and mules.

Labatut had left Shoa in August 1885, commissioned by Menelik to purchase 'arms, ammunition, utensils and sundries'. He had some money from Menelik in advance, and was prepared to venture 'all his own disposable capital'. He went to Obock to obtain permission from the French governor to disembark arms at Tadjourah, a small port a few miles south of Obock, and to form a caravan from there to Shoa. He then went on to Aden and obtained permission, via the French consul, to transit the guns through Aden.

It was at this stage that he entered into an agreement with Rimbaud, who would organize the caravan at Tadjourah and lead it to Shoa. As far as we know they had not met before, though Labatut and Bardey had certainly met some years earlier. Bardey quotes a letter from Labatut, written at Ankober in September 1881 [BA, pp. 298–99], and later refers to Labatut as 'our former contact in Shoa'. This letter of 1881 was itself a proposal for an arms-deal. Menelik had offered Labatut 1,000 thalers to set up a gun-running route from the Somali coast. 'Everyone is making me offers of Remingtons,' Menelik tells him. Labatut thus writes to Bardey:

> I remembered what you told me, as you left Zeilah: that is, that we should do some business next time around. The moment is propitious, M. Bardey. If, with your influence, we could get some rifles and cartridges landed at Zeilah, I would leave immediately and be the first to arrive here . . .

He suggests a consignment of 'twenty double-barrelled piston-rifles' [*fusils à deux coups à piston*] to get the thing rolling. However, Bardey comments: 'I have no intention of pursuing this kind of arms-deal . . . The natives have no knowledge of these weapons; it is dangerous for the Europeans, and for the natives, to introduce them.'

These misgivings, typical of Bardey's integrity, do not seem to have troubled Rimbaud a few years later.

*   *   *

The contract between Rimbaud and Labatut was signed, at Aden, on 5 October. It reads:

> I the undersigned, Pierre Labatut, trader at Shoa (Abyssinia), undertake to pay M. Arthur Rimbaud, on or before this date next year, the sum of 5,000 Maria Theresa dollars, at the exchange rate

obtaining today at Aden [= 21,500 francs], and to bear all the expenses of the said Sieur Rimbaud, who is to bring my first caravan to Shoa.

In signing this deal Rimbaud was breaking the terms of his contract with Bardey, which ran through to 31 December 1885, and which required three months' notice of disengagement. A stormy meeting followed a week later. Bardey was furious at the suddenness of Rimbaud's quitting, and 'reproached him' (as he later put it) 'right there in the office, in front of everyone, for not having given us warning'. He advised Rimbaud of the risks of the Labatut venture, but it was too late. He had already put money into it, was already 'in a panic about this trap he'd landed himself in' [letter to Berrichon, 30 November 1897]. A gruff but essentially generous note from Bardey terminates the contract:

I the undersigned, Alfred Bardey, declare that I have employed M. Arthur Rimbaud as an agent and buyer from 30 April 1884 up to November 1885. I have always been satisfied with his service and with his honesty [*probité*]. He is free of all engagement with me.

Aden, 14 October 1885

p.p. P. Bardey

Alf. Bardey

Rimbaud comments more sourly, in a letter written a week later:

I have left my job in Aden after a violent altercation with those pathetic peasants [*ignobles pignoufs*] who want to stupefy me for good. I have done good work for these people, and they seemed to think I was going to stay with them, at their convenience, for the rest of my life. They did all they could to hold on to me, but I sent them to hell, with all their offers and their deals, and their horrible office, and their filthy town, quite apart from the fact that they've made my life so boring and have always stopped me from making any money. So there it is: let them go to the devil! They've given me some excellent references . . . [22 October 1885]

The animosity soon blew over, and there will be further letters and dealings between them. A few months later Bardey notes in his memoirs:

We remain in touch with Rimbaud and, at his request, we furnish

him with some camp-equipment for Menelik's troops. This
consists of bowls and cups of beaten iron, fitting one into the other
in order to be more compact; and some round steel plates intended
for roasting the grain or cakes of *dourah* on camp-fires. This
equipment was supplied to us by Usines Japy of Beaucourt.

This is a piquantly prosaic footnote to the colourful story of
Rimbaud the gun-runner.

* * *

What exactly was the arrangement with Labatut? One learns
something from Rimbaud's letters home, and from an official
document prepared by Labatut and Rimbaud in April 1886.
   This is what he tells his family:

> Several thousand rifles are on their way to me from Europe. I am
> going to set up a caravan, and carry this merchandise to Menelik,
> the king of Shoa . . . The king pays a good price for weapons. If
> things go well for me I expect to arrive, to be paid immediately,
> and to return with a profit of 25 to 30,000 francs, all in less than a
> year . . . [22 October 1885]

> The goods we are importing are guns (old piston rifles which went
> out of use forty years ago). These can be bought from dealers in
> old arms at Liège, or in France, for 7 or 8 francs each. They are
> sold to the King of Shoa, Menelik II, for about 40 francs. But there
> are huge overheads to pay, not to mention the dangers of the
> journey, both there and back. [3 December 1885]

These are the first optimistic computations. The anticipated profit of
25–30,000 francs would be his fee of 5,000 thalers [21,500 francs], as
in the contract, plus some personal profits from other merchandise
he would carry up to, and down from, Shoa. One notes also his belief
that Menelik will buy the rifles at forty francs apiece. This was later
inflated to fifteen thalers apiece (over sixty francs). The eventual
price he got was much less than that.
   He describes the guns as *fusils à piston reformés*, but the actual
consignment turns out to be *fusils à capsules*, or percussion rifles.
(*Reformé* does not mean 'reconditioned', as one might think, but is
used in its military sense of 'unfit for service', hence discontinued or
obsolete.)

The actual consignment, as unloaded at Tadjourah towards the end of January 1886, was itemized as follows:

— 2,040 percussion rifles, priced in Shoa at 15 thalers each ... 30,600 thalers
— 60,000 Remington cartridges at 60 thalers per thousand ... 3,600 thalers
— An order of utensils for the king, which cannot be itemized separately ... 5,800 thalers.

The total value of the caravan, at the point of delivery, is therefore: 40,000 thalers.

Adding 50% on the return, viz. the profits of selling, at Aden, the goods (ivory, musk, gold) given us as payment at Shoa by the king, we conclude that this operation should realize a net sum of 60,000 thalers after a period of one year or eighteen months.

60,000 thalers, at the standard exchange-rate in Aden (4.30 francs) equals 258,000 French francs.

These are the bald figures of Rimbaud's first venture as a gun-runner, though once again these are projections rather than actual profits.

*   *   *

He left for Tadjourah around the end of November. On 22 October he had written confidently:

By the time you receive this, I shall probably be at Tadjourah, on the Danakil coast annexed to the Obock settlement . . . If the affair succeeds, you can expect to see me in France towards autumn of 1886, where I will buy some new merchandise myself. I hope that this will turn out well. Wish me some good luck: I really need some . . . Don't write to me at the Bardey place any more. Those animals will probably cut off my correspondence.

Four weeks later, however, he was still in Aden, and writes: 'My affairs have suffered an unexpected delay, and I don't think I will be able to leave Aden before the end of November.' He tells his family to write him at 'Hôtel de l'Univers à Aden', in other words the Grand Hotel, where he is apparently now lodging after his break with

Bardey. The manager, Jules Suel, is later involved in the Labatut deal, and may already be an investor.

There are hints of misgiving in Rimbaud's mind:

> Now that this business is under way I cannot pull out of it. I don't deceive myself about the dangers. I am quite aware of the hardships of these expeditions; but after my spells at Harar I'm well acquainted with the conditions and customs of these countries . . .

He asks his mother to send him an Amharic dictionary. He specifies – specificity is his forte – the *Dictionnaire de la Langue Amhara*, with pronunciation in Latin alphabet, by 'M. d'Abbadie of the Institute'. He 'cannot do without' it in Shoa. 'No one there speaks any European languages, since there are, up till now, hardly any Europeans there.'

He expects to stay a month or two in Tadjourah, 'in order to find camels, mules, guides, etc. etc.'. He hopes to leave Tadjourah around 15 January 1886, and reach Shoa two months later.

These predictions are, like the computations of profit, absurdly optimistic. It would be a whole year before he would finally set out for Shoa, and he would return from there richer in experience but not in thalers or francs.

Time and money: they are both running short. 'It is easy to be a millionaire in Africa', he jokes: 'a millionaire in fleas!'

On 23 November he hands over to his associate Labatut the sum of 800 thalers, and gets a receipt from him promising repayment, at zero interest, within a year. This appears to be some kind of deposit or side-investment in the venture.

Not long after this Rimbaud embarks on a *boutre* or a steamer from Aden to Obock, and thence to the little port of Tadjourah. He was there sometime before 3 December 1885, the date of his first letter home.

18

THE AIR OF DJIBOUTI

To REACH TADJOURAH today you must first come to the louche
Red Sea port of Djibouti, now a city of 400,000 people, the
capital of the tiny republic of Djibouti, and one of the last
outposts of the French Foreign Legion.

In 1885 Djibouti was, in Rimbaud's own words, 'nothing but
desert'. It was a sandy promontory or cape, with a cluster of bare
coral islands linked by sandbars at low tide. Its 'sole inhabitant', an
early settler remarked, 'was a jackal dying of hunger under a thorn
tree'. The name is said to derive from an Afar word, *jabuti*. A *jabuti*
is a platter of woven palm-fibre on which the staple East African
fare of *dourah* pancakes is served; the islands being compared to
this. (The Somalis say that it derives from Somali *jabode*, meaning
sterile, an apt description of the surrounding terrain; while the
Oromo claim that it is an old Galla formulation, *ijibuti*, the 'eye of
the eagle'.)

The site stood on the southern edge of the Bay of Tadjourah. The
French, precariously implanted at Obock and Tadjourah on the
north side, were already aware of its potential for a settlement.
Rimbaud makes some prescient comments on the subject in a letter
written to a Cairo newspaper in August 1887. Djibouti has 'good
sources' of water, and is just three days' journey from Hensa, on the
current Harar–Zeilah route:

> We [i.e. the French] would thus have an outlet on the route from
> Harar and from Abyssinia. . . . The formation of caravans can be
> accomplished at Djibouti once there is some establishment
> supplied with native merchandise, and some armed garrison
> [*troupe*]. The place is, at this point, nothing but desert. It goes
> without saying that the place must remain a free port if it is to
> compete with Zeilah.

Here is forming, in his mind's eye, the French enclave we see today, with its commercial 'establishments', its free port, and its garrison of soldiers (currently about 4,000 of them, of which a quarter are *légionnaires*). The chief difference is that the principal trade-route from Ethiopia is not the caravan-trail via Hensa, but the train-line via Dire Dawa.

In March 1888 the town of Djibouti was officially founded by the French Governor of Obock, Léonce Lagarde: a market-place, a garrison, a customs house, and a straggle of shops and houses. Its earliest settlers include several French traders known to Rimbaud, among them Armand Savouré, Eloi Pino, Maurice Riès and the Brémonds. In the 1890s, when the colonial map of the region was finally drawn, Djibouti became the capital of French Somaliland, a small colony sandwiched between Italian Eritrea to the north and British Somaliland to the south. Rimbaud did not live to see this.

In 1967 French Somaliland became the French Territory of the Afars and the Issas, with a measure of autonomy. This was the same time that the British pulled out of Aden. Ten years later the country became – nominally, at least – the independent Republic of Djibouti. But independence was not impartial: power was vested in the hands of the Issah, the Somali tribe which provided the bulk of Rimbaud's native *caravaniers*. This is resented by the Afar or Danakil of the north, and a small but debilitating civil war has split the country since 1991.

*   *   *

Rimbaud never lived in Djibouti Ville, but he was there at the very inception of the place, was part of that first wave of French settlers which built the town, and for the follower of his footsteps a hundred years later this oddly charming hell-hole is perhaps as near as one will get to the 'feel' of Rimbaud in Africa.

In Aden and Harar one walks the streets he walked, but Djibouti is in a sense Rimbaud's creation out here: his colonial legacy.

In Djibouti one sees the last decaying remnants of the French in East Africa – the crumbling colonnades, the pitted grey walls, the street-signs in that peculiarly French shade of blue – and one hears it too, in that lovely flattened-out African French, a version of the street patois or *radio trottoir* ('sidewalk radio') that can be heard in Algeria and Senegal and Zaire, and indeed in the creole of Haiti and Martinique and Cayenne.

He would recognize it. He would even recognize some of the names. The descendants of Maurice Riès are still here, running a major shipping line (Savon Riès) and the Peugeot concession, and much else besides. The city's Toyota agent, Luc Merrill, is also descended from an original Djibouti settler. The line is unbroken back to Rimbaud *négociant*.

His connection with the place was honoured by the French in 1938, when Djibouti's central market-place – then simply called the Place des Chameaux or Camel Square – was renamed Place Arthur Rimbaud. The scene was witnessed by another French adventurer, a man in the Rimbaud mould, the journalist and smuggler Henri de Monfried.

The dignitaries assemble in their tropical whites – Governor Hubert Deschamps, Chef de Bureau Paul Zerbib, the guest of honour, the famous foreign correspondent Jérôme Tharaud, and 'various native chiefs in their best turbans'. The schoolchildren parade past. Tharaud begins his speech, 'amid the gargling of the camels, who seem to be protesting against the object of all this solemnity'. The Europeans listen respectfully,

> . . . but the noise of the crowd drowned his voice, and the natives, amused for a moment by the orator's mouth opening and closing without seeming to produce any sound, soon fell to talking among themselves. Their voices got louder and louder. Indignant 'Ssssh's' put an end to this palaver, but the native schoolchildren, impatient to get on with the songs and dances of the ceremony, mistook these calls for silence, and in the midst of the most moving part of the speech they struck up with the *Madelon* and began dancing their zambas.
>
> The workmen and sailors and coolies shouted encouragement, and the frightened camels gargled even louder, accompanied by braying asses and an ever-growing chorus of wild dogs. The police had to intervene, not without violence, and the ceremony ended in chaos. Poor Deschamps, very crestfallen, contemplated the grandeurs and miseries of power.
>
> Who can say that this wasn't the ghost of Rimbaud, the scorner of all established order, whistling like a wind of misrule among these official puppets who serve the mountebanks of international politics?

In the end the crowd dispersed, some more angry, some more amused, some more puzzled than they had come.

When the sun had faded into the redness of dusk, a pale moon lit up Place Arthur Rimbaud, where the indifferent camels continued to chew the bitter grass of the Somali deserts.

[*Le Radeau de la Méduse*, pp. 79–81]

Place Rimbaud has changed its name once more: it is now Place Mahmoud Harbi, after a hero of Djiboutien independence. One must be content now with the Centre Culturel Arthur Rimbaud, and its banner stencilled with the Carjat portrait; and – perhaps the most fitting tribute – the tug-boat *Arthur Rimbaud* which chugs among the mountainous freighters and container-ships at the port.

The sense of the French presence as precarious, tin-pot, faintly comic – as caught here by Monfried – is still strong. There is something almost illusory about Djibouti. As a country it is economically worthless. It covers an area of about 9,000 square miles, roughly the size of Wales. The land is desert: sand and scrub and a kind of volcanic clinker. Nothing is produced here. The dates you buy in the market are from Saudi Arabia; the orange juice you drink on your hotel terrace is from Kenya. The meat and wine in the overpriced restaurants, and often the vegetables, come from France. Consumer goods percolate in from the Gulf States. The *khat* comes up by train and truck and plane from Harar. The bar girls come from all over Ethiopia.

The country is propped up by French money, French soldiers and French cuisine. There are currently about 10,000 French residents, running the businesses and concessions, advising the government, operating what a Djiboutien politican frankly refers to as '*notre économie fictive*' – our fictional economy.

An Air France cargo plane lands daily on the scalding tarmac of Djibouti airport: a lifeline of *filet de bœuf* and canned duck's breast for this beleaguered Gallic outpost. A Djiboutien dream: a procession of chocolate mousses in tall slender glasses dancing down the conveyor-belt *à la* Busby Berkeley.

Djibouti is essentially what Rimbaud envisaged back in 1887: a French sphere of influence, a gateway to and an outlet from the highlands of Ethiopia. Its value is strategic rather than actual. The whole place is a mirage in that sense: a Looking-Glass City, a curious little Tinseltown perched on the edge of this vast African wasteland.

It used to be said that if the French pulled out of Djibouti, the country would last just six hours. That's how long it would take the Ethiopian army to get here. This was in the time of General Mengistu, the expansionist Ethiopian leader who was toppled in 1990, but it suggests the illusory nature of its nationhood, and of this little French enclave, propped up like a stage-set in the desert.

*   *   *

'*L'air de Djibouti égare les sens*,' Rimbaud wrote in 1890, in an acrimonious letter to Armand Savouré, who was then building a house in the new settlement.

The air of Djibouti makes you crazy . . .

The craziness would be one he knew so well: of torpor, of lassitude, of subsidence into heat and humidity.

At dawn Djibouti is like a half-lit shower-room. The steam condenses on you as you walk down the stairs. The dawn chorus of car horns begins at six, as the taxi drivers take up their posts around Menelik Square. There they will gossip and argue and compete all day.

It's a small town: everybody quickly knows your business. The taxi drivers call out 'Hey, *journaliste*!' . . . 'Hey, Cameraman Zero!' The saving grace of Djibouti is its people. It is one of those cross-roads cities where hybrid cultural energies – Somali, Afar, Ethiopian, Yemeni, Armenian, Lebanese, French – rub together to produce a flickering, fragile electricity.

It is not until the sun is up, and has burned off some of the humidity, that activity really begins. The working day runs from about eight until one o'clock, when the heat becomes insupportable. Government offices, embassies and businesses now close: the business day in Djibouti is over. The shops close too, though they will reopen in the early evening. Silence descends on the city. It is the hour of *khat*:

> *Calm houses, ancient passions,*
> *The kiosk of the woman driven mad with love . . .*
> *Boulevard where nothing moves, where no business is done.*

At lunch you succumb to the second beer, the chewy overcooked *bavette* at the Club Nautique. You climb back up the hotel stairs, drift off down the siesta, the slow boat to nowhere via certain nameless anxieties. And then the late, parched awakening, with the taste of the air-conditioner in your mouth.

You would do better, as usual, to follow the local example and dedicate the afternoon to *khat*. Rimbaud would probably have done so: he 'experimented with' *khat*, according to Ottorino Rosa. In Djibouti the taking of *khat* is virtually a national pastime. The cardboard mat; the distended cheek; the watchful eye. A small bundle of the stuff costs 300 francs (a little less than two dollars) and as a way of passing the afternoon it beats the crapulent Gallic siesta all ends up.

Khat – or, to transliterate more correctly from the Arabic, *qat* – is a medium sized shrub (*Catha edulis*, genus *Celastraceœ*) that grows profusely at altitudes above 1,000 metres. The *khat* in Djibouti and Somalia comes from round Harar; in Aden from the Yemen highlands. It contains a mild stimulant which is released when the leaves are, rather copiously, chewed. (A different strain, grown in Kenya, yields its alkaloids by chewing the bark and cortex of the stem.) A field of *khat* bushes looks like an orchard of overgrown privet. Both the plant and the leaf are similar to South American *coca*, though the active principle is weaker than cocaine. Freshness is highly prized. Every day the harvested branches are rushed, as assiduously as a new Beaujolais, from the upland *khat* orchards of Hararghie. The consignments travel by plane, truck and train. They pass through tax-points both freelance and official. In Djibouti there is a government organization – Société Générale pour l'Importation de Khat (SOGIK) – devoted to the taxing of *khat*.

The *khat* markets have something of the *joie de vivre* of a flower market. Great bunches of glossy green foliage are brandished and compared. You are invited to smell them, to bury your nose in the leaves, to lose yourself for a moment as you do in a bouquet of sweet-smelling flowers.

'*Goutez, chef. C'est comme votre whisky . . .*'

The smell is slight, sweetish, herbal: something like the smell of sorrel, Waugh thought. It has a pleasant overtone of summer gardens: the clippings of an overgrown hedge, the tang of snapped wood. The tiny leaflets at the centre of the cluster have a purplish tinge.

I am sometimes invited to take *khat* with Gina in her room

above the Historil. One of the girls who lives with her – a plump Addis girl called Million, essentially the maid of Gina's little household – is despatched to purchase some. She brings it back in a polybag. She washes it, rolls it up in a cloth. It sits at our feet for a bit. There is a thermos of *chai*, and small cups, and a fresh pack of cigarettes on the floor between us. There is the ceiling fan, and Rahel Johannes singing that haunting Ethiopian soul-music: touches of Indian *raga* and Algerian *rai* mixed up with a backing of ghostly Basement Tape keyboards and horns.

Gina unwraps the bundle, holds it up like a bouquet, smooths the leaves. '*Faut pas tomber*', she says, with a faintly lascivious smile. The leaves shouldn't droop. Should they do so, Million the maid will be in for trouble.

There is something pleasantly arboreal about taking *khat*. One browses there on the leaves. Gina uses exactly that phrase: '*on broute le.khat.*' She must have heard that word *brouter*, I think, from her Belgian lover. The smart young French of Djibouti contemptuously refer to *khat*-chewers as 'goats' but to me it's more monkey-like. You lounge on cushions as if high in the forest canopy. You flick the leaf-clusters with your fingers, strip the branch bare, purse the leaves up into a little package about the shape and size of a tulip-bud.

Khat is taken lightly, pensively. There may be some urgency to begin with: you want to get a few sprigs down sharpish. But this soon levels off. The mood is relaxed, herbivorous.

Chewing with men, which is universally the case among Yemenis and Somalis, you are politely but brusquely offered a few branches and get on with them how you choose. With an Ethiopian woman like Gina it is *de rigueur* for her to pluck the first leaves for you, and to hand them to you pursed in her fingers, and sometimes even to place this glossy package straight into your mouth, so you don't have to trouble at all. This action is graceful and touching. You taste the rawness of the leaf, the first hit of juice on your gums, caustic for a moment then faintly numbing. This is how you'll spend the afternoon, desirous of nothing more than what is already here: leaves to eat, tea to drink, people to talk with.

Then the light starts to soften, and the *muezzin* cranks up the faithful for evening prayers.

Now is the exquisite time: to step out into the cooling streets, the hour before dusk, the hour of the promenade. The blind men and their young, smiling guides are working the hotel terrace. The halt and the leprous are grouped around the Indian money-changer's kiosk where you buy another pile of Djibouti francs, another damp hank of hyper-inflated currency, with its picture of the camel train and the thornbush, and the smell of sweat and stale *khat* that wafts up as you pocket it into your shirt. Your spare change must go first to the leper whose handsome young face makes his deformities more gruesome. You place the money in the crook of his elbow, the nearest approximation to a hand. The sour taste of charity: so little given, and now none left, and you must grow a little surly with the last insistent beggars, and rebuff them with *Allah kerim* – God will give to you (but I'm not going to).

In the streets the vendors are out in force. Tall Issah boys roam the streets, open up their little cardboard boxes with a quick, confidential flourish, as if you'll see something special inside, a magic trick, but there's only the usual gum and cigarettes and postcards and lighters, the small accessories of a hot street at dusk. There are sellers of towels and T-shirts, corals and leopard-skins, and those hefty Maria Theresa dollars – real currency when Rimbaud was here – which they fling to the sidewalk to demonstrate the supposed ring of true silver.

We get to know them: the vendors and hustlers, the shoeshine boys and diminutive car-parkers, the security men with billy-clubs and stringy cat-o-nine-tails. Habiba – an eleven-year-old Issah girl, a little darting figure among the land-cruisers of Menelik Square – calls 'Hey Papa!', her customary greeting. There's the old Somali who thrusts at us nightly the same little collection of key-rings and nail-clippers, dangling from his fingers like small fish. There's the stall with the carpet that shows Martin Luther King and the two Kennedys: a prayer-rug of assassinations. And there's the chipper young man in what looks remarkably like a leopard-skin pill-box hat, who plays 'Yankee Doodle Dandy' on his harmonica.

The light is orange and pink down the sidestreets: Rue de Moscou, Rue de Londres, Rue d'Athènes. They are splashing water on the street to lay the dust, there's a smell of frankincense and rotten fruit, and then suddenly it's evening: the first flutters of neon as the bars and *boîtes* open up for business, the St Amour and the Flèche Rouge, Chez Ali and Mick Mack, the Joyeux Noël, James Bar, Intimité, the mythic Semiramis.

Sweet evening is here, the criminal's friend,
Coming in like a sidekick, with wolfish lope . . . [Baudelaire, 'Twilight']

One by one the signs light up, down the rickety streets: small patterns in pastel, pinks and greens and azures, deceptively inviting, invitingly deceptive. Down on Souvenir Row two French soldiers, big and crewcut, pause before the frontage of the Bar Pile où Face. The Heads or Tails Bar. An Ethiopian girl with glazed hair and a tight white dress emerges from the darkness, extends her hand in welcome. The soldiers enter, stooping slightly. The girl looks up and down the street, calls out something to a friend, then turns back into the darkness of the bar.

The lights of Djibouti seem for a moment a blessing, a refreshment after drought: another afternoon survived. You feel a surge of energy, a momentary stalling of the entropy, but you see also how these streets have already a forlorn air, how the neon signs hang in the heavy night air like little scraps of tinsel, how all the promises are made to be broken.

*   *   *

There are two ways to reach Tadjourah from Djibouti Ville. The first is by road along the so-called Friendship Highway, funded by Saudi Arabia and built by Yugoslavians in the 1980s. The Friendship Highway is currently closed, however, due to the civil war, and so one resorts to the slower, more ancient route, the route that Rimbaud himself took so many times – across the shimmering bay in a local *boutre* or dhow.

The dhow leaves from a small wharf below the Club Nautique. The boat is called Fatah Al Kaire, which means 'The Virtue of Happiness'. It looks both ancient and makeshift, with its twisty mast and its stove-pipe funnel. The captain paces the wharf, prods the cargo: a small man in a bright white *calotte*.

The crossing is slow, creaking, mesmeric:

> *It is found again.*
> *What is? Eternity.*
> *It is the sea, gone*
> *With the sun.*
>
> *My sentinel soul,*
> *Let us whisper the confession*

Of the night so void,
Of the day on fire . . .

The three-hour journey is punctuated by a few minutes of excitement as a yellow-fin tuna is hauled aboard. It is thrown down into the hold, onto the crates of Coca-Cola, snaking and dancing on a bed of bottle tops.

Crossing the Bay of Tadjourah one is travelling across a border: a genuine, ethnic divide. We are going into Afar country, indeed the boat is mainly full of Afar: fine-faced, high-boned people in skull-caps and turbans. The Afar – the Danakil or Dankali, also known as the Adal – are the old nomadic tribe of the Danakil desert. They are a very different from the other Djiboutien tribe, the Somali Issah. The Issah hold much of the power, and since 1991 the Afar have been fighting a small, stagnant and largely unreported war of independence. One of their sources of income, I am told, is gun-running. They are shipping old Ethiopian weapons across the Red Sea to the Yemen, where yet another civil war has erupted. Nothing much changes in the Horn of Africa. Guns are, as they were for Rimbaud, a staple currency of the region.

The deserts of the north are effectively under Afar control. Tadjourah itself was briefly taken but is now back in government hands. Soldiers are everywhere, Djiboutien and French (though the French have not, officially, taken any military role in the conflict). Further up the coast, 'the sad colony of Obock' is off-limits.

The passengers are silent. The boat creaks and pitches. For a long time we can see the little town of Tadjourah – a low frontage of houses, dirty white like a row of carious teeth; and above them the dry, buff-coloured hills – but the sun hammers down and the boat seems hardly to move.

19

TADJOURAH

O N 3 DECEMBER 1885, recently arrived, Rimbaud gave his first impressions of Tadjourah, written in that flat, spare, sardonic vein which is the timbre of his African writing:

> This place Tadjourah has been annexed to the French colony at Obock for a year now. It is a little Danakil village with a few mosques and a few palm trees. There is a fort, built some time ago by the Egyptians, where half a dozen French soldiers snooze under the orders of a sergeant, the commander of the post. The area has its minor sultan and its native administration, which have been left in place. It is a protectorate. The business of the place is slave traffic.

Apart from the slave traffic, not a lot has changed since he wrote this. The mosques and the palm trees continue to be noteworthy, *faute de mieux*. The place is still a French 'protectorate', in all but name, and there are still French soldiers here to prove it. The old Egyptian fort still broods over the village, and is now the seat of regional government, where the governor, or *commissaire*, lives in a manner not unlike a 'minor sultan'.

For Rimbaud, Tadjourah was the place of stasis and stagnation. He spent eleven months here. His business partners died on him, and the 'native administration' – principally Muhammad Abou Bekr, the eldest son of Abou Bekr Pasha whom Rimbaud had met at Zeilah in 1880, and who had died earlier in 1885 – engaged in the usual backsliding and baksheesh. He waited and waited and waited.

> Things are not moving very fast, as always here, but I expect to be leaving, finally, around the end of January . . . [3 December 1885]

> I am still at Tadjourah, and will certainly be here for some months more . . . [2 January 1886].

I have a long wait still, perhaps till the end of May, before getting away from the coast . . . [31 January 1886].

And so on. The letters become a litany of frustration and impatience: 'in Africa the smallest enterprise is beset by senseless obstacles'. . . . 'You need to have superhuman patience in these places.' He dreads the onset of the hot season, around March, when the heat 'takes hold'. This will be the 'fever season', a time of danger:

> The soldiers [of the French garrison] . . . are relieved every three months, and sent on convalescent leave back to France. None of the detachments has lasted for three months without being totally gripped with fever. It will be the fever-season in a month or two, and it certainly looks like I'll be here.

He fusses *ad nauseam* about the Amharic dictionary, first ordered back in November, and still not here.

He reacts angrily to something his mother has written (in a letter received in early January): 'Yes, it is true that I am exposing myself to many dangers and, even worse, to indescribable quarrels. But we're talking about a profit of around ten thousand francs, by the end of the year, which I couldn't make in three years elsewhere . . .'

This is a characteristic priority. He finds the 'dangers' of the road preferable to the 'quarrels' of negotiating with the local sultans.

He is gloomy; he is thinking about chucking it in and returning to Aden, where 'I can always find something to do'. He is petulant again on the subject of the Amhara dictionary, still not received. He writes bitterly:

> People who keep on saying that life is hard should come and spend a bit of time out here, to take a lesson in philosophy!

> So in the end a man has to spend three-quarters of his life suffering, in order to rest up for the fourth quarter; and most often pegs out along the way, no longer knowing where he is or what he's supposed to be doing [*sans plus savoir où il en est de son plan*].

This sounds like a faint, exhausted echo of that stirring sentence in the 'Lettre du Voyant', where the poet also 'pegs out' (*crever* in both cases) on his heroic journey into the unknown: 'let him peg out on his last leap into the unknown and the unnameable; other grim

199

workers will come; they will begin at those horizons where the other fell.'

*   *   *

Towards the end of January the guns arrive at Tadjourah. On the 31st he writes home: 'My goods have arrived.' This is a relief, but not an advance: he has no camels to transport them, no agreement with the sultan. At the same time, we later learn, two other consignments of arms arrived. They too would sink into this miasma of delay, and eighteen months later, in mid-1887, Rimbaud would comment:

> Another caravan [Franzoj's], whose merchandise was landed at Tadjourah with mine, finally succeeded in getting on the road after a delay of fifteen months; and the thousand Remingtons brought in by the late Soleillet, on the same date, are still lying, eighteen months later, under the village's only grove of palm trees.

He does not write for another four weeks. It is now two months since he last heard from home, and six months since he asked for the Amharic dictionary, which is still not here.

> All my goods are unloaded and I am awaiting the departure of a large caravan so that I can join it. I am still here, with the prospect of staying here another three months. It's extremely disagreeable, but in the end it'll end up happening, and I'll get on the road . . .
> [28 February 1886]

Even his grip on language is weakening. '*Cela finira cependant par finir.*' He is sapped.

At this point a new cross is laid on him, in the form of French officialdom. On 12 April he and Labatut received a visit. They describe it in their joint letter of complaint to the Ministry of Foreign Affairs in Paris:

> On 12 April, the Governor of Obock [Lagarde] came to tell us that a government despatch had ordered an immediate halt to the importation of arms into Shoa! Order was given to the Sultan of Tadjourah to prevent us from setting up our caravan. Thus, with our goods sequestered, our capital tied up in the costs of the caravan, our personnel subsisting indefinitely at our expense, and

our equipment deteriorating, we wait in Tadjourah to learn the purposes and effects of this most arbitrary measure.

This letter – undoubtedly written by Rimbaud: Labatut's much rougher style can be read in his letter to Bardey of 1881 – is a masterpiece of thin-lipped, business-like anger. He sets out various (self-serving) reasons why the arms-traffic will not have the dangerous effects which the French government fears. He provides accounts (as quoted in the previous chapter). Their venture expects an estimated profit of some 60,000 thalers, or 258,000 francs, and they consider they should be compensated by the government for this sum.

In fact the ban was lifted. (This was not the result of his letter: a distant political decision, rather, part of the constant jockeying between France, Britain and Italy for trade and influence in East Africa.) But new problems would assail the becalmed trafficker.

* * *

While Rimbaud sweats out the fever-season in Tadjourah, back in France, quite unknown to him, the first edition of his *Illuminations* is published. It appeared in two issues of the literary magazine *La Vogue*, in May and June 1886, edited and arranged by Félix Fénéon from manuscripts which he described as 'scattered leaves without pagination'. The provenance of the manuscripts is complex and in part unknown: Verlaine, Germain Nouveau and Charles de Sivry are variously involved in the rescuing of these fugitive masterpieces, composed over some years – *c*. 1872–4 is conservative – and then cast to the winds of oblivion and indifference by the fugitive poet. The title is first mentioned in a letter of Verlaine's in 1878.

The publication caused a sensation. Few had read the *Season in Hell*: most of the exemplars were gathering dust in Brussels. Rimbaud was a name, a rapidly fading legend. Here now was the work, or at least a substantial part of it: thirty-eight prose-poems (five others surfaced shortly after, and were incorporated into the first complete edition of Rimbaud's poems, the Vanier edition of 1895).

Rimbaud knew nothing of it, and had he known would have cared nothing for it. 'Poetry was dead for him,' said the Aden trader Tian. And he was in a sense dead for poetry – in the introduction to the *Illuminations*, the author is referred to as 'the late Arthur Rimbaud'.

The report is exaggerated, but not entirely inappropriate.

A couple of later letters found their way out to him, giving him a taste of the fluffy chatter he was causing back in France. One was from Paul Bourde – he who had met Bardey aboard an eastbound steamer; and told him about Rimbaud's previous career as a poet – who now wrote to him:

> Living so far from us, you are doubtless unaware that in Paris you have become, among a little coterie, a sort of legendary figure, one of those people whose death has been announced, but in whose existence certain disciples continue to believe . . . Certain young people (whom I find naive) have tried to base a literary system on your sonnet of the colour of letters [i.e. 'Vowels']. This little group, who claim you as their Master, do not know what has become of you, but hope you will one day reappear, and rescue them from obscurity. [29 February 1888]

Another was from the owner of a literary magazine Laurent de Gavoty:

> I have read your beautiful poems. This is to tell you that I would be happy and proud to see the leading figure of the Decadent and Symbolist school contribute to *France Moderne*, of which I am the publisher. [17 July 1890]

Rimbaud did not deign to reply, but the magazine considered the very fact of having Rimbaud's address to be a scoop, and in the issue dated 19 February 1891 trumpeted the following:

> This time, we've really got it! We know where Arthur Rimbaud is, the great Rimbaud, the true Rimbaud, the Rimbaud of the *Illuminations*.
>
> This isn't another Decadent hoax.
>
> We affirm it: we know the abode of the famous fugitive!

*   *   *

By coincidence, it is at just this time of renewed literary interest in Rimbaud that we get a series of marvellous verbal snapshots of him in Tadjourah – our first visual knowledge of him since the self-portraits taken in Harar three years before.

The Italian explorer Ugo Ferrandi met him there in about May 1886. They had known one another the previous year in Aden. Ferrandi was attached to an Italian caravan under the colourful adventurer and journalist Agosto Franzoj. Nearly forty years later [letter to Ottone Schanzer, 1923] Ferrandi recalled the meeting, and his impressions of Rimbaud – a precious first-hand glimpse of him.

> Around the middle of 1886 I found Rimbaud at Tadjourah; he had not yet been able to set off for the interior . . . A tall, thin man, his hair already beginning to go grey at the temples, he was dressed very simply, in European clothes: a pair of rather baggy trousers, a vest [*tricot*], and a loose-fitting, grey-khaki jacket. On his head he wore nothing but a little skull-cap [*calotte*], also grey, and he braved the torrid Danakil sun like a native.

Ferrandi also gives us an idea of Rimbaud's daily circumstances at Tadjourah:

> The Soleillet caravan and the Franzoj caravan, to which I was attached, were camped out in tents in the palm groves near the Danakil village. Rimbaud, however, was living in the village itself, in one of the houses there.

> He frequently visited our camps, and although he had cordial relations with his compatriots, he also enjoyed our [i.e. the Italians'] company.

> Franzoj, a well-known journalist and polemicist, was an enthusiast of French and Latin literature (he was constantly reading Horace, in the original, not something most of us could manage) and he and Rimbaud had long literary discussions, ranging from the Romantics to the Decadents. For my part, I bombarded Rimbaud with questions of a geographical nature, and also questions about Islam. It must be remembered that Rimbaud had, some years earlier, during the Arab [i.e. Egyptian] occupation of Harar, tried to penetrate into the Ogaden. He was an Arabist of the first order, and at his house he would have learned discussions about the Koran with the local elders [*notables indigènes*].

This is a fascinating corrective to the letters' drone of complaint. Rimbaud is not a part of the European encampment – he visits it, but he lives in the village itself, in one of the low white houses gridded up from the bay in narrow, sandy streets. He is a marginal figure, moving between these two worlds. In both he features as a learned talker. With the cultured Franzoj – the man to whom he had written that teasing note about sending l'Abyssine back home – he discusses poetry. With the elders of Tadjourah he discusses the Koran; he is something like the *wodad*, or itinerant Muslim scholar. So Ferrandi remembers it, anyway: there may be seepage of Rimbaud's literary status into this. Whether Ferrandi knew of this at the time is uncertain: it is possible – Bardey had got wind of it in 1883. The use of the term 'Decadents' seems anachronistic: this was not really a literary label until the 1890s, when Rimbaud was retrospectively canonized as a pioneer Decadent.

Ferrandi also, it seems, rode out with Rimbaud.

> Although he had a mule, he never made use of it on his expeditions, and always went on foot, with his hunting rifle, at the head of the caravan.

> An intimate detail: when he had to answer a certain call of nature, he squatted like the natives. The natives considered him to be something of a Muslim. He advised me to imitate this course, seeing that I had some knowledge of Islamic customs, acquired during my earlier travels across the Fayoum : . .

Rimbaud is, once again, *like* the natives. He is hardly a European at all.

The pagan blood rises . . .

Ferrandi concludes, tantalizingly: 'Rimbaud provided me with some precise and lucid observations about Tadjourah which I once intended to publish, along with some notes of my own, but fate did not decree this to be. I still have several pages of these notes by Rimbaud.' No trace of them has been found.

This meeting between Ferrandi and Rimbaud was certainly before 16 June, on which date Ferrandi delivered to Jules Suel, at the Grand Hotel, 600 thalers entrusted to him by Rimbaud in Tadjourah [OC, p. 421], and probably before Rimbaud's brief return to Aden in mid-May.

The explorer Jules Borelli also met Rimbaud at Tadjourah. He later recalled:

I met Rimbaud . . . at Tadjourah, where I was setting up my caravan, at the very time when Savouré and Barral were attacked by Danakil [i.e. April 1886].

He never spoke of his previous life, and I had better things to do than to question him, and anyway I knew absolutely nothing about it . . . He came into one's tent, sat down without saying a word, stayed for half an hour, and then went away again. He was, it was plain to see, an embittered and irascible man . . .

[Letter to Enid Starkie, *c.* 1936]

Another visitor to Tadjourah at this time was a medical man, and enthusiastic traveller, Dr L. Faurot, virtually here as a tourist. He arrived in Tadjourah on 31 January 1886, and stayed some months. Later in the year he published an account, *Voyage au Golfe de Tajoura*, in which he notes:

The French merchants are accustomed to setting up their camps a kilometre from the village, under a clump of date palms. There we meet M. Brémond, who gave us a warm welcome . . . In his camp the goods are concealed under tents, and arranged in such a way as to occupy as little space as possible. Twenty stalwart Abyssinians, very well-disciplined and armed with Remingtons, are constantly ready to rally round him at the slightest alarm.

We also visited another of our compatriots, M. Rimbaud, who had been striving to get his means of transport together for the past three months. The Sultan agreed to come to his assistance, but not without first exacting baksheesh.

These notes are dated by Faurot to May 1886. They record Rimbaud at just the same time as Ferrandi's and Borelli's reminiscences: he makes this sudden brief emergence from the heat-shimmer and then slips back out of view, 'without saying a word'.

*   *   *

In mid-May, after six months of fruitless negotiation in Tadjourah, Rimbaud made a brief return to Aden. He found there – at last – the Amharic dictionary. He wrote home on 21 May: 'I am still well. Things are going neither better nor worse.'

On 1 June he and Labatut sign a receipt for 'various sums' they have received from Suel of the Grand, who was probably an investor to begin with. They acknowledge a debt of 11,518 rupees on account of money and goods received; and they agree to repay the sum within a year, or to pay an interest of twelve per cent on it thereafter. On 4 June, Rimbaud receives a written authorization from Suel as follows:

> I authorize M. Rimbaud to take from *chez* P. Soleillet [i.e. from his camp at Tadjourah] the 1000 piston rifles belonging to me. M. Rimbaud is free to sell them together or singly, but not for less than 6 thalers each. He will be glad . . . to take the remainder of them with him to Shoa and deliver them to M. Pino, for whom I intend them.

Rimbaud returns to Tadjourah. He entrusts 600 thalers to Ugo Ferrandi, who delivers them to Suel in Aden on 16 June. This presumably represents the proceeds of selling some of Suel's rifles in Tadjourah, since Suel's next letter refers to 600 rifles rather than a thousand:

> If we leave the 600 rifles with Soleillet, and if he leaves after you, see what a loss of time and money for me. M. Pino is waiting for these guns, and of course cannot return until he has received them, which is keeping me here for an eternity. I am very tired and would like to be able to go and spend some time in France . . .
>
> Do it, I beg you, and sell as many of the rest as you need to, to pay for the camels . . .
>
> M. Henry leaves tonight on the *Météore*. He will bring you this letter, written in haste . . . [3 July 1886]

In memoranda like these, quite unintended for posterity, one sees Rimbaud in his métier: guns and camels, the eternity of waiting, the arrival of letters on the tramp-steamer *Météore*.

On 27 June Rimbaud signs a *bon* or IOU for 150 thalers to Monsieur Audon, 'as payment for ten rifles delivered to me'. This is another little side-deal; Audon is the French consul at Zeilah.

*   *   *

But it is now, in Suel's letter of 3 July, that we get the first indication of a major change in Rimbaud's situation. Pierre Labatut has fallen

gravely ill, in Aden. A tumour on the brain is diagnosed. He has
returned to France. This happened in June, though whether before
or after Rimbaud's return to Tadjourah is uncertain. The phrasing
of Suel's letter shows that Rimbaud already knew of it, in fact their
main interest seems to be focused on Labatut's belongings, for Suel
writes: 'I'll have a look at the suitcase and tell you what's in it, and
then if you want I'll send it to you.'

Suel's next letter is dated 16 September:

> Since my last letter there has been a noticeable improvement in
> poor Labatut's condition, but the sickness remains incurable. It is
> more than likely he will read your letter before his death, which is
> not expected for some months . . . I am sending you Labatut's
> effects. There isn't much left, but you will have some clothes for
> the journey, some new and some old. The black umbrella with the
> green lining I cannot find . . .

There is a coldness about it all. Labatut on his deathbed back in
Paris, and his old partners picking over his meagre trunkful of
belongings at the Grand. (Subsequent events put this in context:
Labatut's demise brought big financial problems for Rimbaud.)

One regrets the missing umbrella, with its green lining, which
cannot quite be added to the list of known props – field-glasses,
saddle-bags, cartridge-belt, money-belt, guns, knives, books, etc. –
of Rimbaud en route in 1886.

With Labatut suddenly removed, Rimbaud returned to an idea
previously aired in his letters from Tadjourah. He would annex his
caravan to that of Paul Soleillet, a big-bearded man of immense
experience, a founder of the Obock colony, an old hand.

But it seems he is jinxed. On 9 September Soleillet suffers a
stroke in the streets of Aden, and dies.

Rimbaud is more decidedly alone than ever. He is holed up in
Tadjourah with his caravan nearly ready, and this horrendous
journey to make, and no one to travel with. On 15 September he
sums up the situation with extraordinary crispness:

> My partner has fallen ill and returned to France. The news from
> there is that he is near death. I have power of attorney [*un
> procuration*] over all his goods, so I have no choice but to go. I will
> go alone, as Soleillet (the other caravan I was intending to join)
> has also died.

In early October, after nearly eleven months on this 'cursed coast', after extortions and arguments and official embargoes, after fatal illnesses and sudden deaths, he is ready to leave.

'So now I see that existence is just a way to use up your life . . .'

20

THE DANAKIL CROSSING

A T LAST RIMBAUD is on the move again: *'Let's go! The march, the burden, the desert, the boredom, the anger . . .'*

He sets off on what he has known all along will be a 'terrible journey':

> From Tadjourah to Shoa it is a journey of about fifty days, on horseback, across burning deserts . . . [18 November 1885]

> There are huge overheads to pay, not to mention the dangers of the route, both there and back. The people on the route are Danakil, bedouin herdsmen, fanatical Muslims: they are to be feared. It is true that we travel with firearms and the bedouin have only spears, but all the caravans are attacked . . . [3 December 1885]

He sets off, also, in the knowledge of the massacre a few months previously of Barral's caravan. This had been attacked on its return journey from Shoa, in April 1886. The rumour that the attack had been a mistake, and that another French trader, Léon Chefneux, was the intended target, did little to dispel the danger. Henri d'Orléans pondered the matter as he prepared to follow the same route a few years later:

> The memory of the unfortunate Barral, massacred with his wife and twenty Abyssinians, having used up in their defence all the bullets they had at their disposal, still haunts me. . . . His murderers took him for Chefneux. I am told that the latter had a price on his head in parts of the Somali region. One wonders who might have such a strong interest in the elimination of a man who was working on behalf of France at the court of King Menelik.

Chefneux himself passed close by the scene of the massacre. He found 'the remains of corpses half-devoured by beasts and birds of prey, mutilated beyond recognition'. He thought he recognized, by a gold tooth shining in the sun, the severed head of Barral's young wife.

*　*　*

The precise composition of Rimbaud's caravan to Shoa can be found in certain documents he later drew up for the French vice-consul at Aden [Declared Accounts of the Labatut Caravan, June 1887, comprising 'Inventory', 'Liquidation' and 'Account of Expenses'].

The *chef de caravane* was a Somali named Mohammed Chaim. He is listed as receiving 'backshish' totalling forty-six thalers. He 'signed and approved' Rimbaud's expense account when they reached Ankober. A certain Habib is also described as a *chef de caravane*.

There are fourteen camel-suppliers named, plus a further note of camels supplied by '*divers de Tadjoura*'. These suppliers would typically be camel-drivers on the expedition. Three men – Moussa Dirio, Said Massa and Abd El Kader Douad – head the list, and supply between them thirty-six and a half camels, over a third of the total. (The halves represent young camels.) These three also receive single payments, in which list they are described as *chefs*. The payment of sixty thalers to Moussa Dirio is described as a *gratification*.

All these names are Muslim – they are Danakil, Issah, and perhaps some Galla. Rimbaud also had thirty-four Abyssinians, his 'escort' as he calls them. He refers to these in a separate letter to Vice-Consul Gaspary:

> At Sagalo, before my departure, they made me sign an agreement to pay each of them 15 thalers for the journey and two months back-pay, but at Ankober, irritated by their insolent demands, I grabbed the contract and tore it up in front of them; complaints were thereupon made to the Azzaz, etc.

The aggrieved Abyssinians won the argument, for in the 'Liquidation' account Rimbaud lists among the outgoings:

> 34 Abyssinians @ Th 15 for the journey, and two months backpay @ Th 3, payment promised on arrival:
> $$34 \times 21 \dots\dots\dots\dots\dots\dots\dots\dots \text{Th } 714$$

These are essentially a bodyguard. He seems to have hired them at Sagalo, which is the first stop west of Tadjourah, still on the coast of the bay. They are parallel to the 'twenty stalwart Abyssinians' who guarded Brémond's camp at Tadjourah, as described by the sightseer Dr Faurot in the previous chapter.

The accounts also mention a *chef des domestiques*, who is paid 180 thalers 'back pay'; it is not impossible that this is Djami. There is also 'my Arab-Amharagalla interpreter', who receives 130 thalers. (However, these may belong to his entourage in Shoa itself, and on the return journey, rather than on the Danakil crossing.)

The number of camels on the caravan, for accounting purposes, was ninety and a half (more loosely, 'a hundred camel-loads'). They are reckoned at seventeen and a half thalers per camel – an extortionate rate compared to the five thalers paid by Bardey at Zeilah in 1880. Expenditure on camel-hire was thus 1,584 thalers, but this was only a fraction of the overall cost of expedition:

> When all the expenses were paid out, on my arrival at Shoa, the transport of my merchandise, a hundred camel loads, proved to have cost me 8,000 thalers, that is 80 thalers per camel, over a distance of only 500 kilometres. This makes it more expensive [i.e. per kilometre] than any other caravan route in Africa, despite my making every possible economy on the journey and despite my considerable experience of these regions.

When it eventually set off, the caravan was carrying 1,755 rifles. Of these twenty were Remingtons, fourteen 'elephant guns', and the remainder old percussion rifles [*fusils à capsules*]. They had 450,000 rounds of military ammunition, and 300,000 rounds of hunting ammunition. A further sixteen camel-loads of 'utensils and furnishings' – probably including those cunning cooking pots and *dourah* grills supplied by Bardey – completed the cargo.

It was, in short, a very considerable caravan, consisting of about a hundred heavily-loaded camels, and probably about the same number of men – Abyssinians, Somalis, Danakil. As far as we know, Rimbaud was the only European, 'surrounded by a thousand dangers'.

*　　*　　*

Rimbaud predicted that the journey would take fifty or sixty days, a distance he described accurately enough as 500 kilometres. His expectation was based on an assumption of ten kilometres per day. This obtained on the flat but was very optimistic for the steep and rugged ascent to Ankober.

In fact the journey took him much longer. Exactly how long one doesn't know, because there is no precise record of when he left Tadjourah. His intended travelling companion Soleillet died on 9 September 1886. His last letter from Tadjourah – 'I shall depart alone' – was written on 15 September. Suel, however, writing to him on the 16th, expects he will still be at Tadjourah at the end of the month. He probably set out in early October. This ties in broadly with his statement that he had spent eleven months in Tadjourah. He arrived in Ankober on 9 February 1887. The journey took him about four months, therefore, or twice what he had predicted.

The route he took can be reconstructed from his own brief account of it [letter to *Bosphore Égyptien*, June 1887]; and from the account given by Jules Borelli in his *Éthiopie Méridionale*. Rimbaud notes that the route 'was surveyed astronomically for the first time by M. Jules Borelli in May 1886'. He did not have the benefit of this survey when he travelled, as Borelli was still in Ankober when he arrived there.

This is the 'Gobat Route' – 'the route we took is called the Gobat route, from the name of its fifteenth station'.

From Tadjourah the caravan winds along the northern shore of the bay, skirts the inner bay of the Goubbet Kareb, and descends to the salt lake of Assal:

> After six short stages from Tadjourah, that is about 60 kilometres,
> the caravans descend to the Salt Lake, along dreadful routes
> which recall the presumed horror of lunar landscapes . . .

The description is both dramatic and punctilious. This is indeed a lunar landscape: sharp-edged and bleak. Vistas of hot, shimmering scree stretch off to distant hills. There are echoing ravines and strange black dunes. The only vegetation of any size are the low, knotty, yucca-like 'dragon trees'. Lake Assal itself, lying at 500 feet below sea level, is the lowest point of the African continent. Its shores look like sand, but are in fact a ridged crust of fossilized coral which cuts the soles of your feet. The wind blows in your face as hot as a hair-dryer. The salt crystallizes on your clothes.

This is an archetypal, pared-down landscape. It has a sense of profound antiquity. It is like a skeleton.

The sense of antiquity is more than a metaphor. It is precisely here, in the Afar Triangle at the northern extremity of the Great Rift Valley, that the earliest remains of our pre-human ancestors have been found. The famous one is 'Lucy', discovered by Donald Johanson in 1974, at Hadar in the Lower Awash valley, not far north of Assal. (She got her name from the Beatles' 'Lucy in the Sky', which was playing in camp that night.) Lucy – or *Australopithecus afarensis* – lived about 3.2 million years ago. She predated *homo erectus*, that is, by a million and a half years. She had an ape-like jaw, and a locking knee-joint that permitted upright walking. The Ethiopians call her 'Dinkenesh', which means in Amharic 'wonderful one'. The earliest known stone tools (2.5 million years old) were also unearthed at Hadar. A later find, at Aramis on the Middle Awash, may be even older. These are the teeth and bone-fragments of *Australopithecus ramidus*, a small hominid about the size of a pygmy chimpanzee. The carbon dating on these is over four million years old.

These ridged, scorched, volcanic badlands across which Rimbaud struggled in 1886–7 are, in the old cliché, the 'cradle of mankind'. And if Rimbaud's years in Africa seem like a flight from what he was – from Europe, from poetry, from himself – then it is surely here, on this desolate desert trek, that he reaches the furthest point of that arrow-flight, arriving at this utter privation, at this landscape of nothingness, which is also – in a quite scientific sense of which he would surely approve – the very beginning of humanity.

From Lake Assal they turn south-west, into the desert, towards Erer or Herer. They are following the salt road here. Down this trail, Rimbaud says, Danakil tribes carry several thousand camel-loads of Assal salt to Menelik, 'something approaching a thousand tons a year'. This stretch is controlled by a Danakil clan called the Debne. It is 'extremely dangerous' here, Rimbaud says, because the Debne 'are constantly at war, on the right-hand side with the Moudeitos and the Assa-Imara, and on the left-hand side with the Somali Issah'. Their chief, Sultan Loita, is friendly to the French, however: he gets a monthly payment of 150 thalers from the French government in return for leaving travellers alone. Rimbaud calls the Debne, a little ironically, 'our allies'.

We have glimpses of Rimbaud *en caravane*, though one is not quite sure how and when they were gained. There is Ugo Ferrandi, who says that he didn't use his mule, choosing to go 'on foot, with his hunting rifle, at the head of the caravan' – but there is no evidence Ferrandi was with him on this trek. A later reminiscence from certain French settlers in Obock [Dufaud *et al*] describes Rimbaud in similar terms:

> He never left his caravan or his merchandise unguarded, and slept in the midst of his beasts of burden. On the route he was astonishingly active, with an eye on everything. Though he had a mount, he did three-quarters of the route on foot. He was an indefatigable walker, who knew how to put up with thirst and hunger if he had to. His commands were clear and precise, the tone singularly forceful without being brutal. He knew how to make himself obeyed without unnecessary rudeness. Perfectly versed in Arabic, he conversed with the camel-drivers in the bivouac. He knew how to discuss their religion, and read the Koran fluently.

One of the sources of this document is Athanase Righas, whose brothers Constantin and Dimitri certainly travelled with Rimbaud at certain times.

The caravan rests at Gobat, the fifteenth stage, an oasis where 'the Debne generally graze their herds', then presses on south to Erer:

> It is altogether about twenty-three stages to Herer, passing through the most terrible landscapes in this part of Africa. At Erer, pasture-land at an altitude of about 800 metres, about 60 kilometres from the foot of the Itou-Galla plateau, the Danakil and the Issah graze their herds in a state of neutrality.

From Erer they continue south to Tollo, climbing steadily to about 3,000 feet, then turn west towards the Awash (or Hawach) River, a journey of eight or nine days. The journey leads through 'bush'. The caravan follows 'elephant trails'.

He is disappointed by the Awash, because he had heard about projects to build a canal here, and imagined the river much bigger:

> Arriving at the Awash one is dumbfounded to think of the canalization projects of certain travellers. Poor old Soleillet had a special pontoon [*embarcation*] under construction, in Nantes, for

just this purpose. The Awash is a small, twisting little river [*rigole*], obstructed at every step by trees and rocks. I crossed it at several places, over a distance of several hundred kilometres, and it is clear that it would be impossible to descend it even during the floods. Besides it is everywhere bordered with forest and desert.

They cross a bridge, one of two built across the Awash by Menelik:

These are simple foot-bridges [*passerelles*] made of tree trunks, intended for the passage of troops during the rains and floods, but nonetheless remarkable works for Shoa.

All the land on either side of the Awash, for two and half days, is called Careyon. Bedouin Galla tribes, owners of camels and other animals; at war with the Aroussis . . .

You are in bedouin country, in *Konella* or the hot country.

Judging from Borelli's route Rimbaud probably crossed the Awash at Boulohama, south-east of Farré. On the west side of the river there is scrub and mimosa forest, and then the land begins to rise sharply. The trail is hemmed in [*encaissé*]. Slowly the caravan begins to climb up the steep, dramatic escarpment that leads to the Abyssinian highlands he had dreamed of so long: 'the domain of the powerful King Menelik'.

They arrived, probably in late January, at Farré, 'the point of arrival and departure for the caravans, and the end of the Danakil tribe's territory'. Farré (or Farra) is north-east of Ankober. It stands at an altitude of just over 4,000 feet, well below Ankober itself, at about 8,000 feet.

At last Rimbaud's ragged caravan pulled into Ankober, the capital of Shoa. The date was Wednesday 9 February 1887. His arrival was witnessed by Jules Borelli, who had made the journey a few months previously and was still kicking his heels at Ankober, awaiting permission to travel on. He notes in his journal:

M. Rimbaud, French merchant, arrives from Tadjourah with his caravan. He has not avoided difficulties en route. Always the same story: the bad behaviour, greed and betrayal of the men; the mischief and ambushes of the Adal [i.e. Danakil]; the lack of water; the extortion of the camel drivers . . .

Our compatriot has lived in Harar. He knows Arabic, and speaks

Amharic and Oromo. He is tireless. His facility for languages, his great strength of will, and his patience in the face of every trial, class him among the accomplished travellers.

[*Éthiopie Méridionale*, p. 200]

This is the kind of gruff accolade which sums up the intense exertions and privations of Rimbaud's life in Africa. Borelli, the old Africa hand, accounts him '*parmi les voyageurs accomplis*'. After four months of travel through desert and mountain this is an anti-climax, but has also something honourable about it. One contrasts this hard-won acceptance with the fickle caresses of literary fame.

21

AT THE COURT OF
KING MENELIK

IGHLAND ABYSSINIA: PALE green pastures, brown earth, roughly terraced hillsides: a big spacious landscape like a rumpled cloth opened out to the sky and the wind. Tall herdsmen wrapped in white woollen cloaks lead flocks of hump-backed zebu cattle and fat-tailed Somali sheep. The thatched, hive-shaped dwellings are almost indistinguishable from the tall hay-stacks beside them. There is heather and daisies and what look suspiciously like buttercups. There is wild sage blooming on verdant weed-plots. There are stands of eucalyptus, the wind rattling the young leaves.

All this – with the exception of the introduced eucalyptus – he saw. After all those years on the 'cursed coast', after all those weeks in the 'lunar landscapes' of the Danakil, he felt this freshness on his face.

Abyssinia is 'the Switzerland of Africa' in Rimbaud's oddly brochuresque phrase, with its reminiscence of that first great hike from Stuttgart to Milan in the spring of 1875 ('I slept in the heart of Tessin in a solitary barn'), and of the rich pastoral vein of his early poems:

> *Far from birds and herds and village girls*
> *I drank, crouching in the heather . . .* ['Tear']

For me it is a reminiscence of the upland pastures of the Andes: something about the thin, seemingly rinsed air; something about the ancient smell of sun and sweat and loam on the skins of the men pressed up against me in the truck, in the cloud of chalky dust, on the thin white road between Debre Birhan and Ankober.

Ankober was never much, and now it is almost nothing. It had been the capital of Shoa since the eighteenth century but had never grown to any size. Engravings in Borelli's *Éthiopie Méridionale* show it as it was in 1887. The royal compound on the hill, surrounded by a tall palisade; the king's *guebi* or palace of wood, rectangular; and around it the cluster of conical houses where lived the officials and soldiers and silversmiths and weavers of the Shoan court.

The place is now a ruin, almost vanished: another empty inn. A few foundations are visible amid tall yellow grass and brambles. At the bottom of the hill there is a pair of low, round churches: the Church of St Michael and the Church of Mary. They are the only buildings to have survived: a third, the Church of the Saviour, was destroyed by fire some years ago.

Other than these all that remains of the court of King Menelik at Ankober is the path that winds up to the top of the knoll, and the expanse of green and tawny hillsides spread out below.

*   *   *

For Rimbaud too it was another empty inn. He was here, but King Menelik was not. Menelik had founded a new capital, further west: Entotto. His retinue had decamped. Ankober was already obsolete, was slipping into that somnolent silence which one discerns here a century later.

At Ankober, besides Borelli, there were a few other Europeans, among them a certain Monsieur Henon, a former cavalry-officer who was to cause Rimbaud considerable problems. But the chief participants during his stay at Ankober were two locals: Labatut's Abyssinian widow, and her friend the *azzaz* (variously described as a royal attendant or the town magistrate: at any rate, a powerful local figure).

After the hell of the journey, comes the curious black comedy of *l'affaire Labatut*: a modulation not unfamiliar in Rimbaud's poetry.

It begins with the *azzaz*, who actually came down to Farré to meet him. He is the first of Labatut's Abyssinian creditors fastening onto Rimbaud. This is Rimbaud's laconic description of the meeting:

> This toady the *azzaz* arrived at Farré with his donkeys at the same moment as I arrived with my camels. After greeting me, he immediately insinuated that the *ferenji* in whose name I was coming [i.e. Labatut] had run up an immense account with him, and he seemed about to demand my entire caravan in settlement

of it. I soothed his ardours, temporarily, with the offer of a pair of
my field-glasses, and a few bottles of Morton syrup . . .

The *azzaz* was 'bitterly disillusioned' and from then on was an
implacable enemy of Rimbaud's. He assisted Labatut's widow in her
lawsuits against him (a 'thorny process'), and laid various other
impediments in his way, for instance forbidding the local priest to
pay Rimbaud for a consignment of grapes he had brought for the
brewing of communion wine.

His confrontations with 'Veuve Labatut' – one hears perhaps a
faint reprise of 'Mère Rimbe' – have an almost lurid, comic-book
quality. To begin with, after various 'odious' legal arguments,
Rimbaud won an order to seize Labatut's goods in payment of the
moneys owed to him. He arrives at Madame Labatut's 'shack'
[*baraque*], only to find that she has already taken away all the
valuables left by Labatut – 'several hundred thalers' worth of goods,
effects and curios' – and hidden them. Thus,

> accomplishing the seizure of his goods, not without some resist-
> ance, I found nothing more than a few old pairs of underpants,
> which the Widow clasped to her with tears of fire; some moulds for
> making bullets; and a dozen pregnant slave girls . . .

He also found there some old notebooks [*calepins*] of Labatut's.
These were a record of his business deals, but also something more
than that:

> Labatut was in effect compiling his *Memoirs*. I found altogether
> thirty-four volumes, that is thirty-four of these notebooks, at his
> widow's house, and despite the latter's imprecations, I burned the
> lot. This was a great misfortune, I later learned, as certain
> property deeds were shuffled in among these confessions, but after
> quickly skimming through them, they had seemed to me unworthy
> of serious examination.

An extraordinary vignette: this moment of characteristic anger is
also an expression of literary disgust. These writings are 'unworthy
of serious examination' and he consigns them to the bonfire. (How
precious now would be those thirty-four 'volumes' of Labatut's
reminiscences of his years in Shoa.)

It was also at Ankober, one recalls, that he 'tore up' the
agreement with those Abyssinian soldiers who accompanied him

across the Danakil. He did so 'in their faces', just as he burned the Labatut notebooks in front of the widow. (There were, by coincidence, thirty-four Abyssinians as well!)

Thus Rimbaud's war on literature, his desire to efface the record, is played out in this little mountain village in Abyssinia – and is then, paradoxically, recorded by Rimbaud himself in what is perhaps the most purely literary text he has left from all his years in Africa, the long *relation* or newsletter written to Vice-Consul Gaspary, from which I have been quoting. This letter was written in Aden in November 1887, and remained undiscovered in the French consular archives for nearly half a century: it was first published in the *Revue de France* in 1935. In it Rimbaud turns the whole Labatut affair into a series of humorous sketches of Amharic rapacity and trickery:

> A *dedjatch* [official] arrived at my lodgings, and sat drinking my *tej*, and singing the worthy praises of his great friend, the late Labatut, and telling me how he hoped to find in me the same virtues. Spotting a mule which was grazing nearby he cried: 'Why, that's the very mule I gave to Labatut!' (He omitted to mention that the very bernous on his back had been given to him by Labatut!) 'And besides,' he added, 'he died owing me 70 thalers (or 50, or 60, etc!).' And he'd go on insisting that I should repay it, to the point that I dismissed this noble bandit [*malandrin*], saying 'Go to the King!' (That's much the same as saying 'Go to the Devil!') But the King made me pay a part of the debt, adding hypocritically that he would pay the rest.

At his arrival at Ankober Rimbaud enters a web of African trickery and opportunism, centred on these real or imagined debts he has inherited from Labatut. Some of these he considered just:

> For instance, I paid to the widows the wages of those servants who had died during Labatut's last expedition. Then again there were reimbursements of 30 or 15 or 12 thalers, sums taken by Labatut from certain peasants, promising in return a few guns, or some materials, etc.

He exercises that charity which everyone agrees was his great virtue. 'These poor people are always in good faith,' he says. 'I allowed my heart to be touched by them, and I paid up.'

Among the Frenchmen in Ankober was 'a certain M. Dubois'. He also claimed to be owed money by Labatut. It was a small sum: twenty thalers. 'I saw that he had a fair case, and I paid him, adding as interest a pair of my shoes, the poor devil complaining that he had to go barefoot.' An unknown trader – a Monsieur Dubois as faceless as the Mr Browns of his earlier travels – and this unrealized benediction: the gift of a pair of Rimbaud's shoes.

*   *   *

Meanwhile news of King Menelik was percolating up to Ankober. He was off fighting. He was, in fact, already celebrating the success of his latest campaign, which was – ironically enough – the conquest of Harar.

The decisive battle had been fought on 6 January, a month before Rimbaud's arrival at Ankober. It had been won with the help of European firearms – though not, self-evidently, Rimbaud's – but mostly it had been won by sheer force of numbers. Menelik had mobilized a fearsome force of 30,000 warriors. The Emir of Harar, Abdallahi, had only 3,000 men, Gallas and Somalis, plus about 200 Turks, Sudanese and Egyptians who had stayed on after the Egyptian withdrawal from Harar. The battle was fought at Chalanko, in the hills forty miles to the west of Harar. It was a rout. It lasted about a quarter of an hour. A couple of days later, the Abyssinians entered Harar through the Shoa Gate.

There were alarming rumours of a massacre within the walls – it was said, Rimbaud laconically reports, that 'the King's warriors were bringing back the testicles of all the Frenchmen in Harar' – but in fact the taking of the town was swift and bloodless. After a period of comparatively mild looting, and after his symbolic desecration of the mosque, Menelik left a garrison of 3,000 riflemen, handed over administration to the emir's uncle, Ali Abu Kebir, and returned to Shoa.

He entered Entotto in triumph, his soldiers blowing inexpertly on looted Egyptian trumpets. His booty included two Krupp cannons, each hauled by a team of eighty men.

Much of this I take from Rimbaud's excellent account of the campaign [letter to the *Bosphore Égyptien*, August 1887]. It is possible he was already in Entotto when Menelik returned, and that details like the trumpets and the cannon are first-hand.

It was at Entotto that Rimbaud finally met *'le puissant roi de*

Shoa', King Menelik II. Named after the legendary King Menelik – the son of Solomon and Sheba, the 'Conquering Lion of the Tribe of Judah' – he was a shrewd, autocratic, physically powerful man of about forty. Borelli gives a picturesque description of a royal audience at Entotto. Entering the long rectangular *guebi*, one is ushered in to the 'council chamber', where the King is seated on a large divan scattered with rugs and cushions. He wears a flowing bernous of black silk with gold trimmings, and the traditional Amhara head-dress – the white cloth called a *rass masseria* – on top of which is perched a tall, black hat of the kind worn by Quakers. Borelli describes him as 'a robust man, with very black skin, bright eyes, his face pitted by smallpox and framed by a short, bushy beard'. A later visitor, Henri d'Orléans, says:

> What strikes one straightaway is his look. Menelik looks often; he observes; he has a lively, curious eye suggestive of his desire to be abreast of things, to be instructed. He speaks simply, neither raising nor lowering his voice, nor seeming at all flustered, and he is often humorous. [*Une Visite*, p. 124]

Always at Menelik's side – confidential, moustachioed, somewhat stocky – stands a European gentleman. Swiss by birth, an engineer by training, he had been in Abyssinia for ten years now, and had become Menelik's right-hand man in all political and commercial dealings with Europeans. He is the fixer *par excellence*. The Swiss consul in Aden, Herr Furrer, summed him up as 'the man who knows everything'. His name is Alfred Ilg. He will be Rimbaud's champion in the long weeks of negotiation now beginning; and will become a close associate and friend (that is probably the right order) of Rimbaud's during his last years in Africa.

Menelik bargains hard. He sees Rimbaud isolated and disadvantaged, a *ferenji* caught in this web of Abyssinian litigation. He is himself, or so he claims, one of Labatut's creditors. He had furnished Labatut with lands and houses and other benefits to the tune of – a figure no doubt plucked out of the air – 3,500 thalers. The arms trade is, moreover, a buyers' market. He has other suppliers; they can offer him the latest Remingtons, *les plus perfectionnés*. These aged percussion rifles of Rimbaud's are of little use to him.

The King holds all the cards, as befits a king, and in particular he holds the trump-card, time. Rimbaud's impatience is perhaps his great shortcoming as a businessman, but anyone who has stumbled into the snares of Ethiopian bureaucracy, who has stared at the peeling *eau-de-nil* walls of the Ministry of Foreign Affairs, who has rattled the padlocked gates of the consular official, who has waited in drowsy antechambers for the signings and countersignings and stampings and frankings of florid-looking documents quite indispensable until finally issued and never once demanded or perused thereafter – they will know just a little of the knuckle-whitening frustrations that Rimbaud underwent during the spring of 1887. It is sometimes said that Ethiopia's labyrinthine bureaucracy is a legacy of the Marxist regime of General Mengistu, but it is a habit of secrecy and complication far older than that. As the Victorian traveller, Major Cornwallis Harris, remarked: 'Abyssinians despots sully not their dignity by divulging even the smallest of their designs.' Or as the old Amharic proverb goes: 'The belly of the master is never known.'

After much prevarication, and much discreet remonstrance on Rimbaud's behalf by the ever-busy Ilg, Menelik makes his offer. He will take the entire stock off Rimbaud's hands at an all-in price of 14,000 thalers. He subtracts from this the supposed sum of Labatut's debt to him, which with great show of generosity he rounds down to 3,000 thalers. Also subtracted was a further 2,500 thalers, covering the still unpaid wages and costs of the Danakil crossing. (The entire personnel of Rimbaud's caravan is caught up in this limbo of waiting as well.) The bottom line of Menelik's offer is therefore 8,500 thalers. This would not be paid in cash, however, but in the form of signed bonds redeemable from a third party – in this case from the governor of Harar, Ras Makonnen. This would be a further test of superhuman patience, a further area of dispute and potential diminution.

Exhausted and outmanoeuvred, Rimbaud accepts the offer. A year ago, writing to the French Foreign Ministry, he had anticipated a net profit of 40,000 thalers (about 170,000 francs) from the Shoa expedition. The deal he concluded in Entotto a year later was worth little more than a fifth of that, and it is doubtful he ever got this sum anyway. Over a year later he is still railing about the difficulties of converting these 'Shoa payments' into hard cash:

> Write it down in your notebooks, and get others to write it down in theirs, that one of the nastiest tricks they can play on you in Shoa

is to land you with these *Orders of Payment at Harar* ... It is better to accept goods in Shoa, at whatever price, than a payment here. These payments *here* are tortures, disasters, tyrannies, an abominable slavery. The cash-box is in the hands of Makonnen's slaves, who behave like hydrophobic monkeys and don't let a single piastre slip out. [letter to Ilg, 20 December 1889]

He had, as he puts it rather bluntly, been *roulé* – fleeced, conned, done over – by the King.

*   *   *

Rimbaud spent about ten weeks in Entotto, Menelik's new capital. It was at this point even more rudimentary than Ankober. But the future lies here. Below Entotto stood the village of Finfine, the site of the hot springs called Filwoha. Here, in 1887, Menelik began to build a new settlement. In the Ethiopian chronicles it is said that he was fulfilling a prophecy made by his ancestor King Sahle Selassie:

> One day, sitting under a great tree here, King Sahle Selassie was given a hornful of *tej* [mead], while he was playing chess, and he suddenly said: 'The day will come when my grandson will build his house here, and make you a town'.

More sceptical historians suggest that these frequent shiftings of Menelik's court were due to shortages of fuel-wood.

The town he built here became Addis Ababa, the 'New Flower', now a strident, sprawling metropolis of two million people. The hot springs of Filwoha are piped into the swimming-pool of the Addis Hilton. From this base Menelik expanded his territory: into Hararghe, into Eritrea, and – on the death of his neighbour and rival, King Joannes – into the ancient Christian heartlands of Tigré. In 1889 he proclaimed himself Emperor of Ethiopia. Ethiopia had long been a general name for this part of Africa – the name derives from Greek *aethiops*, 'burnt face', hence black face: this is found in Homer and Herodotus – but the nation-state of Ethiopia is Menelik's creation. He resisted Italian attempts to annex the country as a protectorate (attempts supported by France and Britain, and based on a fraudulent treaty) and routed Italian troops at the Battle of Adwa in 1896. He died in his late sixties, in 1913.

Menelik's dynasty continued down to Haile Selassie. He was the son of Menelik's cousin Ras Makonnen; he was born in Harar, where his father was governor, in 1892; he lived his childhood in a house near, and very similar to, the alleged Bet Rimbo. His given name was Tafari, and until his coronation in 1930 he was simply Ras [roughly 'Duke'] Tafari. From this name comes Rastafarian, the cult which venerates Selassie as the 'supreme being and only ruler' of all black people, which promises a return to Africa from the 'Babylon' of the black diaspora, and which prepares for this eventuality on a tonic regime of reggae, ganja and general good cheer.

The deposing of Haile Selassie, on 12 September 1974, signals the end of Menelik's imperial dynasty.

*   *   *

Rimbaud makes some prescient comments about Menelik's political intentions [letter to the *Bosphore Égyptien*, August 1887], and he recounts with gusto the saga of his financial problems in Abyssinia [letters to Vice-Consul Gaspary, August-November 1887]. But of the sights and sounds of Entotto; of his personal impressions of Menelik; of the antiquity and beauty and barbarism of Abyssinia – of all we might value a hundred years later – he says nothing. The only letter he actually wrote while he was there [7 April 1887] is almost hyperbolically brief: he is in good health; letters addressed to him via Aden will eventually reach him; he hopes to be back in Aden in October. It contains just one descriptive comment about Abyssinia: 'Things take a long time in these filthy places.'

Meanwhile the tentacles of the Labatut affair continue to embroil him. 'The news of my virtuous proceedings spread far and wide', he says sarcastically – in other words, the citizens of Entotto took up where those at Ankober had left off – and

> there arose on every side a whole series, a whole bunch, a whole horde of creditors, with stories that made your hair stand on end. This soon altered my charitable disposition. I became determined to leave Shoa as quickly as possible.

> I remember that on the morning of my departure, already trotting towards the NNE, I was confronted by a man who represented the wife of a friend of Labatut, who jumped out from behind a bush and demanded in the name of the Virgin Mary the sum of 19 thalers. A little further on, a creature in a sheepskin cloak leapt

down from a high promontory, demanding to know if I'd paid his brother the 12 thalers Labatut had borrowed from him.

I just shouted at them that they were too late . . .

He rode out of Entotto, in the company of Jules Borelli, on Sunday 1 May 1887.

22

THE WAY BACK

RIMBAUD HAD KNOWN Jules Borelli in Aden, had spent long weeks with him in Tadjourah – sometimes just sitting in his tent 'without saying a word' – and had been much in his company over the last three months, first at Ankober and then at Entotto. They had, as travellers do, the bond of shared knowledge: two *ferenji* stuck in the time-warp of Shoa.

A Marseillais of Italian extraction, Borelli was intelligent, resourceful, egocentric: a scientific 'explorer' who disdained the distractions of trading and politicking which most others engaged in. With his dark, close-cropped hair and beard, and his pince-nez, he has an austere look. His memoir of the region, *Éthiopie Méridionale*, resembled something that Rimbaud might have published one day: precise, perceptive, and very knowledgeable about the indigenous people. Borelli had always liked Rimbaud, or so he later claimed:

> When I first knew Rimbaud in Aden, I immediately felt drawn towards him. His way of life, which some saw as grotesque and others as an obscure kind of originality, was essentially the product of his independent and rather misanthropic personality.
> [letter to Berrichon, *c.* 1897]

They always got on well together, though this was despite having 'absolutely opposite ideas in certain important respects'. On one occasion, perhaps in Entotto, there was a flare-up between them, an incident Borelli recalls *en passant* the following year: 'I have completely forgotten' – apparently not – 'how you lost your temper with me, and wanted to make me sweep out the house. It was stupid of me to take this badly. Anyway, I hope you will forget forthwith the unpleasant words I directed at you' [26 July 1888]. An image of Rimbaud furiously waving a broom at the great explorer flickers across the screen.

In his journal for 30 April 1887, Borelli writes:

> I at last receive authorization from Menelik to travel, without
> having to wait for anyone or anything else. It is midnight. I write
> these lines harassed by fatigue, but I am determined to leave at
> dawn tomorrow with M. Rimbaud, and not to wait any longer for
> the fulfilment of doubtful promises, or for a caravan more suited
> to my plans.

This has the characteristic sniffy note, implying that Rimbaud's
caravan was not entirely 'suited' to Borelli's more scientific purposes.
Rimbaud confirms the last-minute decision: 'It was only when I had
asked Menelik's permission to make this journey that M. Borelli had
the idea of joining up with me' [letter to Bardey, 26 August 1887].
Borelli's intention was to make a full geodetic survey of the route;
Rimbaud's to get himself and his few camels of Shoa merchandise
down to Harar as quickly as possible: this is the 'unsuitablity'.
Borelli's reservations turn out to be unfounded. He did survey the
route, and when they reached Harar he entrusted his log-books to
Rimbaud, who carried them down to Aden: a physical contribution
to Borelli's text.

Though Borelli's attitude here seems condescending – the
explorer looks down on the trader, however 'accomplished' – he
would prove an ally to Rimbaud. He variously describes Rimbaud as
'irascible', 'embittered', 'tireless', etc, and later summed him up in a
clear-headed way: 'He deserves, I believe, neither all the bad nor all
the good that is said about him.' And he said, in terms that
specifically recall this journey from Entotto in mid-1887: 'Rimbaud
was travelling for business purposes, and I for scientific ones. How
much better would science have been served had our positions only
been reversed!' This, coming from the self-esteeming Borelli, is a
real tribute.

It was claimed by Borelli, and is often said of Rimbaud, that they
were the first Europeans to travel this route from Entotto to Harar.
This is not quite true. Two of the Italian 'advisers' currently
battened on Menelik – Vincenzo Ragazzi and Raffaele Alfieri – had
travelled with the king on his campaign against Harar, four months
earlier than Borelli and Rimbaud.

Rimbaud also kept a journal of the itinerary. He wrote this up in
August, and sent it to Alfred Bardey, who sent it to the Société de
Géographie. It was read at the Society's meeting on 4 November

1887, and published in the annual *Comptes Rendus* shortly afterwards, thus predating Borelli's account by three years. This is the
second, and the last, of Rimbaud's 'African texts' to be published in
France during his lifetime.

* * *

Setting out on 1 May, 'trotting to the NNE', shaking off the last
straggle of creditors and beggars, they soon turn east, and begin to
skirt Mount Herer. Both teams lose some men who abscond on the
first night. After two days they have covered thirty-five miles and
rest at a Galla village called Abichu. They cross the high plateau,
then descend along the course of the Chankora river to the plain of
Mindjar. Rimbaud notes punctiliously:

> The Mindjar has rich soil, assiduously cultivated. Its altitude must
> be 1,800 metres. (I judge the altitude by the type of vegetation; I
> am certain this is accurate, even though I have not travelled much
> in Ethiopian regions) . . . The Mindjar lacks water. Rainwater is
> conserved in holes in the ground.

And so down to the Awash, which they cross at an altitude of 800
metres, and into the hotlands. The route is designed to cut this
lowland stretch to a minimum: they have about fifty miles to cross
before the trail starts to climb towards the Itou plateau. It is a better
route, in this respect, than the modern road from Addis, which
follows the line of the railway further east, as far as Mieso, before
going up into the Tchercher Hills. (This section of the road was built
by the British firm of Marples-Ridgway in the 1950s.)

In these uplands – the scene of the massacre of Henri Lucereau's
expedition seven years earlier – Rimbaud is moved by the spectacu-
lar beauty of the landscape. This reaction is found, unusually, in the
terse measures of his *itinéraire* –

> We swiftly climb up to the Itou by shady trails. A beautiful
> wooded countryside, not much cultivated . . .

> The Tchercher stretch: magnificent forests. A lake called Arro.
> You walk on the crest of a chain of hills. The Aroussi, to the right,
> parallel to our trail, is higher than the Itou. Its great forests and
> lovely mountains are spread out in a panorama.

[Between Goro and Herna] splendid valleys crowned with forests in whose shadows we walk . . .

– and again in the letter to the *Bosphore Égyptien*, though now tending to more practical considerations:

The Itou plateau [is] a region of magnificent pastures and splendid forests, at an average altitude of 2,500 metres. It enjoys a delicious climate . . . This most salubrious and fertile country is the only area in Eastern Africa suitable for European colonization.

It is his expressing of this exhilaration that is unusual, not his experiencing of it. The language quickens: one is reminded how much is removed, drained off, in the bulk of his letters home. His passion for nature and landscape – the young man wandering 'like a gypsy' through the countryside, 'as happy as if with a woman' – is undimmed, but now unspoken. Mgr Jarosseau said of him:

Tracing the rocky paths of the countryside around Harar, he carried his luminous spirit high above the servile preoccupations of commerce . . . If he adopted this life of the commission-agent, it was undoubtedly because it placed him in contact with the contrasts of Nature: the solitude of the desert, where the absence of men brings one closer to God; the high fertile plateaux of the interior, where all the living creatures fill the air with sound . . . [letter to Enid Starkie, 1936].

And the poet Mallarmé, pondering the riddles of the African years, concluded that Rimbaud 'cared little for the trash [*pacotille*] he sold, but much for the landscapes which he drank down, thirsty for emptiness and for freedom'.

The journey took three weeks, though Rimbaud notes that the Abyssinian couriers can do it, on foot, in ten days. On the last day, 21 May, the caravan camped at Arro. There Rimbaud left Borelli and rode on, alone, anxious to reach Harar before nightfall:

And me hurrying on to find the place and the formula . . .

*   *   *

It was three years since he had been in Harar, and he found it very different since its defeat by the Shoan army of King Menelik. 'In Harar,' he wrote to Bardey (now back in France, but one who knew the place almost as well as he did), 'the Amhara continue with confiscations, extortions, *razzias*. It's the ruining of the country. The town has become a cesspit' [26 August 1887].

Rimbaud remained there for a few weeks, trying to sort out his affairs with Ras Makonnen, the new *dedjazmatch* (governor) of Harar, installed in the palisaded *guebi* close to the former Bardey depot on the 'upper square'. This was the occasion of his first meeting with Makonnen, whom he would come to know well during his last years in Harar. Makonnen (or as he writes it, Meqonnen) was the first cousin of King Menelik. They were both grandsons of King Sahle Selassie of Shoa. (Menelik was the son of Sahle Selassie's male heir, King Hyla Melekot; Makonnen of his daughter Princess Tenange Warq.) He was born in May 1852, and was thus a couple of years older than Rimbaud. At the age of fourteen, according to the autobiography of his son Haile Selassie, he was introduced to the court of Menelik, who made him 'his special companion'. As governor of Harar he had the rank of Dedjazmatch; it is as such that Rimbaud refers to him in letters to Ilg, often abbreviating it to 'the Dedj', and sometimes simply 'the D'. It was not until early 1890, after Menelik's 'anointment' as Emperor of Ethiopia, that Makonnen was formally granted 'the dignity of Ras'.

Photographs of Makonnen show that delicate, fine-featured, limpid-eyed look, at first glance more Indian than African, which his son also had. Though Rimbaud's comments about him are often acidic, it is universally said that the two men got on extremely well. Letters between them, after Rimbaud's return to France, confirm this, as does Savouré [15 August 1891], who says Makonnen was 'deeply affected' by Rimbaud's unhappy departure from Harar: 'He has told us all this *twenty* times over, saying that you were the most honest of men, and that you had often proved yourself to be his *true friend*.'

While here Rimbaud writes to Menelik, and receives a courteous reply, in Amharic: 'How are you? I myself am well, God be thanked, as is all my army.' He left for Aden around the end of June, bearing a much sealed and stamped letter from Makonnen to the French consul at Aden, which concludes: 'I would be most obliged if you would favour M. Rimbaud in his plans to return: he is handling certain commissions for King Menelik and also on behalf of us.'

This has a certain ring to it, but the first extant document from after his arrival in Aden has a more familiar note. It is a receipt from

Suel of the Grand, dated 27 July. Rimbaud has paid him the sum of 4,000 thalers, in the form of a promissory note [*bon*]. This represents payment of all money he owes Suel, both 'personally' and 'on account of *l'affaire Labatut*', and makes a sizeable hole in the sum of 8,500 thalers he had squeezed out of Menelik.

There was surprise and welcome as he climbed those three flint-block steps into the Grand, haggard and dirty after this latest traversing of the Somali desert and then the dhow-ride to Aden; bearing the indefinable scars of his experience from the mountains of Shoa; throwing down his bag and sinking into a chair. This is the first time they had seen him for year.

But business is business out here, and Suel has waited long enough for his money.

23

CAIRO

HE SHOA FIASCO has an aftermath: a recuperation which is also
a period of unexpected literary activity.

In early August, after just a couple of weeks in Aden, he
is on the move again. The heat of the Aden summer is especially
fierce this year. He leaves Steamer Point on the weekly mail-boat,
heading northwards up the Red Sea. He is heading for Cairo, 'to rest
up for a bit'. He plans to stay there two or three months: this 'will
put me on my feet again'.

On 4 August he arrives at the little Eritrean port of Massaouah.
He is promptly arrested.

The following day the French consul at Massaouah, Alexandre
Merciniez, sends a despatch to his counterpart at Aden, M. de
Gaspary, requesting information:

Dear Sir,

A certain Sieur Rimbaud, who claims to be a trader at Harar and
Aden, arrived in Massaouah yesterday, on board the weekly mail-
boat from Aden.

This Frenchman is tall and skinny, with grey eyes and a small
moustache, almost blonde. He was brought in by the police.

M. Rimbaud has no passport, and no means of proving his identity
to me . . . I would be much obliged, Monsieur le Consul, if you
could give me some information about this individual, who
appears to be a rather shady character.

(I have translated the consul's word *sec*, literally 'dry', as
'skinny'. It is used in this physical sense, as in the phrase *sec comme
un hareng*, 'as thin as a herring'; Rimbaud will later use it to
describe his own 'long, skinny leg'. *Sec* is also used to describe
someone's manner, just as we use the term 'dry'. This would

certainly be true of Rimbaud's curt, sardonic style, but Merciniez is giving a physical sketch here, for identification purposes, so the visual meaning is probably uppermost. Also, it is *carabiniers* who bring Rimbaud in – 'police' in general, but probably Italian *carabinieri* in particular. Massaouah was principally occupied by Italians at this point.)

And a curiosity: Merciniez describes Rimbaud's eyes as grey while everyone else who looked into them described them as blue – 'a pale unsettling blue' according to Verlaine; 'eyes of forget-me-not and periwinkle' from a florid Delahaye; 'my whitish blue eye', says Rimbaud. Eyes are in the eye of the beholder: the truly remarkable aspect of Rimbaud's appearance is not the greyness of his eye, dazed by the Dankali sun, but the greyness of his hair. Rimbaud says it a couple of weeks later, in a letter to his family: 'my hair has gone totally grey'. An exaggeration perhaps, though by no means a figure of speech. He is thirty-two years old: in the brief curriculum of his life he is already an old man.

This is a snapshot of Rimbaud en route in 1887: a shady character, a man under escort, a man with no alibi.

In fact he had business to attend to at Massaouah. He had with him two 'drafts' or money-orders (*traites*), drawn on local traders to the tune of 7,500 thalers: doubtless a part of the elusive 'Shoa contract'. These, and a few documents relating to the Labatut affair, are the only papers he has on him.

And while the anonymity of the moment is perfect, the sequel is characteristic too. A week later the consul has a very different view of Rimbaud – perhaps from Gaspary's bona fides, but also from his own impressions. On 12 August he writes a handsome letter of introduction, addressed to an old friend of his in Cairo – a marquis no less – recommending Monsieur Rimbaud as 'a very honourable Frenchman, a trader and explorer in Shoa and Harar, countries which he knows extremely well, and where he has lived for more than nine years'. (A typical Rimbaldien exaggeration lies behind this. Rimbaud had actually been in East Africa less than seven years.)

Rimbaud is next in Suez, where he once more charms his diplomatic host. The vice-consul there, Lucien Labosse, will later write to him [22 April 1888]: 'We all have good memories of your short stay in Suez, and we hope to shake you by the hand when the Gods bring you back to Egypt.'

*   *   *

He is in Cairo by 20 August. He puts up at the Hotel Europe. He presents his letter of introduction to Merciniez's friend, the Marquis de Grimaldi-Régusse. The Marquis is a lawyer in the Appeal Court of Cairo. Rimbaud also meets Octave Borelli, the brother of Jules, who is the editor of Cairo's French-language newspaper, *Le Bosphore Égyptien*. Jules Borelli himself was also in Cairo some of the time.

After seven years in which Aden (pop. 60,000) was the largest city he had lived in, Cairo hit his senses with its dense sprawl of humanity, its clogged traffic ways, its throbbing twilights and its great attenuated souks which are themselves the size of small towns. As stingy as ever, he complains about the inflated city prices; 'life is *à la européenne* and very dear'. He is very anxious about money here: 'I am scared of losing the little I've got. Imagine this – I continually carry around over sixteen thousand *francs d'or* in my money-belt; this weighs about eight kilos and it's giving me dysentery.' Another image: this tall, greying figure with the money-belt sagging off his gaunt frame. After a few days he deposits the money in the bank, the Credit Lyonnais: another reason for coming here. He comes into town like a prospector, bringing gold from the hills.

And so now he rests amid the raggedly genteel comforts of the Hotel Europe, and listens to the comforting wash of the street-sounds below, and smells the peachy smoke of the *shisha* pipes on the corner, and he sees this life of hardship he has lived as if with surprise, as if seeing it whole for the first time, as if this brief taste of life *à la européenne* was indeed a return to Europe, and a chance at last to see what all these travels had meant: 'Seven years of unimaginable fatigues and abominable privations ...' Physically exhausted, 'enfeebled', 'excessively tired', he is also now 'tormented by rheumatism' – a faint anticipatory death-knell, though it is the left thigh and knee afflicted, not the right leg he eventually lost. His friend Savouré will later speak of Rimbaud's *étrange dégaine* – his 'strange gawky gait' with 'his left shoulder always in advance of the other'. He feels himself battered by his travels:

> Just imagine what shape I'm in after the following sort of activity: sea crossings and land journeys, on horeseback, in open boats, with no clothes, no provisions, no water, etc., etc. [23 August 1887]

Sans vêtements, sans vivres, sans eau . . . The echo answers back, across the years, quite unmistakable: *'sans gîte, sans habits, sans pain'*. It is the line from 'Bad Blood' in the *Season in Hell*, probably an evocation of those foot-journeys to Paris in early 1871:

> *Those winter nights on the road, no shelter, no clothes, no*
> *bread, a voice clutched my frozen heart: 'Weakness or strength?*
> *Of course, choose strength'* . . .

These brief catalogues of deprivation seems to lock together: the freezing nights in the ditch and the desert sun at midday, the absence of bread and the absence of water, as if these are negative and positive of a single endless journey, a single drastic experiment in the physics of hardship. The hardship is one of exposure, of nakedness: 'no clothes' in either case: naked as a baby, naked as a pagan.

*   *   *

Of course! Choose strength . . .

But can he still choose strength? He is in very bad shape, *'excessivement fatigué'*. Yet his spell in Cairo is marked by a spate of unexpected activity – with his pen.

Within a few days of arriving he is working on an article for Octave Borelli's newspaper, *Le Bosphore Égyptien*. (It is framed as a letter to the 'director', but is essentially a piece of reportage.) The *Bosphore Égyptien* was 'a daily journal of politics and literature' for the growing French community in Cairo. It had been closed down briefly in 1885, amid rumours that Borelli was being paid by the French government to 'stir up trouble in Egypt'. Rimbaud's report details the circumstances of his journey to Shoa, the political and commercial situation there, the merits or otherwise of the two routes he had travelled (the Danakil route via Tadjourah, and the Itou route via Harar), and offers a few piquant and pessimistic remarks about other French operations in the area, such as the concession won by Chefneux and Brémond to transport salt from Lake Assal. It was published over two days, 25 and 27 August 1887. It is, broadly speaking, the only prose text apart from the *Season in Hell* to have been published under his control.

The *Bosphore* article is about 5,000 words long: in journalistic terms, a major piece. At the same time as he was working on it he wrote three letters home (23, 24, 25 August), and the day after the first portion appeared, he sat down and wrote to Alfred Bardey, giving a precise account of the itinerary between Entotto and Harar, together with some trading notes about Shoa.

Some of this material was already written in note form, but this is by any standards a busy week, and by Rimbaud's post-Parnassian standards a positive furore of creativity.

On 26 August he also wrote to the Société de Géographie. The letter is lost, but the reply from the Secretary-General, Monsieur Maunoir (who had written to Rimbaud in 1883, fruitlessly requesting a photograph), shows its import:

> It is unfortunately not possible, at present, for us to respond favourably to your proposal . . . It is to be feared that the sum you ask for in your letter is too much . . . I remain most disposed to assist you, within the limit of my means . . .

The kind of work he was offering, one gathers, was a 'memoir' based on his 'notes and recollections' of the tribes of East Africa and the 'routes and topography' of their lands. It would include 'new facts, useful information and precise descriptions'. He is apparently talking of a new expedition as well – the Secretary says: 'the countries you intend to travel in are very dangerous'. In a letter home Rimbaud talks of going to the Sudan. This is perhaps the intended journey he hoped the Société would back.

The Secretary suggests, without much optimism, that Rimbaud applies to the Ministry of Public Information to get funding for a proper scientific 'mission'.

*　　*　　*

In the event it seems he spent the next few weeks doing what every visitor to Egypt does: some sightseeing. His last letter from Cairo, to Bardey on 26 August, gives his customary poste restante address, and says he will be here until September. Nothing further is heard from him until 8 October, by which time he is back in Aden.

There seems to be just one piece of written evidence concerning Rimbaud's whereabouts in September 1887. It is a carving of his name, in large capital letters, on the west wall of the birthplace of Amenophis III in the Valley of the Sphinxes at Luxor. The inscription stands about nine feet from the ground. There are a couple of smaller scratchings on a nearby pillar, one of which trails off leaving RIMB, a contraction he used in his letters.

Those who believe this *graffito* was done by Rimbaud will tell you it is at a height appropriate to the 1880s, before excavation, when the sand was of course higher. This seems borne out by some dated doodles and signatures nearby. Those who do not believe it point to the fact that nothing was heard of this inscription prior to 1949, in which year it was suddenly and independently spotted by no less than three travelling writers, Jean Cocteau, Henri Stierlin and Théophile Briant.

It might seem uncharacteristic of Rimbaud: leaving his mark is exactly what he strives not to do. (It might also seem vandalistic, but this is a more recent perception. It was perfectly *de rigueur* to deface monuments like this: at the top of the Great Pyramid of Chiops, Gérard de Nerval reports, was an inscription by a shoe-polish manufacturer in Piccadilly, advertising his new 'improved patent'.) Perhaps in the antiquity of Luxor, in these pagan stones, Rimbaud felt he had found a page worth his name.

*   *   *

It is about this time that we get another brief narration of what it was like actually to be around Rimbaud. These are certain recollections gleaned in Obock and Djibouti by a French traveller who spent two years in the area, 1911–13. They were first published in an obscure French periodical in 1934. The compiler asked to remain anonymous – and still is – but among the sources he names are Athanase Righas, Ato Joseph, then the Ethiopian consul at Djibouti, and various French and Greek settlers in Obock, including a couple called Dufaud who ran a hotel there. Apart from Righas, none of the names occur in other records of Rimbaud. Much of it is probably at least second-hand, but the reminiscences of the Dufauds appear to be an eye-witness account of Rimbaud as their hotel-guest in Obock. He probably first visited the French settlement of Obock in 1884 – his first reference to the place is in a letter dated 10 September – but certain internal details suggest that these reminiscences mainly refer to his periods of transit there *after* the Abyssinian adventure. He may have called in there en route from Egypt to Aden in 1887; he was certainly there in early 1888, to pick up a consignment of rifles

of Savouré's; he probably stayed there at some points during his last
years at Harar, though there is no precise documentation of this.

The flavour of these reminiscences is often rather barbed. The
following extract appears to be based on the Dufauds' testimony.
This is some of what they had to say, some twenty years after the
event, about their strange guest:

> Physically Rimbaud was a rather slender man, of above average
> height, quite thin, and with an unattractive face, indeed rather
> ugly, which made his *hôtelière* [i.e. Madame Dufaud] say:
> 'Abyssinia isn't going to get a very good impression of the French
> race from him' . . .

> Rimbaud spoke well, his words were fluent and well-chosen. He
> could discourse on any subject whatever, though he did not often
> do so. In politics he showed himself to be uncompromisingly anti-
> clerical, a lover of freedom and independence, a rebel who readily
> mocked laws and rules, which he seemed to disdain to an
> extraordinary degree. He liked to read *Le Rappel* and *La Lanterne*
> [radical journals] and he claimed he had been imprisoned with the
> Communards in Paris . . .

> He was by turns exuberant and taciturn, 'following the moon' as
> he put it. Having dazzled his fellow-guests with his odd sallies,
> peppered with slang and with literary quotations, and sometimes
> with spirituality too, he would then fall into a mute silence for
> several days, shutting himself up in his room, where he did
> nothing but smoke pipes and cigars, and perhaps also hashish, for
> his memories of Egypt were very vivid! . . .

> Although active when dealing with a caravan, he was very
> different when resting. Alcohol of every sort, tobacco, hashish and
> even opium were familiar to him. In his hours of spleen and cafard
> he debased himself with prolonged use of all these drugs. He
> emerged from these 'bad moons' downcast, haggard, morose,
> hardly eating at all, but always drinking a great deal.

> His favourite meals, when he came down to the coast, were
> peppery dishes, outrageously spicy. He liked shrimps, lobster, crab
> *à l'américaine*, clams, cod *rouguaie*, curried rice, and always had
> on his table some of the powdered red pepper which the
> Abyssinians call *Berberi*, much hotter than all the pickles and
> mustards of Europe. This was a taste that Rimbaud's stomach had

not quite got used to; like many, he sometimes repented afterwards for having tasted these spices of the devil!

Some of this, like the puzzling shifts from eloquence to silence, is
amply confirmed elsewhere, is indeed a paradigm of his life. In the
matter of drug-taking, it is at odds with other evidence. Various
witnesses – Ottorino Rosa, Dimitri Righas, Mgr Jarosseau, etc. –
describe him as profoundly ascetic: he used *khat*, according to Rosa,
and drank a lot of coffee, but nothing stronger. However, these
describe his life up in Harar, and it is possible that his periods 'down
on the coast' were rather different: rest and recreation. The allusion
to Egypt, then famed for its hashish, is suggestive.

I cannot resist this untrustworthy memoir and the images it
proffers. We are in this meagre little hotel on the Red Sea, *circa*
September 1887. Rimbaud is in the dining room tucking in to 'crab
American-style'; Rimbaud is locked in his room in an aromatic cloud
of Cairo hashish; Rimbaud is in the khazi with the shits from too
much Abyssinian pepper.

*   *   *

Back in Aden Rimbaud once more toys with the idea of journalism –
though tending also, in his letters home, to shrug the idea off as a
scam to drum up some travel money. Writing home in November, he
announces that he has sent some articles off to *Le Temps* and *Le
Figaro*, and that he even intends to send something to the *Courrier
des Ardennes*. He describes these articles as 'interesting reports
[*récits*] of my travels in East Africa'.

These are evanescent pieces. Scholars have put in time among
the back-catalogues and microfiches, and nothing resembling an
article by Rimbaud has been found in these journals. They are not
entirely weightless, though. Two of Rimbaud's associates, Alfred Ilg
(whom we met in Entotto) and Armand Savouré (whom we shall
meet shortly), were in Europe at this time, setting up various African
deals, and anxiously scanning the newspapers for the latest
developments in East Africa. There was trouble brewing between
Menelik and the Italians in the hinterland of Massaouah. On 13
February 1888, Savouré writes to Ilg, from Paris:

Like you I'm still waiting for news, and nothing serious arrives . . .
I still only know the tall stories [*racontars*] in the newspapers,

Self-portrait, 'with my arms folded', Harar, 1883.

Self-portrait, 'on the terrace of the house', Harar, 1883.

Self-portrait, 'in a coffee plantation', Harar, 1883.

Constantin Sotiro.
Photograph by Rimbaud, 1883.

Harar trader. Photograph by Rimbaud, 1883.

The house of Raouf Pasha in Harar, where Rimbaud lived between 1881 and 1885.

'Bet Rimbo', 1994.

The tug *Arthur Rimbaud*,
Djibouti port, 1994.

The dhow to Tadjourah.

Caravan inventory,
Harar, 24 August 1889.

Rimbaud's Abyssinian mistress.

Alfred Bardey, Rimbaud's employer.

Jules Borelli, explorer.

Abou Bekr Pasha, sultan and slaver.

Danakil *chef de caravane*.

King Menelik of Shoa.

Alfred Ilg.

Ras Makonnen, Governor of Harar.

Rimbaud shortly before his death. Sketch by Isabelle Rimbaud.

Commemorative plaque, Hôpital de la Conception, Marseille.

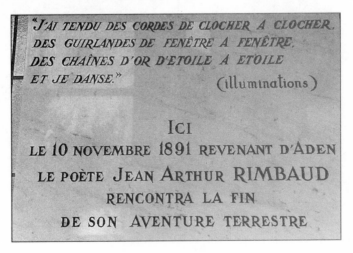

"J'AI TENDU DES CORDES DE CLOCHER A CLOCHER,
DES GUIRLANDES DE FENÊTRE A FENÊTRE,
DES CHAÎNES D'OR D'ETOILE A ETOILE
ET JE DANSE."
                                        (illuminations)

ICI
LE 10 NOVEMBRE 1891 REVENANT D'ADEN
LE POÈTE JEAN ARTHUR RIMBAUD
RENCONTRA LA FIN
DE SON AVENTURE TERRESTRE

which grow more and more improbable, and which every morning contradict the news of the previous evening. It's Rimbaud having fun in Aden, sending hoaxes [*fumisteries*] to the press.

The fine-tuning of this comment is difficult to get. It shows that Savouré knew of Rimbaud's journalistic interests; it suggests that he didn't take them very seriously, though this may just be his general, joshing tone. It may or may not suggest that he had actually read something by Rimbaud in the Paris press. Though no identifiable article by Rimbaud has yet been found, there is one teasing reference in *Le Figaro* of 9 February. This has a news piece about the Massaouah crisis: Savouré would certainly have read it, and he would have noted that one of its sources was an 'unofficial cable from Aden'.

Is this Rimbaud's last and most ghostly publication? An unofficial cable to *Le Figaro* written – if Savouré is to be taken literally – for the 'fun' of misinforming: a hoax, a *blague*?

As it happens, we do have Rimbaud's comments about the so-called Massaouah crisis, in a letter he wrote to Ilg on 1 February (received by Ilg, at Zurich, on the 19th). I quote it briefly to give the flavour, and to show what the Paris news-sheets of the 1880s missed out on:

> Your predictions about the Massaouah saga are shared by everyone here. They [the Italians] are going to make a *conquest* [underlined] of a few volcanic hillocks, scattered as far as 30 kilometres from Massaouah, and join them up with a scrap-metal railway line. Having planted themselves in these hinterlands, they will let loose a few volleys of mortar-fire to scare the vultures, and launch a light aircraft [*aèrostat*] garlanded with heroic devices. This will soon be over. It will then be time to sell off the last few hundred of the several thousand donkeys and camels they brought, and the timber of the camp-huts, etc., all that shoddy stuff which the military factories toil so proudly to produce.

> And then, after this moment of legitimate delirium, what will happen? The charming plain of Massaouah is going to need a lot of people to guard it. This conquest will prove expensive, and will be dangerous to maintain . . .

This is the first of his news-letters to Ilg (it was unpublished, like most of them, until the 1960s). Its sarcastic, magnifying, almost vaudevillian 'take' on colonial politics is perhaps what Savouré means by a *fumisterie*.

At the end of February, Paul Bourde – the Charleville-born journalist who had first told Bardey about Rimbaud's poetic past – wrote to Rimbaud urging him to send 'some reports on these regions which you know so well'. He is sure he can get them 'placed' in *Le Temps*. (Bourde does not apparently know that Rimbaud has already sent some pieces to *Le Temps* – if indeed he really had – though he may know from Bardey or Savouré of Rimbaud's intentions that way.) Writing these articles, he tells Rimbaud airily:

> . . . would be no trouble at all for you, and would be a link by which to reattach yourself to civilized life, something from which you could draw a moral profit. You would be paid fifty centimes a line. This is the rate we offer to our freelance correspondents, who are not special envoys. If you like the idea, perhaps you can send something in your first letter . . . [Argelès, 29 February 1888]

Bourde later told Paterne Berrichon that Rimbaud wrote back demanding the exorbitant sum of 4,500 francs, in advance, and so the idea was dropped. The acutely patronizing tone of Bourde's letter, with its talk of 'civilized life' and 'moral profit', cannot have helped. The letter also contains the kind of smug literary froth which froze Rimbaud to the heart. He reads: 'You have become, among a little coterie, a sort of legendary figure . . .' He reads: 'Certain young people, whom I find naive . . .' He reads: 'This little group, who claim you as their Master . . .' And he throws the letter aside.

Paul Bourde (whose surname translates as 'blunder' or 'boob') has a brief and slightly baleful presence in this story: the ghost of Parisian chit-chat.

Nothing tangible remains of this last spark of literary ambition, this faint outline of Rimbaud the foreign correspondent which emerges for a moment – another of those spectral photographs – only to vanish. *Tout est devenu blanc*. From what he did write in this vein – the published pieces for the Société de Géographie and the *Bosphore Égyptien*, and more particularly the news-letters to Ilg and others, which we will look at soon – he would have been a good journalist, in the wider 'feature' sense of today, though not a great one. He has the intrepid courage, the acute scepticism, the eye for detail, but he lacks the compassion and empathy of the great foreign correspondents. He is not a Cameron or a Kapuscinski. He is too 'closed up', in Bardey's phrase.

What perhaps emerges from all this is a sense that he is *enjoying* writing. Another piece from this time, which also remained unpublished for decades, is his long letter to Vice-Consul Gaspary [9 November 1887]. This *relation*, as he calls it, gives that convoluted and often comic account of his trials in Shoa from which I quoted earlier. It has an easy narrative pace, a flow of incident and detail. He seems almost surprised to have written it, and concludes: 'Forgive me for doing it in this style.' He has written it as a 'diversion', he says, to keep his mind off the 'memories which this affair has left me, which are, in brief, very disagreeable'.

To write as a mere *diversion*? He lays down the sweat-greased pen, thinks of the wild fulminations of his *voyance* – the poet who 'seeks inside himself all forms of love, of suffering, of madness', who 'swallows down all the poisons' – and he almost smiles at this latest hoax he has played on himself.

But the affair he speaks of – *l'affaire Labatut* – rumbles on. He is back in Aden with things to attend to. There are accounts to be drawn up, procurances and inventories. A certain Monsieur Deschamps is looking for him, further to some moneys still owed up in Shoa, and writes huffily to the consul:

> Since my return [to Aden] from France I have tried in vain to establish his whereabouts; no one has been able to tell me, though I am quite positive that he is living in Aden. Considering this attitude of M. Rimbaud, who systematically hides himself away, I am asking you, Monsieur le Consul, to be so good as to demand his presence before you. [28 October 1888]

The whingeing Deschamps has it just right: Rimbaud '*systematique-ment se dérobe*' – he slips away, shies away, hides himself, evades the issue: the phrase carries all these meanings – and this brief dream of fame and fortune as a journalist disappears along with him.

PART FOUR

THE AFRICAN

*'I might come [to the Paris Exhibition] next year,
and exhibit some of the products of the region.
Perhaps I could exhibit myself, as I'm sure I
look excessively baroque after so long here . . .'*

– Letter from Harar, 18 May 1889

24

RIMBAUD'S CIRCLE

A FTER THE LONG ardours of the Shoa trip and the brief recuperation at Cairo, Rimbaud was once more installed at Harar in May 1888. He was there as a 'commission agent' for César Tian, another French import-export merchant based at Aden; and was working increasingly on his own account as well.

He remained continuously in Harar for nearly three years. These were his last years in Africa and – until the very end – his happiest. Perhaps a certain air of defeat hangs over them: a diminution of his strength and will. There are no more big journeys planned, no more talk of being an explorer or photographer or journalist. His horizon becomes more limited. He is no longer that young man who wants 'so much to escape from reality'. He is no longer hurrying to find 'the place and the formula'.

What the formula was one cannot say, but the place he found – or anyway ended up in – was Harar.

In these last years, Rimbaud attains a certain status. He is a respected figure, valued by Europeans and Africans alike. Among the European expats and explorers of the region he is considered a man of experience, an 'old hand', and indeed something of a 'character'. He is also a voluminous correspondent, a vigorous purveyor of news and views in among the traders' shop-talk. He has, one might almost say, a 'circle' of friends and admirers.

I would distinguish two or three different types of 'circle'. There are the business partners of these years, chiefly Alfred Ilg and Armand Savouré. They are based elsewhere: Ilg in Entotto, Savouré shuttling between Abyssinia and Djibouti (the latter founded as a French settlement in 1888). They correspond with him, and occasionally visit him. And then there is his daily circle of acquaintances in Harar: the Italians Ottorino Rosa and Ugo Ferrandi, and the Swiss-Italian Pietro Felter, who all worked for the Trieste-based firm of Bienenfeld & Co; the French traders, Bidault

(first name unknown) and the two Brémonds; the French missionaries Mgr Taurin-Cahagne and Mgr Jarosseau; the Greeks he had
worked with back in the early days, Constantin Sotiro and the
Righas brothers. And then there was his African circle: the governor
of Harar, Ras Makonnen, with whom he had very cordial relations;
his servant Djami, and his chief *abban* Farah Kali; and his unnamed
mistress who is either Tigrayan or Galla but not, curiously, one of
the 'radiant' Adari of Harar.

I do not want to tint this too rosily. Rimbaud's moods are as
black as ever. The sense of isolation and ennui continues to haunt
him:

> I'm always very bored; in fact I've never known anyone be more
> bored than I am. And isn't this indeed a miserable existence,
> without any family, without any intellectual activity, lost in the
> midst of these negroes whose lot one would like to improve, and
> who themselves seek to exploit you and to prevent you from
> realizing any money without long delays? Obliged to speak their
> gibberish, to eat their dirty food, to endure a thousand frustrations
> on account of their laziness, their treachery and their stupidity.

> But that's not the saddest thing. What's worse is the fear of
> becoming brutalized oneself, little by little, isolated as one is, and
> so faraway from any intelligent society. [4 August 1888]

But we have learned to look round the edge of the letters, to see their
negativities as in part conditioned by the shadows of his childhood,
by his relationship with his mother. They travel down a narrow
band of emotion in which so much of his African life remains
unspoken. We also have, for this period more than any other,
alternative texts: the letters he wrote to others like Ilg and Savouré,
so different in mood from the letters home; and the views which
those others give of him in their letters and memoirs, which speak of
him as such good company. He was 'one of the most charming
raconteurs I have ever met,' said Savouré. 'He could make us all
laugh until we cried.'

His thoughts turn more and more to France, to home, and even
to marriage – 'settling down' – but always with a wistful note, as if
these were places and states he would never quite reach, impossible
destinations. It is the paradox of the last years: Roche has become a
kind of distant dream, like Zanzibar or Panama. If he has a home it

is here, in the twisted streets of Harar, where he is Abdoh Rinbo, trader in gold and servant of Allah: Rimbaud the African. No one in France would recognize him now: the grey hair, the shambling gait, the buttonless cotton tunic, the disappointments etched in the bones of his face. You would indeed think this was 'somebody else'.

Only the eyes tell a different story. They are the same as always, burning and beautiful, staring out of this now-perfect disguise.

*　　*　　*

Let us meet briefly this gallery of little-known traders and travellers which constitutes the 'circle' – as it were the *salon* or *cénacle* – of the great Rimbaud.

The best-known is Alfred Ilg, the mercurial Swiss fixer, 'the man who knows everything'. Borer calls him 'the true No. 2 of the story'. We met him briefly at Entotto, in the entourage of King Menelik, in a role which might nowadays be described as 'technical adviser' (though Ilg himself was heard to use the designation *Biho Added*, or prime minister).

Ilg was born in Basle in 1854: an exact contemporary of Rimbaud's, as were Alfred Bardey and Ottorino Rosa. He had studied at the Technical Institute in Zurich and worked in Europe as a civic engineer. He designed the Berne waterworks and the cupola of the Berne observatory. He first travelled to Abyssinia in his early twenties, and in 1878 – on the advice of Rimbaud's future partner Labatut – he was engaged by Menelik. He swiftly became a valued member of Menelik's entourage, both for his engineering skills – he constructed the small pontoons over the Awash river which Rimbaud's caravan had used – and for his diplomatic and financial skills. He was Menelik's chief broker with the European powers who were jockeying for influence in the region. 'Because of his knowledge of languages and his honesty,' Rimbaud told Vice-Consul Gaspary, Ilg 'is generally employed by the King in all the court's dealings with the Europeans'. With him worked two other Swiss whom Rimbaud came to know: Ernst Zimmerman ('Zimpi') and L. Appenzeller.

Photographs of Ilg show him in a Ruritanian garb – uniform, medals, pendant badge of office – which may relate to his Shoa days. He has a strong, squarish face: 'the cuboid head and the scrubbing-brush hair' [Borer]. The eye is alert, the thin smile all but obscured by a florid, *belleépoque*, circus-master moustache. He sometimes wears spectacles, sometimes a monocle in his left eye.

The monocle and the moustache give him a dandified air, a Germanic fastidiousness which makes him incongruous among the mud and thatch dwellings of Entotto, and indeed among the shabbier traders like Rimbaud, who looked more like a 'building worker'. The biographers have mostly warmed to Ilg, 'with his comforting corpulence, his drawling accent, and his talk vaguely tinged with humour' [Steinmetz]. Borer calls him a man of 'scrupulous honesty' in whom Rimbaud 'found a rare opportunity for intellectual commerce'. Only Enid Starkie, with the prejudices of an Oxford bluestocking in the 1930s, strikes a sour note, seeing in him a 'common-looking' Swiss bourgeois.

The other business associate of Rimbaud's last years was Armand Savouré. Rimbaud knew him in Tadjourah, where he was setting up a caravan with Barral (who was killed on the return journey); and again in Entotto, where he was in partnership with one of the Brémonds. He was a somewhat shady character much involved in the arms trade: he had a stockpile of guns at Djibouti. Ilg described him as 'good honest bloke' but in fact never really trusted him. However, Savouré himself wrote to Rimbaud: 'I err in the opposite direction to you: instead of believing that everyone is a scoundrel, I believe too easily that everyone is honest' [10 December 1889].

Of all the Europeans here, Borer says, Savouré was 'the most louche and the best acclimatized'. His servant and *abban*, Ali Fara, was the son of an Issah chief and the envy of other traders. Savouré lent him to Rimbaud on occasions: 'Do not neglect him, he knows the whole region intimately . . . I pay him 10 thalers per month.'

Savouré was a caustic observer of Shoan affairs, and his asides on the subject are much in Rimbaud's own vein:

> Menelik's daughter, who was married to the elder son of Joannes [King of Tigre], has just arrived in Shoa where she's looking for a new husband to console her for the death of the first. Madame Zaoditou – all offers considered! She's no prettier than her father . . . [Entotto, 28 February 1889]

He was a blustery, hot-tempered man. He gives Rimbaud 'a bit of a bollocking' [*je vous engueule un peu*] for selling a few rifles without his permission [20 January 1889], and they had a vitriolic spat over

a consignment of coffee – 'I never needed your wretched coffee,'
Rimbaud writes,

> . . . I only took it to close your account, as you were in a hurry. If I
> hadn't done so you would have *got nothing for it, nothing,*
> *absolutely nothing, nothing times nothing.* Everyone knows this
> and everyone will tell you this. You know it yourself, but I see that
> the air of Djibouti has sent you crazy. [undated, *c.* April 1890]

In early 1891, he commented to Rimbaud: 'we are the only two who
haven't got married yet', but a few months later Sotiro tells
Rimbaud: 'Savouré has gone up to Harar with his money and his
wife, a white woman' [14 August 1891].

After Rimbaud's death Savouré continued to shuttle between
Shoa and Djibouti, and in 1897 he wrote from Addis Ababa to
Rimbaud's brother Frédéric, who had written asking for letters:

> I spent a lot of time with your esteemed brother, both in Harar and
> here [i.e. Shoa]. I hardly ever saw him laugh, though he could
> make all of us laugh until we cried with the stories he told. He was
> one of the most delightful raconteurs I have ever met. I can assure
> you he was also a very serious man, experienced in business
> affairs, and highly trusted and esteemed by the Abyssinian
> authorities in Harar, especially by Ras Makonnen. Even Mgr
> Taurin, who certainly abhorred his ideas, had great respect for
> him, I am sure . . .
>
> All who knew him out here were deeply saddened by his untimely
> death. It is true he was sometimes rather surly [*bourru*] in his
> manner, but not, as far as I am aware, in a way that made anyone
> bear a grudge against him.

And later, nearly forty years after his last acquaintance with
Rimbaud, the image of him springs to Savouré's memory:

> Rimbaud! I knew and was often in the company of this
> extraordinary Original, with his strange gawky gait [*sa dégaine*
> *étrange*], always the left shoulder far in front of the right. He was
> one of the best Arabists that ever lived, and around 1886/7 he went
> off preaching the Koran, as a way of penetrating those regions of
> Africa that were still unknown . . .

And he remembers again, as he did in his letter to Frédéric, the poker-faced humour of Rimbaud as raconteur:

> He was a deadpan type [*pince-sans-rire*]. I rarely saw him very gay, but he had a talent for entertaining his audience with stories and anecdotes, recounted in words so comic that you wondered where he got them from . . . [letter to Georges Maurevert, 1930]

(This was a skill that stayed with him to the end: on his sickbed at Roche, Isabelle recalled, he talked 'in detail' about his life in Africa. 'He explained so much in just a few words, in a style that was precise and charming. Sometimes he made a joke of it, and turned everything to ridicule.')

And then in a postscript in the corner of the letter, in his big garlanded handwriting, Savouré adds a last recollection, a blurred glimpse into the very rooms of Rimbaud's house, in about September 1888:

> Once one of our caravans arrived in Harar at the beginning of Ramadan, and we had to wait there until the end. He gave me hospitality for the month. Quite a nice house, but no furniture. I had nothing to sleep on but my camp-bed from the journey, and during the whole month I never found out where he slept, only seeing him writing, day and night, at a makeshift table.

'One could go on forever about this singular figure,' Savouré concludes. 'Forgive me for speaking of him at such length'.

* * *

It was not just as a trading contact and occasional host that Ilg and Savouré valued Rimbaud, but as a correspondent from Harar. These were the 'news-letters', of great practical value in this region of rumours, but also regarded as prime entertainment. Ilg frequently applauds them:

> I laughed heartily at it [i.e. Rimbaud's letter of 1 February 1888] I can assure you. I perceive, with great pleasure, that behind that terrible mask which makes you seem so horribly severe, there hides a good humour which many would undoubtedly envy. If I wasn't afraid of compromising you, I would have sent your passage about the famous Italian conquest [of Massaouah] to

the newspapers, and we would have made a few others laugh as well . . . [19 February 1888]

You amused us divinely with your details about M. Bidault, and I only regret not being able to paint his portrait in the same style as you. I would undoubtedly have been a success . . . [16 June 1889]

We are completely without any news of the Grrrreat Embassy [i.e. of Makonnen to Italy]. I look forward to interesting details from you. You can tell these stories so well if you want to, but it seems that the delights of doing business here have driven away completely the little bit of good humour you had left. Look, my dear Monsieur Rimbaud, you only live once, so make the most of it and to hell with your heirs. [26 October 1889]

Savouré also cherished the arrival of a letter from Rimbaud: 'Though they were business letters, they were composed in a really amusing [*crevant*] style. We all used to get together to read those letters of his, and we made quite a party of it . . . We were never in doubt that he was a poet of talent.' Subsequently, Savouré handed over these papers to Berrichon, and comments in a typically blustery way:

That animal his brother-in-law pestered me for them, and eventually squeezed them out of me, something I have many times regretted, especially as he only produced that idiotic book [*Vie de Rimbaud*, 1897], which he sent me but which I've never had the courage to read all the way through.

Some of these letters that occasioned such mirth have survived. Rimbaud has a marvellous gift as a sketch-writer. Eddying currents of news and gossip are crystallized into little vignettes – almost one might say into *illuminations*, or 'painted plates' – of expatriate life. A few examples:

Herr Zimmerman has just gone back up to Harar, wearing a kind of three-tiered helmet . . . [29 March 1888]

Good news from up there [i.e. Harar]. Peace and silence on earth and in heaven. The scientists are being scientific (and their wives are being raped, at least that's what has happened to the good Signor Traversi, it seems, who has denounced his dearly beloved and got rid of her brat) . . . [29 March 1888]

Antonelli has smallpox and stays on at Lit Marefia – Traversi is hunting hippopotamus on the Awash – I hear M. Appenzeller is repairing the bridge [over the Awash] – Borelli with the King of Djimma – M. Zimmerman awaiting your pleasure – Antoine Brémond is suckling his babies at Alin Amba – Bidault wandering and photographing in the Harar mountains – Stéphane the skin-dyer stretched out in the gutter in front of our doors, etc etc. It's all much as usual. [25 June 1888]

(Stéphane the skin-dyer is elsewhere described as 'Stéphane Second-Class', as opposed to 'Stéphane First-Class', an Armenian merchant.)

Rimbaud is also trenchant about the political pretensions of the Abyssinian court at Harar. In mid-1889, Ras Makonnen's diplomatic mission to Italy – 'the Grrrreat Embassy' as Ilg put it – comes under the thin Rimbaldien gaze.

The Ras is optimistic, says Rimbaud. He imagines he is going to bring back all sorts of gifts and concessions from Rome:

a quantity of machine-gun batteries, thousands of bales of silk, several millions in *beur* [i.e. *birr*, or cash], and the homage of all Europe prostrated before those varnished boots and silken socks which the intelligent count [i.e. Antonelli] has already ordered for him by special courier.

Poor *tota* [a small monkey]. I can see him from here, throwing up into his boots on the crossing from Alexandria to Naples, and the *djanos* [cloaks] of the Shoan embassy floating on the deck planks . . . [1 July 1889]

I assume they have now left Italy, and are on their way to Jerusalem, Bethlehem, Sodom and Gomorrah – I can't believe they'll turn up a chance to visit the Holy Places. [7 October 1889]

Rimbaud undoubtedly plays up to this idea of the humorous observer, the Harar satirist. His own comment on his letters, and their circumstances, is this:

The couriers from here to Shoa don't actually leave until long after the announcement of their 'immediate' departure, so one has time, in these letters, to accumulate the most eccentric paragraphs, the most dramatic surprises and contradictory stories and anecdotes. [7 October 1889]

He has his audience – a tiny, scattered audience: a score of

Europeans strung out across several hundred miles of African wilderness – and he plays to it. There had always been this intimacy about his writing: it was always *addressed* – to Izambard, to Demeny, to Banville and of course to Verlaine. His acknowledged medium is the prose-poem, but I would say also his medium is the manuscript. As a speaker he was habitually taciturn; as an author he was weirdly indifferent to publication; and between those twin reticences there is this wonderful fluency of the pen – the Douai notebooks, the fugitive leaves of the *Illuminations*, and now these last quixotic bulletins, these 'eccentric paragraphs' brought out by saddle-bag from a hilltop town in Africa.

*　　*　　*

Other Frenchmen flit in and out of view in Rimbaud's daily life in Harar. There are the Brémonds. They were not brothers, as is sometimes said, but uncle and nephew. The Italian journalist Edouardo Scarfoglio, who was in Harar in 1891, describes the nephew, Antoine Brémond, as 'a wretched young man who has ruined his health, having lived for years in native style in Shoa'. The uncle, L. Brémond, he calls 'old Brémond, or Brémond the terrible, as the romancers style him' [*Corriere di Napoli*, 17 June 1891]. Chief among these 'romancers', perhaps, is Rimbaud, whom Scarfoglio also met at this time.

Rimbaud gives this sketch of 'old Brémond' in a letter to Ilg:

M. Brémond has expressed his intention to build a house here, something appropriate to his enormous commercial success and his elegant style of dress.

It seems he has already built something at the place called Djibouti, but it was constructed out of imperfectly petrified sponge, so that it swelled up in the spring, when the rains came to the coast, and then afterwards collapsed in a heap on the ground.

He is still planning to create a caravan service between here and the said Djibouti, complete with timetable, itineraries and fixed tariffs – but only for his own use . . .

He is also promising himself a journey to Shoa in the near future. Perhaps he wants to start building there as well. He's turning into a beaver! [1 July 1889]

255

(The 'sponge' he refers to is madrepore, a type of porous coral abundant in the area, which was indeed used for the first buildings in Djibouti. This house – or if Rimbaud is to be believed, its replacement – was visited by Scarfoglio in 1891: 'we sat with a bottle of beer in the guest quarters at M. Brémond's factory, resting our weary bones in the delightful draught of a *punkah*'.)

Another trader who is mentioned is Bidault: nothing seems to be known about him. Rimbaud has him 'wandering and photographing' in the mountains of Harar in June 1888. A later bulletin had certain 'details' of Bidault which 'divinely amused' Ilg, but the letter [4 May 1889] has disappeared. Another Italian visitor to Harar, Luigi Robecchi-Brichetti, speaks casually of 'Bidault and his friend Rimbaud'. He also refers to Bidault as a photographer.

And there was, of course, the Catholic mission, with whom he had very cordial relations. Savouré notes that the Bishop, Mgr Taurin-Cahagne, held him in great respect, though he 'abhorred his ideas'. (Savouré's phrase, *'blamit ses théories'*, carries a suggestion of actual disputation: that these theories were advanced by Rimbaud in theological argument with the Bishop.) There is perhaps a note of tension in this 'abhorrence'. Bardey has a telling reminiscence: how when Rimbaud heard that Mgr Taurin-Cahagne was 'preparing a study of the Gallas' (this is probably in 1883) he announced fiercely: 'I too am going to do one, and cut the grass from under this Monseigneur's feet!' The churchmen were a little too close to the intellectual world, about which he had such paradoxical feelings; the traders did not trespass that way.

Mgr Jarosseau was also clear that Rimbaud was 'not a good Catholic', but his reminiscences are of a Rimbaud so compellingly ascetic and admirable that the abhorrent 'theories' are immediately forgotten:

> He lived chastely and soberly. Or to be more precise, if I can employ this comparison: he lived like a Benedictine . . . [in Henri d'Acremont, 'En Abyssinie sur les Traces de Rimbaud', 1932]

> From time to time he came to the Mission. Knowing our poverty, he used to bring the samples [of cloth] he received from France. Our sisters sewed them together to make ornaments for the altar. We used to say he had missed his vocation, and that he ought to have been a Trappist or Carthusian monk . . . [in Henriette Célarie, 'À Propos de Rimbaud: Souvenirs d'Éthiopie', 1933]

He lived the most simple life. How many times have I seen him walking behind his mules and his donkeys, carrying for his provisions nothing but a handful of toasted millet in his pocket [in Jean and Jérôme Tharaud, 'Rimbaud à Harrar', 1941].

This last is one of the most enduring images of Rimbaud in Africa – the quaffer of absinthe has become this haggard ascetic trekking off into the hills with a pocketful of grain to eat. (In Starkie's biography she translates it as a handful of rice, but Jarosseau specifies *mil grillé*. This is, of course, African millet or sorghum, the staple of the region, called *dourah* in Somalia, *tef* in Ethiopia.)

Another reminiscence of Jarosseau's, recorded by Pierre Arnoult: 'Yes, I knew Monsieur Rimbaud well. I remember his large clear eyes. What a gaze!'

*   *   *

Rimbaud was also much appreciated by the little Italian clique in Harar – Ugo Ferrandi and Ottorino Rosa, the employees of Bienenfeld & Co; and various Italian visitors passing through, who put up at Bienenfeld depot on the Faras Maghala.

Though he was sceptical about Italian politicking in the region – justifiably so, given their aggressive colonial policies towards Ethiopia – Rimbaud seems to have had an affinity with Italians. (One recalls the charmed and charming widow he stayed with in Milan in 1875; and, more recently, his convivial discussions with Agosto Franzoj and Ugo Ferrandi in Tadjourah.) The journalist Scarfoglio, who knew him briefly in Harar in 1891, singles him out in this respect: 'Among the Frenchmen who trade with Shoa, there is one, Rimbaud, [who] . . . is in continuous and cordial contact with all the Italians working in the Red Sea area.' Scarfoglio's assessment of Rimbaud is rather surprising: 'an absolutely peaceful [*paisibile*] man'. This is not a word one associates with Rimbaud at any stage of his life. It is possible Scarfoglio means it in the particular sense of 'uninvolved', since he adds that Rimbaud is 'a complete stranger to politics and is entirely occupied with his business interests'. (He is rebutting the current Italian suspicion that the French traders in the region were all meddlesome political agents: I will return to this in a later chapter.)

Another Italian who met Rimbaud at this time was the explorer

Luigi Robecchi-Bricchetti, who was often a guest at the Bienenfeld house. He first put up there in July 1888, and there met the man he later recalled as 'Rimbaud *il poliglotto*', the polyglot or multilinguist. In his printed memoir, *Nell' Harrar* (1896), he says of Rimbaud:

> [He] was a man of letters in France until he abandoned the Muses, cast aside criticism, and threw away his pen to come to Africa, plucking out his ideals, and drowning his winged verses, odes, epics and literary articles in the prosaic but lucrative bath of an import-export business. He had a wit, verve and skill in conversation that was truly French [*Nell' Harrar*, p. 152].

It seems Rimbaud also knew an Italian rejoicing under the name of Naufragio ('shipwreck'), to whom he refers in a letter to Ferrandi [30 April 1889] – 'I have communicated your note to Naufragio, who sends his greetings' – though possibly this is a nickname for someone: for Ottorino Rosa, perhaps.

*   *   *

One gets a profile of Rimbaud in Harar in these last years: something of a character, an 'Original' as Savouré puts it, with a capital O. He is a mystery to them – aloof and saturnine, 'very serious and sad', but it appears that this is only his 'terrible mask' (Ilg) or his 'satirical mask' (Bardey) or his 'spiky shell' (Rosa), because when he wants to he can keep the company in fits of laughter with his 'verve and wit' and his satirical accounts of Harar life. He is 'bizarre' (Bardey), 'strange' (Savouré), 'excessively baroque' (Rimbaud himself).

They too had their stories and vignettes about him, as he did about them. The suspected hoaxer of the newspapers, the writer of *fumisteries*, is one. Another (culled second-hand from a young assistant of Savouré's, G. L. Guigniony) has him on a hunting-party, somewhere outside Harar. In the evening he is missing; his companions are worried; it turns out 'he had gone back all alone, without telling anyone' [Pierre Ripert, 'En Marge du Symbolisme', 1952]. Another, from Ottoman Righas, has him assaulting a native girl and threatening to remove her fibula (a kind of clasp fastened to the vaginal labia to ensure virginity) with a pocket-knife – perhaps before inducting her into that multilingual harim, those 'flesh-

covered dictionaries', which the bar-gossip of Djibouti later attrib-
uted to him.

More retrievable historically is the story that surfaces in early
1889 and which earns him the sobriquet, 'The Terror of the Dogs'.
The first mention of this incident is a letter to Rimbaud from
Brémond *vieux* [10 February 1889]. Brémond is in Aden, so the story
has had time to percolate down to the coast. Discussing some
venture between them, he concludes:

> We'll talk about it when I see you, and decide whether we can do
> something together, just as long as you don't go poisoning all the
> dogs in Harar, and then move on to the hyenas, the sheep and
> even the Greeks. The latter would have deserved your vendetta,
> however . . .

(The last sentence probably refers to the Moussaya family, Greek
traders and political meddlers detested by Rimbaud and others;
Rimbaud's relations with the Greeks of the region were generally
cordial.) Savouré gets wind of it up in Shoa, and writes to Rimbaud
from Farré (the trail-head near Ankober): 'Do please tell me what is
behind this news we're getting of your imprisonment. It seems that
everyone is now talking about "Rimbaud or the Terror of the Dogs"'
[11 April 1889].

Many years later the episode was explained by Jarosseau: 'I
remember that as the dogs were fouling the skins he had drying near
his warehouse, Monsieur Rimbaud poisoned two thousand of them.'
However, the poison – 'capsules of strychnine' – also poisoned some
sheep, whose owners had Rimbaud summoned to the Abyssinian
tribunal on the upper square. The chief plaintiff was perhaps an
Abyssinian worthy, the *dedjazmatch* Bantu, whom Rimbaud later
refers to as 'the protector of dogs' [letter to Ilg, January 1891].

From these scattered sources one also gets something richer than
this vein of semi-legendary anecdote: more a kind of mosaic – if a
very partial one: large areas missing, as in an excavation – of
Rimbaud's daily life in Harar.

He is at his simple, bare, single-storey house – 'a little house in
the square' [Jarosseau]; a house with a 'wide roof' [Rosa]; a 'nice'
house but almost totally without furniture [Savouré] – which may or
may not be the house on the south-western corner of the palace
grounds identified by the late Père Émile. It has a 'makeshift table'
where he writes his letters and his ledgers but not, as far as we know,

anything more literary. When he uses the word 'writings' [*écritures*] in a letter of 1891, he clearly means ledgers, accounts, etc. – 'paperwork' – and he speaks of them in the same breath as his 'cash box' [*caisse*]. This place full of goods and crates and bales but without much furniture is more of a warehouse than a home, and is fragrant with coffee, musk, incense – 'transporter of incense' is the *métier* inscribed on his seal – and the rancid tang of half-cured goat-skins.

Outside is the courtyard in which more goods are piled, donkeys and mules tethered, and the pissed-on hides stretched out to dry. Business is done here: both buying and selling. In his sickness he would have his bed rigged up close to a window of the house, and thus 'keep an eye on my weighing-scales on the far side of the courtyard'. These are the heavyweight scales of the kind seen in Rimbaud's photograph of the Harari trader: each of the balances the size of, and looking much like, a child's swing.

In the street outside you might see an ostrich, as in the Rosa photograph; or the drunken skin-dyer Stéphane asleep in the gutter; and then you are out into the milling brilliant diversity of another morning in Africa with that hubbub of sounds and activities which obscures, for a while, the silence and the waiting.

The days are busy, tense, haggled. He must attend the *zapti*, deal with the 'rabid *gorezzas* [monkeys]' who control Makonnen's exchequer:

I had to use menaces to winkle out these last hundred *fraslehs* . . .

To get hold of any thalers here you have to strangle the cashiers and break open the strongboxes, which I hesitate to do . . .

'Presents and prayers' . . . 'cunning and intimidation' . . . 'grindings and grimacings' . . . *'marasmes'* . . . *'accrocs'*. [Letters to Ilg, October–December 1889].

Or perhaps he journeys out, through the sagging rhomboid gates of the city, walking behind his little column of mules and donkeys, or riding out on horseback with his friend Ottorino Rosa, who recalls:

We set aside one or two days a week for excursions into the surrounding areas, trying to go out as far as possible in order to satisfy our curiosity, and to learn about anything of interest in the region, whether from the point of view of the topography, or the flora and fauna, or the memories of former times. It was during these excursions that poor Rimbaud began to feel some pain in his right knee.

Rimbaud's Greek friend Dimitri Righas also remembers going out with Rimbaud: 'He was a great walker. Oh, an astonishing walker! His coat open, a little fez on his head in spite of the sun . . .' Still *le piéton de la grand'route*, the 'tramper of the highway', long after the highways have run out.

And then the quiet nights: at home, or over at the Bienenfeld depot on the Faras Maghala with Rosa, or *chez* Righas. 'Almost invariably,' wrote Rosa, 'and often in the company of the Greek Dimitri Righas, we spent the monotonous Harari evenings together, talking about this and that over a few glasses of the wholesome local beer.'

Righas adds that Rimbaud 'was very sober, never drank alcohol, only coffee, in the Turkish style, as is customary here'. Perhaps the 'wholesome' [*sain*] beer of Harar was too mild to count as alcohol (unlike today's local brew, Bedele) or perhaps Righas is being over-emphatic. Rimbaud had *tej* – the very powerful Ethiopian mead – at his lodgings in Entotto, which his creditors happily drank. He was certainly not a drinker any more, but not necessarily a teetotaller either.

Luigi Robecchi-Brichetti, who arrived in July 1888, paints a more convivial picture of the little 'European colony' in Harar. They met most evenings at sunset, to talk and drink and play cards, and 'to argue over the destiny of Europe, and the colonial expansion of the Powers, while a few piastres and some very scarce thalers circulated in the whirlpool of seven-and-a-half or in the more philosophical baccarat' [*Nell' Harrar*, p.144]. Rimbaud was certainly present at these soirées, displaying that 'wit, verve and conversational skill that was truly French', but they are not perhaps the norm that Robecchi-Brichetti suggests.

There were other visitors. In September 1888, Jules Borelli was 'passing through Harar' after a long sojourn in Djimma. He saw Rimbaud then, 'and never again'. In his journals – unaware of the finality of the meeting – the entries are brusque:

Tuesday 25 September 1888 – I arrive at Harar . . . M. Rimbaud offers me cordial hospitality.

> Friday 5 October 1888 – Arrive at Gueldessah. Thanks to M.
> Rimbaud's efforts, I find the camels ready to leave.

He is Rimbaud's guest for about ten days, receives hospitality and local expertise from his former travelling companion.

A little later Savouré arrives, is caught by the seize-up of Ramadan, and spends a month with Rimbaud, puzzling about the lack of beds. 'I never found out where he slept,' Savouré says. (Because he was an insomniac, and didn't? Because he slept on the floor? Or because he soon tired of Savouré's company, and spent his nights elsewhere?)

And then in December, the Grrrreat Ilg is there, and Robecchi-Brichetti chronicles the gaieties once more: 'We spent Christmas in very good and cheerful company. We celebrated it at my quarters.' The company included Ilg, Rimbaud, Bidault, Rosa, Ferrandi and Father Joachim of the Mission. Ilg does not, probably, stay with Rimbaud, for in the latter's papers is found an invoice to Ilg 'for one month's rent of the Maison Nalin'.

These convivialities punctuate the longer slower rhythms of life at the end of the line. Often Rimbaud is alone – or alone with those two half-seen figures on the periphery of the lamplight, the two people who form his fiercely honed-down version of 'home', or indeed of 'family': his servant Djami, now in his late teens; and his woman, whose name is unknown but who was remembered forty years later by both Rosa and Mgr Jarosseau, a 'native woman' who 'lived with' him and was 'kept' by him and 'returned to her own people' after he was gone.

And sometimes on these quiet domestic evenings – if a later drawing by Isabelle is to be believed – he sits cross-legged on a cushion, with his bernous tossed over his shoulder like a scarf, and strums on an Abyssinian harp, accompanied by the howls of the dogs and hyenas outside.

25

BAZAAR FEVER

'MY INTEREST NOW is in precise things', Rimbaud had written to Ernest Delahaye in 1875. He meant precise things as opposed to poetry, precise things like the books of science needed for a *baccalauréat*, yet the sentiment remains true enough, fifteen and more years later. It is among things as much as people, amid dusty piles of goods and merchandises – *les m'ises*, in the trader's contraction – that we find Rimbaud the African.

There are no poems among that stack of 'writings' near the cash-box, and even the witty and waspish letters are only a small part. (He did not often make copies before he sent them.) The bulk of it is mere papers: inventories, accounts, receipts, bills, bonds, conversions, procurances, memoranda, reports, and so on. Some of these documents have survived the scattering winds and have come to rest in the pages of the *Œuvres Complètes*, in which context they take on a kind of poetic life which is indeed to do with their precision and their thinginess.

An early example is the '*Étude de Marchandises* No. 7'. (This is the only one of the series to have survived. It is undated, but is thought to belong to late-1883, around the time of the Ogaden explorations.) There is a demand at Harar for *sirwal* (cloaks) and *sperraba* (caparisons), he reports, so please supply the following:

> Cotton cloth, closely woven, warm, thick, with the strength of light sailcloth, striped lengthwise with red or blue bands 5 cm wide and 20 cm apart. Have 500 *sirwal* made up, cut to the pattern enclosed . . .
>
> 50 tassels of braided cotton, red or green . . .
>
> 20 metres of long carpet-fringes, of the same colour and the same cotton, to hang in front of horses' chests . . .

I like this terse memo to head office for what opens up behind it: the expert appraising, the thumbing and measuring, this whole sense of Rimbaud's immersion in the jostling, aromatic, tactile circumstances of the African market-place.

The market-place is for Rimbaud, as drink was famously for Ben Jonson, 'the element he lives in'. I include in this both the actual Harar markets – at the Faras Maghala, at the Shoa gate, at scores of other crossroads and clearings – and, in the commercial sense, the local 'market' or demand which he supplied as an importer. This reaches an apotheosis in the last years at Harar. He succumbs, in Alfred Ilg's droll phrase, to *la maladie bazardique* – 'bazaar fever'.

In a letter to Ilg [1 July 1889], Rimbaud scoffs affably at 'old Brémond' and the contents of his newly opened store in Harar:

> Brémond has opened up a 13-sou bazaar [i.e. dime store] where you can buy hairbrushes, ornamental oyster shells, stock cubes for Julienne soup, slippers, macaroni, nickel chains, wallets, boleros, eau de cologne, peppermint, and a host of other terribly practical products ideal for native consumption. That's the sum of his knowledge of Abyssinian products after twelve years in the place!

He cannot leave it at that – the urge to specificity is almost obsessive – and beside the words '13-sou' he inserts a marginal note:

> Not exactly: I saw a hairbrush priced there at $7\frac{1}{2}$ rupees; a carved oystershell at 20 rupees; one enamelled plate, 3 rupees; macaroni 2.50 F per kilo; espadrilles 5 rupees, etc etc . . .

This mordant catalogue has the ring of inside knowledge, because there is no doubt that, as Ilg said, Rimbaud himself had a 'bad dose' of this bazaar fever.

*　　*　　*

Products in general dealt with by Rimbaud, import-export merchant at Harar.

He buys the precious commodities of Africa: gold (in ingots or rings), ivory, musk, gum, frankincense, coffee, and skins of all sorts from panthers' to goats'. These are raw materials, almost exclusively, though there is the odd carpet or tribal curio mentioned here and there. ('Musk' is a generic term for the aromatic glandular secretions of various animals, particularly musk-deer: the word probably derives from Sanskrit *muska*, scrotum. Here the musk is civet, from the animal of that name [Arab *zabad*] which is loosely called a 'civet-cat' but which is actually more like a large weasel. The trade was ancient, and had its own unit of measurement, the *okiete*. The dealer in musk had to be on the look-out for adulteration, typically with a paste of butter and bone-marrow. This gave a whitish tinge: pure musk is a deep tawny red. What Rimbaud calls 'gum' [*gomme*] is not, of course, rubber, but various balsams and resins tapped from trees, notably myrrh and frankincense. These are still traded in Ethiopia and the Yemen.)

These he sends off down the familiar caravan-route, via Gueldessah and Biokobobo, to debouch either at Zeilah or at Djibouti. The caravans travel under the care of trusted *abbans* like Farah Kali; Rimbaud no longer accompanies them himself. They bring back up, a few weeks or months later, the goods he will sell in Harar or distribute onwards to Ilg or Savouré in Shoa.

These are imported products, some specifically manufactured for the Ethiopian market: in particular various kinds of cloth and clothing; kitchenware; foodstuffs; technical goods like balances; and also guns and ammunition. Some of this comes from Europe and some from India. Almost all is transited through Aden, though with Djibouti an alternative entry-point now.

Borelli sums up the basic operation when he recommends Rimbaud as a trading-contact for Abba Djiffa, the King of Djimma, a region rich in ivory and civet. 'I have spoken to the King,' Borelli reports:

> I have told him that you have everything he might wish – sugar, rice, sandals, shoes, cloth, etc etc; and that you would exchange these goods for his musk or ivory, or that you would pay him in thalers if he preferred. [26 July 1888]

He was very much the 'general trader' but of the products he sells the one he knows most intimately is cloth. (This is perhaps partly due to his employment by the Bardeys, trained in the Lyonnais silk trade.) His inventories and order-books are full of the stuff – silk and wool, cretonne and crepe, cotton and canvas. There is 'American Sheeting' and 'Blue Guinea' and 'Turkey Red' (as in 'the Turkey Red is of type no.7140, 5 lbs at 1s 8½d in London'). There is a great deal of blue spun cloth from India suitable for making the Abyssinian cloak called a *djano*; and silk tassels for *matads*, worn by

Christian Abyssinians, and particularly popular among Menelik's soldiers to ensure a Christian burial if they were killed in battle.

Much of this was on his own account. His exact arrangement with César Tian in Aden is unclear. 'He ran [*dirigeait*] our branch office in Harar', Maurice Riès wrote some while later, 'where he was exclusively concerned with buying coffee, and sending it down to the coast by camel, for sale in Aden or France.' This suggests that all the rest fell outside the Tian aegis, though no doubt the company acted as brokers and suppliers for some of the imported goods.

In one case at least, Rimbaud had goods produced to his own specifications. In mid-1889 he tells Ilg he has 6,000 '*brillés*' in his warehouse (the *brillé* or *birilli* is a pitcher, typically used for the Ethiopian mead, *tej*). They

> ... have been made according to my design and specifications, and are not to be found on the market ... They are solid, handsome pieces, with a quick turnover, and you need have absolutely no fear of competition from those of Moussaya. [1 July 1889]

He has them in white, blue, yellow, green and violet. ('I won't send you any violet ones'.) They are brought up from Zeilah: one camel can carry three crates, each crate containing 100 jugs. 'Breakages in the crates I have opened amount to no more than 2 per cent.' He sells them in Harar at four for a thaler wholesale and three a thaler retail. He sold 500 to the Ras's court at Harar, but Makonnen returned them, saying 'he could find them for nothing' in Italy.

* * *

A brief dip into the Rimbaldien ledgers over a few months in 1889 gives a kind of cross-section view of these clanking caravans he sent out from Harar, across the Itou plateau to Entotto, under the eye of Farah Kali, Akadar, Serquis or Cirkis, Jean, Elias and other *chefs de caravanes* (and once in the charge of 'M. Mikael the Russian mechanic', of whom one would like to know more). The men under these *chefs* are unnamed, but surface from time to time in the accounts: '1 bot cognac for the men: 1 Th', 'For a man left sick: 2 Th', etc.

On 20 July he despatches ten 'bundles' [*ballots*] to Ilg. These are carried on four donkeys, under the supervision of 'Jean', annexed to a larger caravan of Savouré's. He itemizes the bundles as follows:

1. 1 bundle of 242 metres of damask cretonne ... which the Abyssinians can make into *marechas* [i.e. *maréchates*, caparisons] for mules, and also shirts. It is tough as well as finely coloured.

2. 1 bundle of coloured wools. The blue merino [a soft wool like cashmere] is good stuff, as is the red flannel, and at the price I am offering it you have nothing to fear, except for worms if it is kept too long, but at present it is in good condition.

3. 1 small crate containing various items in demand among the Abyssinians: scissors, fancy buttons, religious artefacts, etc. If you approve the samples of gilded braid, for the saddlers or for the clergy, please advise. I have also included some stationery, but only a thaler's worth, and no more, as I'm not getting very much stationery.

4. 1 small bundle containing 15 packets of Bloknote [a brand of writing block], which you can use or sell, the narrow line format being suitable for *debdabies amara* [i.e. the Amharic alphabet].

5–10. 6 packages of pearls. The biggest of these pearls currently sell here at 2 for a piastre. But this sort of business is not at all to my taste. Your men will be able to sell them easily at markets. It's retail work, but it shouldn't be difficult.

Ilg writes on 10 September that this caravan is still at Ankober, and that he is going there to find out about it. Six days later he is there, and writes:

I have just paid a visit to the famous bazaar you have sent me. One would think you wanted me to lose my last four sous, but that's the way things are these days.

To go about preaching with these rosaries, crosses and crucifixes, etc, at the very moment when His Majesty is issuing a formal order to Revd Father Joaquin to go back to Harar, would be more dangerous than a journey into the desert. Just for now I wouldn't even dare to give them away as presents – the Abyssinians might very easily take me for a Capuchin in disguise.

As for your famous Decran & Co pearls you would have done

better to go partridge-shooting [*tirer aux francolins*] with them, which would have been more profitable than flogging them several hundred leagues from Harar.

It looks like M. Brémond's bazaar fever is spreading, and that you've got a bad dose of it. To sell writing-blocks at $2\frac{1}{2}$ for a thaler to people who can't write, and who know nothing of the mysterious uses of such implements, is really rather a tall order. It's a great pity you haven't got a few hundred mother-of-pearl carvings and some shoe horns to send me!

I will see what I can do with them . . . but meanwhile, my dear M. Rimbaud, be wise enough to send me saleable stuff, otherwise I will return you your bric-à-brac, at your own risks and charges, and with the thunder of God. [6 September 1889]

Rimbaud replies cheerfully:

As for the goods I sent to you with Jean, your observations are *all right* [in English: a catchphrase he uses elsewhere when writing to Ilg]. But despite it all, I still think you'll have turned a profit when all this 'bric-à-brac' is sold. The large-size pearls are good for Lejkka, etc., etc. I see I'm going to have to give you a few more lessons in the commercial geography of Ethiopia.

Meanwhile more was on its way, for on 24 August Rimbaud had despatched another caravan to Shoa. According to the invoice [duplicate, 7 Oct 1889] this contained a total of eighty-one packages, marked 'ILG', comprising:

30 bales of various *matads* containing altogether 701 *matads*, value Th 621,875

39 packages containing in all 67 cooking-pots and lids, value Th 940,500

2 bales containing 40 packets of 'extrafine red Djano', value Th 140

10 cases of *brillés* each containing 100 *brillés*, value Th 285

The total value of the caravan was Th 1,987,375, or about a quarter of a million francs.

On 8 October Ilg sends news of this: 'The caravan of *matads*, etc is still at the Awash, but should reach us in a few days.' A couple of weeks later it has reached Farré, having lost a camel carrying forty *matads* while crossing the Awash. 'As I understand, Houssein hopes to recover them when the river gets lower.' On 13 November he reports that Menelik has bought 500 *birillis*, but that otherwise the goods are not selling well.

Ilg also 'reproaches' Rimbaud about the state of his caravans when they arrived from Harar:

> You never give them enough provisions. There is not a single caravan that hasn't arrived here half-starved, and with all the men in a deplorable condition, and everyone complains very bitterly about you. It isn't worth the trouble, just to save a few thalers on the provisions, to have all the men sick and worn-out . . .

This harsh treatment also extends to the animals, particularly the donkeys he sent in July. Ilg grumbles:

> I had to pay transport costs of 6 th in the thousand, because the donkeys you supplied were already exhausted before the descent of Arajamo . . . Donkeys cannot march for a long time unless they are very lightly loaded. Those you sent from Harar are all in a very bad state, and I have had to put them all out on my land to recover from their injuries. There isn't a single one I can use. You'll tell me it's the fault of the servants, etc, but it's exactly because one knows how the Abyssinians travel that one has to take precautions. [8 October 1889]

Rimbaud retorts angrily to this. The accusation is 'absurd': *une bonne farce*. 'I am, on the contrary, known everywhere for my generosity in these cases.' He does indeed blame it on the servants: 'This is certainly the measure of the natives' gratitude' [11 December 1889].

As Ilg feared, Rimbaud's bric-à-brac proves problematic, and several months later he reports:

> Unfortunately the goods are hardly selling at all now. The cooking pots and *matads* we can't even sell for 50 th, despite having cut the price considerably. I still have nearly 200 pkts of red yarn which I can't get rid of at 3 th per packet, because the place is full of them. Besides this, I still have all the pearls, four pieces of silk, and all the cretonne, and even a piece of black wool. No one wanted to buy anything except the Arab bernous which Decran is bringing . . .

> Other than the ironware [i.e. cooking-pots] the main problem is
> the last delivery of *djano*. This was packaged up in inferior paper.
> No one wants it at any price. Everyone is after the best quality
> with the 'Moon' brand-mark. [17 July 1890]

Thus the ebb and flow, the delays and losses, of just a couple of
Rimbaud's caravans from Harar.

*   *   *

For all this, Ilg considered Rimbaud a skilled and valuable trading-
partner. He does not actually say so – in fact Ilg, alone of Rimbaud's
associates, has left no memoir or comment about him, other than the
letters themselves – but the relationship implies it. In 1890 he writes
to Rimbaud:

> If you treat him [i.e. Ras Makonnen] carefully he won't cause you
> any more heartache. I have strongly recommended you as the only
> trader worth his time – a bit of a difficult character to deal with,
> but very honest. Try to be nice to him. [17 July 1890]

The phrase Ilg uses is *'un peu raide'* – stiff, rigid, inflexible; hence, in
this context, a hard bargainer. Difficult, honest, not always nice: a
formidable profile in the business world.

Borelli's recommendation of Rimbaud to the King of Djimma is,
similarly, an index of his esteem for Rimbaud's trading skills. Borelli
later told Berrichon:

> He certainly didn't get into this business for the love of it, but his
> extraordinary attainments [*nature d'élite*] meant that, without
> even wanting to, he immediately understood the right way to deal
> with the natives. At Shoa, purely in his capacity as a trader,
> Rimbaud won the respect of the chief Abyssinians by his upright
> dealing and strength of character.

This approval is echoed by his various associates, hard-bitten men
who didn't suffer inefficiency gladly: he was 'an honest, capable and
courageous man' [Bardey], 'a passionate trader' [Maurice Riès], 'a
remarkable trader' [Riès again], 'a good merchant' [Djibouti traders
to Pierre Mille], 'entirely devoted to commerce' [Ottorino Rosa], 'an
experienced merchant as well as a very distinguished traveller and
writer' [Robecchi-Brichetti], 'a very serious man, experienced in

business affairs, and highly trusted and esteemed by the Abyssinian authorities' [Savouré], and so on.

These are, as it were, Rimbaud's 'references' after eleven years in Arabia and Africa. One remembers the pride – half-humorous, perhaps, but only half – with which he showed his first testimonial, from the Cyprus engineers E. Jean & Thial, to Delahaye. 'We have been very satisfied with his services', etc. In his recollection of this Delahaye adds, rather smugly, that this certificate was really 'quite worthless'. It was not so to Rimbaud, who found that in this realm of precise actions and precise things, if not in the realm of love and affection, he could give and receive 'satisfaction'; and who found that the 'other' he had conjured in the wild days of his *voyance*, the 'somebody else' he had to search to the end of the world to find, was nothing more than this rather upright, serious man, this *homme d'affaires* who would be remembered as 'a bit difficult but very honest'. He attains, at the end of his long journey, a kind of luminous ordinariness.

26

'AS FOR THE SLAVES . . .'

RIMBAUD DEALT IN gold and musk, in cloths and cooking-pots, but did he also deal in slaves?

It is loosely said that he did and fiercely argued that he didn't. A lot of emotion and indignation has been generated on the subject. The indignation has a particularly Gallic flavour since the chief culprit – in the eyes of Rimbaud's apologists – is his English biographer, Enid Starkie. She was not the first to raise the question of Rimbaud's involvement in the slave-trade, but she was the first to advance documents in support of the idea.

Either way, it is part of the legend of Rimbaud in Africa, and I think it is best at this stage to put aside one's feelings – the ardent proponent of *la liberté libre* trafficking in slaves? – and take a soberly analytic view. There seem to be two basic historical questions to ask: context and text. First, is it likely that Rimbaud would have dealt in slaves? And, if so, what is the evidence that he did?

*   *   *

The context is East Africa in the 1880s, and the first thing to say is that our whole idea of the 'slave-trade' derives from the West African experience: the terrible pillage of men and women by European slavers, the transportation to Caribbean and American plantations, the shacklings and whippings – in short, an African holocaust. The slave-trade of East Africa was different. (There is a fundamental moral horror about any form of slavery, but this does not preclude such differences.) V. S. Naipaul, not a writer disposed to condoning slavery, makes the distinction in his novel *A Bend in the River*, set in a decaying East African port:

The slavery of the east coast was not like the slavery of the west coast. No one was shipped off to plantations. Most of the people who left our coast went to Arabian homes as domestic servants. Some became members of the family they had joined; a few became powerful in their own right. . ... This was one reason why the trade went on long after it had been outlawed by European powers; and why a secret slavery continued on this coast until the other day. The slaves, or the people who might be considered slaves, wanted to remain as they were.

This states the basic difference. The slave-trade of East Africa was run by and for Arabs, who were originally colonists but who had by now been settlers and petty sultans of the region for centuries. It was something written into the social and cultural fabric; it was accepted by, and even advantageous to, the 'slave' though hardly in the way that it was to the *djellal* or slave-trader.

To bring it nearer to Rimbaud, here are some observations on the subject by his friend Jules Borelli:

The slave's condition is not necessarily as horrible as it is generally represented in Europe. Doubtless they suffer if they have bad masters; but cruelty is not the rule. The lot of these poor creatures is not to be envied, and justifiably inspires our compassion; but more often, when placed in a family, they are well treated . . .

What is said on this question of slavery is often far from the point. Slavery takes many different forms according to the country. Thus in the country of Mima where I have lived, slaves had their own properties, handed from father to son, and were masters of their land. As for corporal punishment, I have never seen it used. Anyway, one never really knew who was a slave and who was not. But it would take a whole book to explain these nuances. . . .

Some of this jars, but see also Alfred Bardey's reaction when encountering a slave-caravan for the first time, in 1880: a hundred Abyssinian women and children, en route from Farré and Harar to the coast. 'We' – Bardey and Pinchard – 'quickly realize we are in a slave-camp', but

. . . like my companion, I am troubled and surprised because no longer sure if I have that feeling of revulsion which is so habitual on the subject of slavery. To report faithfully what we saw, I have

to say that this caravan had nothing apparently tragic about it.
The majority of the girls displayed a gaiety and aplomb, and, it
seemed to us, even a spirit of mockery towards us. [BA, p. 125]

One could no doubt discern covert strains of racism in Bardey,
though for his time he was extremely liberal and enlightened.
Anyway, the point is to register his reaction rather than judge it. He
is predisposed to 'revulsion' about slavery but, like Borelli, finds the
actuality of it quite different: not 'apparently tragic' at all.

Rimbaud's own attitude is more dourly pragmatic. When it suits
him to do so – broadly, when he is trying to run guns through the
territory of the chief slavers of the region, the Abou Bekr clan – he
regards the slave-trade as a given fact of East African life. Thus
from Tadjourah, *tout court*: 'the commerce of the area is slave-
traffic'. Any effort by the Europeans to stamp it out is seen as
woolly-headed interference. The British had been especially busy
persuading the Abyssinians to outlaw the slave-trade, and look at
the result:

> Now one cannot get through [to Abyssinia] without the greatest
> difficulty. All the native people along the coast have become
> enemies of the Europeans since the English Admiral Hewett made
> Emperor John of Tigre sign a treaty abolishing the slave-trade,
> which is the only native commerce which makes any profit.
> However, under the French protectorate, there will be no effort to
> interfere with the trade, and that will work better. [3 December
> 1885]

This is merely expedient, but aligns Rimbaud with that *laissez-faire*
acceptance of slavery which is also expressed, with variations in
tone, by Bardey and Borelli.

Slavery is the *realpolitik* of the region. Like Joannes of Tigre,
Menelik had passed an anti-slavery law in 1884, but the trade
continued unabated, not least because Menelik too needed the good
grace of the Abou Bekrs. This was Ilg's view, as reported by the
British Assistant-Resident at Zeilah in May 1889:

> ... regarding the sale of slaves in Shoa, he [Ilg] told me that
> Menelik could not afford to interfere with the Abou Bekr family, as
> hitherto he had been dependent on that family for communication
> with the coast.

Thus for King Menelik, as for French traders, the slaver ruled the trade-route.

Their acceptance of slavery is perhaps a bit more than a shrug of non-involvement, because many of these European settlers and travellers actually kept slaves. Pierre Labatut, as we know from Rimbaud, had a household of about twenty *domestiques*, still in tow after his death and dependent on his widow. Jules Borelli says: 'I have lost count of how many slaves I have; fortunately Abba Djiffar [King of Djimma] deals with them for me.' And later he chides himself, 'I'm behaving like a slaver [*négrier*] – I have instructed them all to return back home and they are refusing to do so.' It is, oddly, when he tries to dismiss them that he feels like a slaver. Naipaul discerns the same irony:

> Officially these people were only servants. But they wanted it known – to other Africans, and to poor Arabs and Indians – that they were really slaves. It wasn't that they were proud of slavery as a condition; what they were fierce about was their special connection with a family of repute.

Or, in our context, with a European of repute.

So too with Rimbaud. The French commentators tend to call his Abyssinian woman a '*servante-concubine*' (not without a certain relish), but surely 'slave' will do. She was probably purchased by him from a third party, rather than hired; and she was 'kept' by him rather than paid a wage. Ottorino Rosa 'kept' and then 'got rid of' her sister; he also says Rimbaud 'kept a Galla woman' in Harar. (It is curious that one can also call these women his 'mistresses', but this is a sexual paradox outside my present scope.)

Djami is described as a *domestique* and is said by Isabelle to be Harari. If so he would not be a 'slave' when working for Rimbaud in Harar: slaves were from elsewhere, people 'brought' as well as bought (precisely the verb Rimbaud uses about the Abyssinian woman, who was 'brought from Shoa'). But we have no real knowledge of Djami's employment, of the nature of the contract between them. In what sense does Sotiro refer to him, in a letter to Rimbaud, as 'your Djami'? A servant is free to leave, is not owned, but is otherwise indistinguishable from a 'slave'. One notes that Bardey says of those Abyssinian slave-women he encountered: 'they have been sold by their owners or by their relatives, or they have sold themselves.' In the latter case their slavery comes close to a condition of employment: they are paid something, at least. This is not to mitigate the exploiting of these women: I am concerned with definitions here.

The attitude of Rimbaud's circle to slavery was a condoning one. They saw the trade as relatively benign and deeply entrenched; they considered it normal to 'keep' slaves as part of their little African *ménages*; they were sceptical about distant intentions to abolish the trade; they had enough problems with local magnates like Abou Bekr already. Down here slaving was the reality: it was, as Rimbaud says, 'the only native commerce that makes a profit'.

But this question of Rimbaud and the slave-trade is not really about his attitudes. It is about his alleged actions. And here the context for Rimbaud-as-slaver begins to fall apart, for there is no conclusive evidence of *any* Europeans being involved in the slave-trade at this time. If Rimbaud did run slaves in the late 1880s, it seems he did so uniquely. In fact the trade is always described as an exclusively Arab, or anyway Muslim, affair. It was said that 12,000 Arab families ran this human pipeline from central Ethiopia to Arabia and Turkey, of which the sultan Mohamad Anfani was perhaps the biggest. 'All the slave-traders in the vast kingdom of Shoa are Muslims,' notes the Marquis Antinori (one of the Italians hovering around Menelik at this time, not to be confused with Count Antonelli). He contrasts this with the Christian tradition of Abyssinia:

> Throughout Abyssinia the law allows the buying of slaves but not the selling of them, and this law is respected on pain of very severe penalties: at least the amputation of the right hand. Besides, an Amhara slaver or slave-driver would be the object of great opprobrium ... [letter to Professor della Vedova, *c.* 1890, in Matucci, *Dernier visage*]

This is confirmed by others. According to the French traveller and photographer Sylvain Vigneras, in 1897, 'slavery does not exist in Abyssinia'. He witnessed the hanging of four men convicted of the trade.

In this way slaving seems a remarkably poor business opportunity for a European in Rimbaud's position. The trade is a fiercely guarded Arab monopoly. The lead player is Abou Bekr whom he dislikes and distrusts ('the most incorrigible bandit in all Africa'). The caravan-route is controlled by the fanatical, testicle-hunting

Danakil. The chief source of slaves is the domain of King Menelik, who has to tolerate the Muslim slave-trade but otherwise treats slavers to the axe and the halter.

All this makes it intrinsically unlikely that Rimbaud would even consider becoming a slave-trader, and adds weight to his own disavowals. Writing from Tadjourah to the French consul, after the embargo on his arms-caravan in early 1886, he says:

> It simply cannot be argued that there is any correlation between the importation of arms and the exploitation of slaves. The latter traffic exists between Abyssinia and the coast, and has existed without variation since ancient times. But our affairs are entirely unconnected with the obscure traffickings of the Bedouin. No one would dare to suggest that a European has ever sold or bought, transported or helped to transport a single slave, either on the coast or in the interior. [15 April 1886]

This is plainly stated, as is Rimbaud's way. It is not true just because he says it, but the situation I have outlined makes it plausible, and other observers say much the same.

Against this I would add a brief comment of Rimbaud's, not noticed before. In his letter to Vice-Consul Gaspary [9 November 1887] he relates the behaviour of his *chef de caravane*, Mohammad Dankali, after their arrival in Entotto. He 'squeezed 400 thalers' out of Menelik's cashiers, to pay off the men, and instead 'used it to buy some slaves'. These slaves 'he sent with the caravan of Messrs Savouré, Dimitri [i.e. Righas] and Brémond, but they all died on the journey, and he himself ran off to hide in Djimma'. In this case, at least, a European caravan seems to have carried some slaves out of Abyssinia.

*　　*　　*

From this brief overview, the circumstantial evidence is pretty flimsy. Rimbaud is not against the traffic; he thinks it is 'better' not to interfere with it; but there is little to corroborate the idea that he was himself involved in this unpleasant business. His good relations with Menelik and his bad relations with Abou Bekr both argue against it, though the hint of Savouré and Righas's human cargo in mid-1887 is troubling.

Nonetheless, Africa and slavery run together in the European mind, and almost as soon as he died Rimbaud was tarred with this brush of the *négrier*. In 1891 he was described as having been, among other things, '*négrier en Ouganda*'; and in 1897, Edmond Lepelletier described him as a *marchand de nègres* or slave-merchant. These are merely rumours, or rather assumptions. The first is so geographically wide of the mark – 'Ouganda' is Uganda – that it cannot be based on any actual testimony. The second comes from a man who had nursed a grudge against Rimbaud for twenty-five years, and never missed a chance to air it.

These are disembodied accusations, made at a time when little was known of his African life. On the matter of slave-trading, as Borer says, 'Rimbaud is a suspect a priori'. Izambard says much the same, in 1898, when he chides the Decadents for appropriating a feverishly imagined Rimbaud as their role-model: they have made of him 'a thief, a murderer, a trader in human flesh'.

And so it remained until the late 1930s, when Enid Starkie set out more specific charges in her short book, *Rimbaud in Abyssinia* (1937). These have become the basis for the idea that Rimbaud was a slaver. They have also earned her the opprobium of Rimbaldiens, who dub her 'La Miss' in parallel to the baleful presence of 'La Mother'.

The first was her discovery, among the archives of the British Foreign Office, of a report dated 16 June 1888. This states:

> I learn that a large caravan led by Ibrahim Abuker [i.e. Ibrahim Abou Bekr], bringing ivory and slaves in considerable numbers from Shoa via Harar, arrived on the 10th inst at Ambos [near Djibouti]. The French trader Remban, one of the cleverest and most active agents of the French government in those regions, accompanied the caravan. The slaves, intended for the principal places on the neighbouring coast of Arabia, were sent partly to Tapura [i.e. Tadjourah] and partly to Ambadu, to await a favourable opportunity to be conveyed in native boats to the Arabian ports.

This was, on the face of it, a remarkable discovery. There is no doubt, she argued, that this 'Remban' is meant to be Rimbaud. She goes on to say: 'Rimbaud was in Harar early in May 1888 . . . and could easily, at the end of the month, have accompanied a caravan back to the coast.' This is, therefore, documentary evidence of his involvement in the slave trade.

In fact, as further research has shown, the evidence is erroneous. This document is actually a translation of an earlier report filed by the Italian consul at Aden, Captain Antonio Cecchi. This report was passed on to London by the Italian Foreign Ministry, in accordance with certain agreements, and was there translated into the document found by Dr Starkie in the Public Record Office.

The crux lies in the dating. The date given by Starkie, 16 June 1888, is the date of the translation (or perhaps of the receipt) of Cecchi's report in London. The date on the original Italian report is 22 May. And if the report was written on 22 May, then the arrival of the slave caravan at Ambos, given as '10th inst', is 10 May rather than 10 June. And if the caravan arrived at Ambos on 10 May, it is virtually impossible for Rimbaud to have 'accompanied' it.

His actual movements during April and May 1888 are quite well documented. We have his own letters, and we have a brief journal by Ugo Ferrandi, who travelled with him up to Harar. A brief calendar is as follows:

12 April [Rimbaud to Ilg, from Aden]: I am leaving tomorrow for Zeilah, and will be in Harar around the end of the month.

13 April [Ferrandi's journal]: Today we are leaving [Aden] on a British-built steamer of about 200 tons . . . Among the passengers for Zeilah are M. Rimbaud, the two Righas, me, and a young Greek with a black beard, Christos Mussaya.

14 April [Ferrandi]: We are at Berbera. Rimbaud, Dimitri Righas and I go ashore, and go to the native quarter. In a large hut there we drink some very good tea prepared by a Turkish café owner.

17 April [Ferrandi]: I see Messrs Sotiro and Rimbaud in the evening [i.e. at Zeilah].

24 April [Ferrandi]: A Somali brings a letter from M. Rimbaud at Hensa: all goes well.

3 May [Rimbaud to Bardey]: I have just arrived in Harar. The rains are extraordinarily strong this year, and I made the journey through a succession of cyclones.

15 May [Rimbaud to his family]: I am installed here once more, and for a long time. I am establishing a French trading post here.

From this it is clear that Rimbaud could not have 'accompanied' that slave-caravan from Harar to Ambos. The caravan is reported as arriving at Ambos on 10 May; its presence at Danan is noted by the British authorities in Zeilah on the 13th: these independent reports corroborate one another. Given the slow rate of travel, especially considering the storms and 'cyclones' which Rimbaud mentions, the caravan must have left Harar around the end of April. Rimbaud, on the other hand, was at Hensa on about 23 April (Ferrandi received his letter from there, via a Somali courier, on the 24th) and had 'just arrived' in Harar on 3 May. He may well have *met* the slave-caravan, but he was travelling in the opposite direction.

He could in theory have ridden straight out from Harar on 3 May, caught up with the caravan near Ambos on the 10th, and ridden straight back again to Harar in time to write his letter home on the 15th. This unlikely scenario would explain why Captain Cecchi's informers saw Monsieur 'Remban' in this discreditable company at Ambos. The far more likely explanation is that Cecchi's information was wrong. Rimbaun was not at Ambos at all in May; he was, as all the other documents show, newly settled in at Harar, beginning the last and longest chapter of his African years. This misinformation is fairly typical. The Italians were highly suspicious of French traders. As Scarfoglio says, in a parallel case,

> They have always wanted to see these people [Brémond and Chefneux], who are nothing other than honest traders entirely devoted to their own rather uncomfortable affairs, as conspirators against Italy; and have used every means possible to prejudice their reputations and their interests. [*Corriere di Napoli*, 17 June 1891]

And again: 'Queen Victoria and Emperor Wilhelm II have revealed to Crispi and Antonelli [Italian advisers in Shoa] many more French agents than ever existed.'

The Italian report, in short, is no more than another inaccurate rumour serving to discredit a French trader.

*   *   *

Starkie backs up this supposed evidence with some rather vague statements about César Tian's involvement in both the arms-trade and the slave-trade. This drew loud protests from Tian's son André, and from his friend Borelli, and in a subsequent edition she retracted this. Her statement that Tian was involved in the arms-trade was, she admits, 'not based on any document'. It was 'a simple personal supposition'. She also exonerates him from slave-trading: 'This hypothesis is not based on any document, either. The supposition concerning the slave trade came from me alone.'

Tian is exculpated, but not Rimbaud. The erroneous Cecchi report continues to be advanced as evidence against him, and to this she now adds what she claims to be further 'proof' of his dealing with slaves.

This was a passage she found in an unpublished letter from Ilg to Rimbaud [23 August 1890]. The letter was owned by the Rimbaud collector Henri Matarasso; the full Ilg–Rimbaud correspondence was not published until 1967. Ilg wrote, in Starkie's translation: 'As for slaves, I cannot undertake to obtain them for you. I've never bought slaves and I don't want to begin. Even for myself I wouldn't do it.' Here, she says, is the 'proof' that Rimbaud himself 'had tried to purchase slaves', but once again her evidence is flawed.

The extract she gives is oddly pruned by her translation. What Ilg actually wrote is:

> *Quant aux esclaves, pardonnez-moi, je ne puis m'en occuper, je n'ai jamais acheté et je ne veux pas commencer. Je reconnais absolument vos bons [sic] intentions, mais même pour moi je ne le ferais jamais.*

Her translation of this brief extract has one glaring omission, and two other, more minor massagings of the original sense. She has left out the key opening phrase of the last sentence, which should read: 'I recognize absolutely your good intentions, but even for myself, etc . . .' This brief surgery alters the whole tone of the passage. The more minor tidying-away of Ilg's *pardonnez-moi* – 'forgive me' – tends to the same purpose. She has removed all the qualifications, and makes Ilg sound shocked and huffy about Rimbaud's request. This is not the tone of the original.

Her translation is inaccurate in a third instance. This is probably unintentional – it only proves to be wrong in view of an earlier letter from Rimbaud: the one which occasioned Ilg's reply. Starkie did not apparently find this. It shows that when Ilg wrote '*Quant aux esclaves*' he meant 'as for *the* slaves' – specific individuals – rather than 'as for slaves', which presupposes a more general enquiry by Rimbaud.

We can now trace both the beginning and the aftermath of this minor aspect of the Ilg–Rimbaud correspondence. Ilg's mention of 'the slaves' refers back to a request made by Rimbaud eight months previously. On 20 December 1889, at the close of a long, chatty, business-oriented letter, Rimbaud writes: 'I earnestly confirm my request for a very good young mule and two boy slaves [*deux garçons esclaves*]'. Ilg refers to this request in a letter to his sidekick Zimmerman ('Zimpy'): 'As for Rimbaud's requests (mule, slaves), do what seems to you best. I think one could, without any remorse, entrust him with the destiny of two poor devils' [22 January 1890]. Rimbaud repeats the order for the mule, urgently, on 16 March: 'send me the young mule or she-mule, a good trotting mule, very well-built, very strong, young, the best animal you can find, well-harnessed, at any price . . .' but does not mention the 'boy slaves'. Zimmerman writes back ten days later; the mules he has looked at were not 'the Numero 1 you're looking for'; he too says nothing about the slaves. There is nothing more on the record about them until Ilg's letter of August, disengaging himself of the task: '*Quant aux esclaves* . . .'

The whole business concerns two young Amhara or Galla boys to work for Rimbaud: underlings for Djami or Farah Kali, toters of bales. It is a slave transaction – hence Ilg's misgivings about it – but it is not the evidence of slave-trafficking that Starkie claims it to be.

'Did Rimbaud deal in slaves?' asks Jules Borelli, turning it over in his mind forty years later. 'I do not believe so.' Rimbaud, he says, 'did not talk very often, but when he did talk he sometimes used unpleasant language [*écarts de langage*], which could be taken wrongly by people who did not know him'. Besides, it was a time of uncertainties and antagonisms: the European powers were squabbling over the Somali coast: 'this was the origin of all these rumours, a few true but most of them false' [letter to André Tian, 31 March 1939].

This is probably all it is: a rumour, a misreading, an exaggeration. Rimbaud the slave-trader is a legend, like Rimbaud the wrecker off Cape Guardafui. If the word *esclavage* recurs in his letters, it is usually to describe his own conditions of employment, his own strange sense of existence as a kind of captivity.

He never got the two boys, or anyway not from Ilg. It seems he never got the mule either. 'As for the mule you were asking me for', Ilg writes in early 1891, 'I have tried but I just can't find one.' Soon Rimbaud will no longer need one.

27

THE HAMMER BLOW

'Iᴛ ᴀʟʟ ꜱᴛᴀʀᴛᴇᴅ with something like a hammer blow, so to speak, under the kneecap, repeated very lightly about once a minute.' This was the beginning of the end, in the first days of 1891.

There is a drastic sense of exertion throughout Rimbaud's life – he tramps along the high roads of France, he trudges across the Alps, he criss-crosses the globe from Siena to Stockholm, from Java to Queenstown, always *'pressé'* – and this physical driving of himself reaches a climax in Africa. He sweats across the desert on his mule or horse, 'braving the Danakil sun like a native' as Ferrandi puts it. He is 'tireless', an 'astonishing walker'. That punishing of his men and beasts which Ilg complains of is no more than the punishment he metes out to himself.

There is an element of iron will-power in this, because his health was always vulnerable. One recalls the fevers and sunstrokes of the first European wanderings; the typhoid that brought him back from Cyprus in 1879, and which still had him by the back nearly a year later. He pushes himself, punishes himself, to the point of exhaustion and beyond, and now, as the shadows lengthen on his life, these hardships and fatigues begin to exact a terrible cost.

He had suffered frequently from the common diseases and complaints of a European in the tropics: that punctuation of sickness. He was suffering from fever when he arrived in Aden in 1880; he contracted syphilis in Harar the following year; and he battled against dysentery and malaria throughout.

'I wish you better luck and a more settled stomach than mine,' he wrote from Harar in 1883.

The first hint of more serious problems occurs in a letter from Cairo in 1887, after the long and exhausting escapade in Abyssinia. He is 'enfeebled' and 'excessively tired', but that is not unusual. He is also suffering from dysentery, brought on, he claims, by carrying that heavy money-belt round his waist. But most ominous is the onset of rheumatic pains:

> I am tormented these days by a rheumatism in my side [*reins*], which is giving me hell; another in my left thigh which paralyses me sometimes; a pain in the joints of my left knee; and a rheumatism (which I've had for a while) in my right shoulder. My hair has gone completely grey. I feel that my life is going under . . .
> [23 August 1887].

(*'Que ma vie périclite'* – this verb is usually used to describe the collapsing of businesses.)

This rheumatic condition has antecedents: as early as 1876, one of Verlaine's *'vieux coppées'* [i.e. parodies of François Coppée] imagines Rimbaud complaining of *'les avant-goûts d'un rhuma-tisse'*, the first pangs of rheumatism. This may record an actual condition. His sister Vitalie died, at the age of seventeen, from a tuberculosis that began with a rheumatic or synovitic condition. However, the symptoms Rimbaud describes in Cairo are not a premonition of his fatal condition, since that affected his right leg.

In Harar in early 1889 he is talking of illness, but it seems this is specifically in response to a letter from his mother, urging him to make some financial provision for his repatriation in the event of illness or death. He says:

> If one day I found myself seriously ill, I would entrust my will to the Christian mission hereabouts, and by this means it would reach the French consulate at Aden in a few weeks . . . If I was badly ill, I would liquidate the agency here and go down to Aden, which is a civilized place where you can put your affairs in order immediately . . .

But he does not like to dwell on this:

> Why do you always talk of sickness and death, and all those other disagreeable things? Let's keep such thoughts far from our minds, and try and live as comfortably as we can, within the limit of our means . . . [10 January 1889]

In fact he did not write a will, as far as is known. The legacy for Djami is nuncupative: an oral instruction to Isabelle. The remainder of his African earnings were subsumed into the family coffers at Roche, where his mother lived on until 1907.

*　　*　　*

The beginning of the end is in February 1891, and the letter of the
20th, addressed perhaps significantly (though not uniquely) to his
mother alone, rather than to his *chers amis*:

> I am not well right now. I have these varicose veins in my right leg
> which are causing me a lot of pain. That's what you get for toiling
> away in these forsaken places. These varicose veins are compli-
> cated by rheumatism . . . For the last two weeks I haven't had a
> moment's sleep on account of the pain in this damn leg.

He requests a stocking for the varicose veins. As always he is precise
in his demands. 'Buy me a stocking for a long skinny leg (my foot is
shoe size 41). The stocking must go up over the knee, because I have
a varicose knee above the back of the knee.' He specifies silk woven
with elastic, rather than cotton. He believes they can be purchased in
Vouziers.

His mother despatched them a month later: two elastic stockings
made in Paris, and 'a jar of ointment to rub on the varicose veins'.
She would have sent them sooner but her doctor said one of the
stockings should be laced. The doctor recommends total rest, 'not
just sitting but lying down', because 'he can tell from your letter that
the ailment has reached a stage very worrying for the future'. This
package reached Rimbaud, in Aden, towards the end of April – too
late, for by then the condition had worsened. The varicose veins
were only a symptom. The leg was now virtually paralysed; the knee
had swollen till 'it looked like a *boule*'; the knee-cap was immobile,
'drowning in secretions'. Every step 'was like a nail driven into it',
and even when resting and bandaged the pain did not let up.

The condition, as diagnosed by an English doctor in Aden, was
'synovitis'. In Rimbaud's words (presumably echoing what the
doctor told him), 'synovitis is a disease of the liquids of the knee
joint; it can be caused by heredity, or by injury, or by many things'
[30 April 1891]. More technically, it is an inflammation of the
synovial membrane, and thus an impeding of the flow of synovia, 'a
viscid albuminous fluid secreted in the interior of the joints and in
the sheaths of the tendons'. Without this lubricant, the joint seizes
up. Contemporary medical opinion on the subject asserts 'that 85
per cent of the cases of synovial inflammation occur in the knee' and
'that the pain of synovitis is caused by the distension of the fibrous

elements of the joint' [St George's Hospital, London; report of 1879]. In Fagge's *Principles of Medicine* (1886) there is a reference to 'synovial rheumatism', which ties in with Rimbaud's symptoms.

Later, in France, the diagnosis (as echoed in his first letter from hospital, 21 May 1891) was: *'une synovite, une hydarthrose, etc, une maladie de l'articulation et des os'*. This adds the *'hydarthrose'* element, which seems to be 'water in the joints': 'arthrosis' is an obsolete synonym for arthritis. The word 'neoplasm' – in other words, cancer – does not appear until his last spell in hospital, and is probably not yet the case.

The causes of his synovitis are variously interpreted. Alfred Bardey implies that it was syphilitic in origin; in other words, he links it to the illness which Rimbaud 'picked up' in Harar ten years earlier, and which he (but not Rimbaud) identifies as syphilis. A sexual peccadillo would, therefore, be the ultimate cause of Rimbaud's death.

More frequently the cause is thought to be a specific injury. There is talk of a fall from his horse during a hunting trip with the Righas brothers; of a wound from a thorn-tree which festered – but these are late testimonies. Savouré seems to favour the latter when he says, in 1930, that Rimbaud died because of a 'tiny [*infime*] wound in one of his knees', but then he erroneously adds that Rimbaud was 'dead on arrival [in France] from gangrene'. The most authoritative independent source is Isabelle Rimbaud's friend Nicolette Hennique. In her 1921 edition of Isabelle's writings, *Reliques*, she appends a long note entitled 'Pathology of Arthur Rimbaud, based on the memories of his sister'. For the year 1891 she writes:

> Violent pain of the right knee. One day, to overcome this pain, he makes a mad dash on horseback. The horse, out of control, dashes his bad knee against a tree. Dreadful suffering, total insomnia, immoderate use of narcotics which are anyway ineffective. No doctor in Harar.

This suggests a damaging injury, but only *after* he had already begun to suffer from 'violent pain' in the knee.

Though Isabelle's 'memories' presumably echo what Rimbaud had told her, he himself makes no mention of any injury in his letters. His comments on the cause of his affliction are highly generalized. He blames the sheer hardship of his life. The ailment is 'caused by too much work on horseback and also by exhausting journeys on foot'. He says the rheumatism is caused by the 'dry winds' of the Harar region, 'very unhealthy for the whites'. Even young Europeans – apparently no longer including himself in this category – 'suffer from rheumatism after two or three years here'. He turns the matter over in his head, restlessly seeking an explanation:

> This is what I have concluded about the cause of my illness. The climate in Harar is cold from November to March. Out of habit, I wore very light clothes: simple canvas [*toile*] trousers and a cotton shirt. Dressed like this, I made long journeys on foot, anything between 15 and 40 kilometres a day, and went on wild horse-rides across the steep mountain ranges of the region. I think I must have developed an arthritic condition caused by fatigue, heat and cold.
> [Letter to Isabelle, 15 July 1891]

In his own judgement, his suffering was caused by – was written into – the life he lived out in Africa. It was his destiny. *Mektoub*. It was as the *voyant* had foreseen, all those years ago:

> an ineffable torture, which will require all his faith, all his superhuman strength, which will make of him the great Invalid, the great Criminal, the great Outcast – and the supreme Philosopher! – for he has arrived at the *Unknown* . . .

*   *   *

Up in Harar in early 1891, none of these diagnoses had yet been made. All he knew was that something was very badly wrong. By mid-March, it was so bad that he was unable to move:

> On about 15 March I decided to take to my bed, or at least to stay in a horizontal position. I rigged up a bed between my cash-box, my ledgers, and a window from which I could keep an eye on my weighing-scales on the far side of the courtyard, and I paid people more money to keep the business going for me, while I stayed stretched out . . .

> For about three weeks I was laid up at Harar, unable to make a single movement, suffering atrocious pain, and never sleeping . . . Having no remedy nor any advice, since in Harar you are in the midst of negroes and there are no Europeans there at all, I decided

to leave. I had to abandon my business, which was not at all easy, since I had money dispersed all over the place. [30 April, 15 July 1891]

Thus, crippled with pain, Rimbaud set about 'liquidating' his interests, and those of César Tian, at Harar. He did so with difficulty, and at a loss. According to the journalist Scarfoglio he was much beholden to 'an Italian company' – undoubtedly Bienenfeld – which 'stood guarantor for him, and generously helped him' in this hour of need.

He had a stretcher or litter [*civière*] made up for him. His sketch of it survives: two long carrying-poles, a low wooden frame lashed onto them, a canvas cover or 'curtain'.

He hired sixteen porters, at the rate of fifteen thalers each, to carry him. He travelled down with a caravan, though whether it was his caravan or not is unclear. Travelling with him was a British trader, whom he refers to either as M. [i.e. Monsieur] Donald or as McDonald (his handwriting is very poor by now), together with his wife and their two children. And, of course, Djami. His woman remained in Harar, and later returned to her own people.

And so, at six o'clock on the morning of Tuesday, 7 April 1891, Rimbaud left Harar, by the Bab el F'touh or Zeilah Gate, and embarked on the last and most dreadful of his African journeys.

The journey took twelve days. For the first ten days he kept a fraught and increasingly brief journal or '*itinéraire*'. Borer calls it his *carnet de damné* – the condemned man's notebook: Rimbaud's own phrase for the *Season in Hell*. Extracts from this, and from a couple of later letters, provide the stages of this infernal journey.

Day 1. They move north from Harar to the summit of Egon. From there, around midday, they begin the steep descent towards Ballaoua [Ballawa]. This is 'very painful for the porters, as they stumble over every stone; and for me, as I am almost overturned every minute'. The litter is soon 'half-broken' and the men exhausted. 'I try riding on a mule, with my bad leg tied to its neck, but after a few minutes I have to dismount and get back onto the litter, which has already fallen a kilometre behind.' They reach Ballaoua at 3.00 p.m. and make camp. It rains. A furious wind blows all night.

Day 2. They reach Geldessey [Gueldessah] after four hours. 'The porters get the hang of things, and I suffer less than on the Ballaoua descent.' They camp at Gueldessah. A storm blows up at 4.00 p.m. A cold night with heavy dew.

Day 3. They move on to Grasley. The *abban* [guide] and the camels of the caravan fall behind. That afternoon at Boyussa [Bussa] they find the river swollen and impassable. He camps with Mr McDonald and his family.

Day 4. Rains; difficulties getting the camels loaded. He goes on ahead in his litter, through the rain, arriving at Wordji [Voji] at 2.00 p.m. Here they wait for the camels, and the provisions, but they do not come. 'It rains non-stop for 16 hours, and we have neither provisions nor the tent. I spend the time under an Abyssinian skin.' This was a dreadful night. He singled it out in his later account of the trip to Isabelle, though wrongly saying it was the second day:

> The second day of the trip, having got far ahead of the caravan, we were caught in open country by a rainstorm. Here I stayed, flat on my back in the rain, for 16 hours, without shelter and without any possibility of moving. This was very bad for me.

The utter helplessness is anathema to this most self-sufficient of men:

> Throughout the journey I was unable to get out of the litter. They set up a tent over me wherever they put me down. I dug a hole with my hands at the side of the litter, and managed with difficulty to hoist myself over the side so I could relieve myself [*aller à la selle*] in that hole, which I then covered over with earth. In the morning they lifted the tent off me, and then lifted me up.

Day 5. In the morning he sends back eight of his men in search of the straggling caravan. He waits immobile at Wordji. Finally the caravan hoves into view at 4.00 p.m. 'We eat after 30 hours of total fasting.' (One notes that even here, *in extremis*, he gets the right word – the MS of his journal shows he first wrote *abstinence*, then amended it to *jeûne*, a 'fast' rather than mere 'abstinence'.)

Day 6. Slow progress; they camp at Dahlamaley.

Day 7. They arrive at Biokobobo, the well-watered half-way stage of the journey. They camp for the day and replenish their canteens.

Day 8. 'The bearers march very badly.' After four hours they reach Arrouina [Arrowina]. 'When we arrive they throw me down on the ground: I impose a 4 thaler fine.' The names of the four bearers, each fined a thaler, are listed in the margin:

Mouned Souyin	Th 1
Abdulahi	Th 1
Abdullah	Th 1
Bakir	Th 1

They proceed to Samado.

Day 9. Samado to Lasman, four hours; rest up, four hours; Lasman to Kombavoren, four hours.

Day 10. From Kombavoren to Hensa to Doudouhassa. A cryptic notation: '*Trouvé là 10½ das 1 R*' – presumably means he purchased ('found') 10½ *daboulahs* of coffee for 1 rupee. Again that evening, at Dadap: '*Trouvé 5½ chx 22 das 11 peaux*': a purchase of camels, coffee and skins.

Day 11. Long and scarcely noted. They left Dadap at 9.30 a.m. and were at Warambot seven hours later. The unspoken stretch is the crossing of the desert of Mindao, meaning (according to Bardey) 'only a madman stops here'. This is the last entry of his *itinéraire*. It dwindles to this hieroglyphic of numbers, times, figures. All that's left: these last precisions; a man counting the hours, counting the seconds of pain.

They reached Zeilah on about 19 April. He is 'worn out, paralysed'. He rests there, on the wharf, but only for four hours, as there was a boat leaving for Aden.

> Dumped on the bridge of the boat on my mattress (they had to hoist me on board in my litter!). I then had to endure three days at sea with nothing to eat. At Aden I was unloaded once more, in my litter.

Loading and unloading: he has become an item of merchandise, transported down from Harar to Aden.

*   *   *

According to this schedule, he arrived in Aden on about 22 April. He spent a couple of days *chez* Tian, 'to organize our affairs', and then went into hospital. There he was put in the care of an English doctor whose name, according to Isabelle, was Dr. Nouks (perhaps Nokes?) On 30 April he writes home:

> I have been admitted to the European hospital. It has only one room for paying patients; I am in it. As soon as I showed him my knee, the English doctor told me it was a synovitis that had reached a very dangerous stage, brought on by lack of care and by fatigue. He immediately talked off cutting the leg off, then he decided to wait a few days to see if the swelling would diminish a little under medical care. It has been six days now, but there has been no improvement.

So here he waits, immobile on the narrow bed, in the 'European hospital' of Aden. According to a local historian, Dr Masoud Amshush, this hospital was the building which now houses the Crater police station. This stands on the southern slopes above the town, with some slight freshness resulting. It is a low, rectangular building in Aden brownstone, built up on a small bluff, with a balconied verandah.

On the night before I visited it, during my stay in Aden in 1991, the building was gutted by fire. They were carrying out heat-warped filing cabinets when I arrived; I was not allowed in. I have no real memory of the place except of a pair of crows sitting on the burned-out hulk of an air-conditioning unit. They nested there. 'They have always been here,' a policeman told me, and perhaps their forebears were there to bring some wintry solace to Rimbaud as he lay there:

> *Strange army of harsh sounds,*
> *The cold winds attack your nests.*
> *Along the yellowed rivers,*
> *Past the roadside calvaries*
> *Above the ditches and the pits,*
> *You must scatter, you must rally.*

He lies stretched out on his back, his leg 'bandaged, bound, rebound, chained', his back rubbed raw from sweat-sores, the food both expensive and awful, and the heat mounting with every day.
'I am scared . . .'

His thoughts are now only of getting back to France, where 'the care and the medicines are up to date, and the air good'. The steamers are all full – everyone comes back from the colonies at this time of year – but he is not without contacts.

On 10 May 1891 he leaves Steamer Point aboard a Messageries Maritimes passenger ship, *L'Amazone*. The great adventure is over.

28

RETURNING

After 'THIRTEEN DAYS of sorrows', he arrived at the Vieux Port of Marseille on Wednesday, 20 May 1891. He set foot on French soil for the first time in eleven years, though not literally, as he was probably carried ashore on a stretcher. His leg was now 'enormous'; his knee 'looks like a giant pumpkin'.

The last irony – '*I will return with limbs of iron . . .*'

He was taken to the Hôpital de la Conception, down in the Italian quarter of the city below the wide-open space called La Plaine (now Place Jean-Jaurès). The original hospital, built in 1858, already a bit old-fashioned, was a three-storey building ranged around a central courtyard. There were eight sections or wings, each divided into three wards. The men's wards were on the eastern side; Rimbaud was in the *pavillon des malades payants*, or private ward, ten francs a day, including medical care.

The hospital was entirely rebuilt in the early 1980s, and no trace remains of the buildings where Rimbaud was tended.

The following day he summons the strength to write home: 'I'm very sick, very sick, I'm reduced to a skeleton by this affliction of my left leg . . .' The mistake – it was his right leg – is poignant. There has been talk of amputation; the mistake is a kind of desperate shielding of the wounded limb.

> This is going to take a very long time, unless complications force them to cut off the leg. Either way I will be left a cripple. But I doubt if I will wait. Life has become impossible for me. How wretched I am! How wretched I have become! [21 May 1891]

The following day his wretchedness is confirmed. The doctor makes the fatal decision. At 2.50 p.m. Rimbaud sends a telegram home:

TODAY YOU OR ISABELLE COME MARSEILLE BY EXPRESS TRAIN. MONDAY MORNING THEY AMPUTATE MY LEG.

DANGER OF DEATH. SERIOUS MATTERS TO ATTEND TO. ARTHUR.

Less than four hours later his mother wires from the post office in Attigny:

LEAVING NOW. WILL ARRIVE TOMORROW EVENING. COURAGE AND PATIENCE. VVE [i.e. *Veuve*] RIMBAUD

She arrived as promised. One hears the stifled gasp as she sees him for the first time, the son she had lost all those years ago: his ravaged face, his grey hair, '*a dark skin, a furious eye.*'

The operation was delayed. It was not until Wednesday 27 May that Rimbaud was etherized upon a table, and his right leg was amputated, 'very high up'.

He knew it was necessary, but later he would tell Isabelle:

If someone in this condition asked my advice I'd tell them this: never let yourself be amputated. Let them butcher you, flay you, slice you to pieces, but never allow anyone to amputate you. If it means death this will always be better than living without one of your limbs. Many have made this choice, and if I had another chance I would make it too. Better to suffer a year in hell than to be amputated . . . [15 July 1891]

*   *   *

Even now he had not, in his mind, left Africa for good. On the contrary: he was only back in France for this pressing medical emergency; he was on that sick leave, that cool climate recuperation, which all his colleagues took and which he was certainly due.

The first letters he wrote after the operation (or anyway the first that are now known) were to his associates in Africa – to Ras Makonnen and Dimitri Righas, and probably to César Tian. The only one that survives is the letter to Makonnen. It is dated 30 May; however, it says the operation was six days ago. Perhaps time has blurred for him, but nothing in the letter suggests confusion: it is clear and concise. Perhaps, rather, he is showing that characteristic *haste* in the only way that it remains to him, as a mental hurrying onward from that dreadful day of amputation.

It is a wonderful letter under the circumstances:

Excellency,

How are you? I wish you good health and complete prosperity.
May God vouchsafe you all you desire. May your life flow
peacefully.

I write this to you from Marseille, in France. I am in hospital. They
cut off my leg six days ago. I am doing well at present, and in
about three weeks I will be healed.

In a few months I expect to return to Harar, to carry on my
business as before, and I thought I would send you my greetings. I
remain your devoted servant,

Rimbaud

Also on 30 May he wrote to his Greek associate Dimitri Righas in
Harar. The letter did not reach him for six weeks. Righas's reply is
very touching, both in what it says and in the way it is phrased.
Written in a kind of stripped-down *pied-noir* French, with the
childlike quality of its misspellings and phoneticisms, this heartfelt
document seems like a last signpost on Rimbaud's long flight from
the ornate portals of French Literature.

'*Mon cher Monsieur Rimbaud*,' writes Righas,

> *Set aujourduy saliment que jai recu votre lettre du 30 mai et du 17*
> *juin sur lequel vous manonsé que on vous a fet loperation, savedire*
> *que on vous a coupé votre jambe et sama frapé beaucoup insi que*
> *tout vot conesance du Harar. J'oré preferé que on me coupe la*
> *mien pluto que le votre. Enfin jai vous suit une bone guerison . . .*
> *Moi, depi que vous et parti du Harar, j'ai croi que j'ai perdu le*
> *mond. Jai ne sort jammé de se moi que jousque au Zaptie . . .*

[It is only today that I have received your letters of 30 May and 17
June, in which you announce that they have operated on you, that
is to say they have cut off your leg, and this has been a blow to me,
and to all of your friends in Harar likewise. I would have preferred
that they cut off mine rather than yours. Anyway, I wish you a
good recovery . . . As for me, since you left Harar I have felt like I
have lost the world. I never go out of my house, except as far as the
Zapti . . .]

On the same day, probably, Rimbaud wrote to César Tian in

Aden; at any rate, Tian has had a letter from him by 11 June, and writes, in his rather buttoned-up way: 'I was very saddened to learn that amputation has proved necessary.' He too talks as if Rimbaud were returning soon, and makes some veiled comments about their future dealings together, and about Maurice Riès, and the state of the markets in Harar.

With that optimism that still has not left him, that desperate belief in the future, these letters of 30 May say: Business as Usual.

*   *   *

La Mother remained at his bedside for two weeks. On 8 June she wrote to Isabelle: 'I wanted to leave today, but Arthur's tears touched me. But to stay means I will have to stay at least a month: that is not possible.' She left the following day.

It is understandable, but for Rimbaud it seems a terrible reprise of those earlier rejections, real or imagined, of his childhood. Arthur's tears were in vain once more. 'I was very angry when mother left me,' he wrote to Isabelle a few days later. 'I didn't understand the reason for it.'

He never wrote to his mother again. There begins now this last and most poignant relationship with his young sister Isabelle that had been strangely foretold by the teenage prophet of the *Season in Hell*:

> *Women nurse these fierce invalids back home from the hot countries . . .*

She was thirteen years old when he wrote *A Season in Hell*, nineteen when he left Europe. Through her teens Arthur had been an unpredictable presence, departing suddenly, returning unexpectedly, and one day departing and never returning. She knew of, but did not know, his poetry: her reading of the *Illuminations* after his death was a revelation to her. And now, as Rimbaud recuperates in Marseille, it is to Isabelle that his letters are addressed – *'Ma chère sœur'* – and to her that he recounts the agonizing progress of his recovery. It is a curious apotheosis of Rimbaud's personal life: intimacy and distance, this stranger who is his sister.

She has herself been ill -- this was one of the reasons for Madame Rimbaud's return to Roche – and must have mentioned this rather melodramatically in the letter to which he replied on 17 June:

But what do you mean by all this talk of burial? Don't be so fearful, have patience like me, take care of yourself, have courage. I would so like to see you! What can it be that you have? What illness? All illnesses are healed by time and care. In any case one must resign oneself, and not despair . . .

His counsel to her, with its stern Islamic fatalism, was hard to follow himself. On 23 June, nearly four weeks after the amputation, he is close to despair: 'I do nothing but weep day and night; I am a dead man; I am crippled for the rest of my life. In a couple of weeks I will be recovered, I think, but I will not be able to walk without crutches.' He is tormented by neuralgia in the stump of his right leg, and he is terrified by discomforts and 'congestions' in his left leg, 'my only support in the world'. Perhaps it is his destiny to become a *'cul-de-jatte'* ('a basin-bum', or a legless cripple).

The crutches present their own problems. He writes about this with the obsessive detail that he had once written about his profits and losses at Aden, or about the customs and topographies of the Somali bedouin or about the exact width and spacing of the stripes on the cloth the company should send to Harar.

The crutches are an affront to this greatest of walkers, the tramper of the highway, *le piéton:*

I am trying the crutches once again. What ennui, what exhaustion, and what sadness to think of all my past journeying, and how active I was only five months ago. Where are the treks across the mountains, the riding and the walking, the deserts, the rivers and the seas? And now just this legless cripple's life . . . [10 July 1891]

Night and day I'm thinking about ways of getting around. It's a real torture! I would like to do this and do that, go here and go there, to see, to live, to depart: impossible, impossible at least for a long time, if not forever! Beside me I see nothing but these cursed crutches: I cannot take a step, cannot exist, without these sticks. I cannot even dress myself without the most dreadful gymnastics.

His eye is still merciless: he sees his own state as a kind of grotesque comic turn:

I sit, and from time to time I get up, and hop a hundred paces or so on my crutches, and then sit down again. My hands cannot hold anything. When I am walking I cannot look at anything but my solitary foot and the ends of the crutches. Your head and shoulders

297

slope forward, and you slump along like a hunchback. You tremble at the sight of objects and people moving around you, frightened they're going to knock you over and break the other leg. People sneer at the way you hop along. When you sit back down you have lifeless hands, and armpits rubbed raw, and the face of an idiot. Despair overwhelms you once more, and there you sit, utterly impotent, snivelling away, waiting for the night, which only brings constant insomnia and another day even sadder than the last. To be continued in the next issue . . .

He has a wooden leg made – 'very light, varnished and padded, very well made, price 50 francs' – but after a few days of trying to walk with it he has inflamed the stump of his thigh and has to put it aside, and return to the crutches. He is impatient for a 'mechanical leg' [i.e. articulated] but will have to wait months.

He is 'very low'. He wishes for death, but 'however stupid his existence, a man keeps clinging onto it'.

On 20 July he writes announcing his imminent departure for Roche. Much persuaded in this by Isabelle, he has so far resisted. The difficulty and cost of travelling; his fear of the cold (it was wet and chilly that summer of 1891) – these are the reasons he gives. But he fears also that last return, that interment in the 'hole' of his Ardennais home.

This is the last surviving letter that he actually wrote (later letters were dictated to Isabelle). He can hardly write at all because of the pain in his right shoulder from the crutches. He concludes this final manuscript: '*Au revoir*. Rimbaud.'

*   *   *

He is back in Roche on about 23 July. He has asked for an upstairs room to be prepared for him ('*je préférerais habiter en haut*'), an indication of his frame of mind, as he has specified several times that he cannot get up and downstairs with his crutches. He is returning to Roche with the intention of rest, of inertia: his status as invalid is confirmed by this desire for an upstairs room.

The room – 'the nicest in the house', says Isabelle – was prepared for him with 'naive diligence'. When he saw it he gratefully exclaimed, 'It's like Versailles here!' La Mother is presumably present, but is nowhere mentioned in Isabelle's account – the only account – of the prodigal's return. She is excluded from the intimacy of these last months. She wrote the epitaph of her relationship with her son, unwittingly, many years later: 'My poor Arthur, who never asked anything of me . . .'

Isabelle fusses around him, her eyes bright with this new mission of caring for him. 'His bags were unpacked, his curios set out; his needs as an invalid and his desires as an exhausted traveller had all been taken care of.' These 'curios' [*bibelots*] might include the few meagre belongings now on show at the Musée Rimbaud: the lengths of Ethiopian cloth; the seal which styled him Abdoh Rinbo; the books of science and geography sent by his mother;' and perhaps the harp which features in one of Isabelle's sketches of him.

Insomnia and fever; dreadful sessions with the crutches and the artificial leg; unseasonable chill and rain. But there are outings:

> Staying in was very disagreeable to him, and often he went out in an open carriage. Every day, despite his exhaustion and despite the bad weather, he spent the afternoon out and about. He liked to be taken to places where there were crowds of people enjoying themselves, on fête days and Sundays; and without joining in with them he took pleasure in observing the movements and gestures of the people, as also the changes in fashion over the last ten years

This viewing of scenes, from his silence, from his '*voiture découvert*', is as near as he comes to re-entering France. It plays before him like a movie. His sole interpreter is Isabelle, from whose journal [*Reliques*, p. 103] all this comes. He thinks also of marriage, still:

> He had not abandoned his marriage plans. On the contrary: his recent misfortune had rather exacerbated in him the desire to start a family. But at present he would not 'expose himself to the scorn of some bourgeois girl: he would look in an orphanage for a girl of irreproachable breeding and education; or indeed he would marry a Catholic woman of noble Abyssinian race'.

These last comments are given as verbatim (though this memoir of Isabelle's did not appear until 1897).

Rimbaud's fear about being laughed at by women is not particular to his current state, but a perennial feeling expressed in his early romantic poems ('Novelette', 'Set to Music', etc.). The woman of 'noble Abyssinian race' is also a figure from his past: a

'masquerade' that had once passed before his eyes and now does so
again.

His condition worsens; paralysis in the right arm; agonizing
neuralgias. The carriage rides become too painful and are discontinued; 'a mortal ennui pervades him'. His only respite was opium
[*tisanes de pavot*]:

> For some days he lived in a strange waking dream ... This
> illuminated his memory and provoked in him an irresistible desire
> to confide. The doors and the shutters hermetically sealed, all the
> lights and lamps and candles lit, to the soft and soothing sound of
> a little hurdy-gurdy [*orgue de barbarie*], he went back over his
> life, evoked his memories of childhood, developed his intimate
> thoughts, discussed future plans and projects ... His soft, slow
> voice took on an accent of penetrating beauty. He often mingled
> his sentences with Oriental phrases and even with expressions
> borrowed from other European languages; but the whole very
> clear and comprehensible ...

Then the hallucinations begin. One night, imagining himself
'nimble' [*ingambe*] once more, he tried to pursue some 'imaginary
vision that had appeared and then fled', and which he believed had
'taken refuge in a corner of the bedroom':

> He tried to get out of bed unaided and pursue this apparition. We
> heard the sound of his tall body crashing down, and we came
> running. He was stretched out on the carpet completely naked ...

From this time on, Isabelle says, he 'renounced' opium, because the
relief it gave him 'modified his moral state to the point where he,
Arthur Rimbaud, had been able to give intimate confidences'.

Try to recount the story of my sleep and fall ...

*   *   *

All the while there are letters coming in from Africa: from Tian, from
Dimitri Righas, from Sotiro, the latter full of his homespun
philosophizing and humour, and the old familiar shop-talk on which
life depended out there:

> I know well, dear friend, that you are not used to staying put,
> without getting up and moving and learning to dance ...

Always remember that over here there is someone who speaks in your favour, and who knows you, and that fate will bring you back here if God gives you health . . .

I read with pleasure that you are with your mother in your homeland. You are happy. I seem to see this. It was the same for me when I went back home. I too had the pleasure of seeing my parents and sisters and brothers, etc. I didn't once think about this wretched life here, or about the business . . .

Dimitri has put in another order for liquor from Deschamps, but at the same moment Makonnen has forbidden it . . . Procopis has come back from Abyssinia with a loss, he brought back some silks . . . Ilg and M. Pino are on the coast. Brémond has unloaded 2,000 *fraslehs* of coffee at Aden. Savouré has gone up to Harar with his money and his wife, a white woman.

Be sure to come back soon, and ready to learn how to dance. My poor friend, what bad luck! But God is great! He it is who thinks of us all, always. [Zeilah, 25 July and 14 August 1891]

The weather is cold, he is prey to a 'mortal ennui', and more and more he is possessed with the idea of returning to Harar and 'resuming, at least for a while, his active life'. He said simply: '*il faut absolument que je retourne . . .*' He *must* return.

It is on this note – not so much the desire as the necessity of returning to Africa – that he sets out on his last journey.

29

THE LAST JOURNEY

'23 AUGUST 1891,' writes Isabelle. 'Exactly a month after his return to Roche, he's leaving us once more.' And she is leaving with him, his constant companion and nurse, and our sole source for the last weeks of his life.

'The idea of returning to Harar, even just for a while, haunted him. But as it became clearer every day that such a long journey was impossible for him, he resolved to leave for Marseille.' There at least, he said, 'there would be sun and warmth.' There also, 'he could be tended at the Conception by the surgeon who had operated on him'. In the surgeon one glimpses the last of those fallible fathers and pathetic brothers in whom he placed something approaching his trust.

He lives, as always, '*dans l'expectative*'. He will be 'ready to be embarked for Aden at the first sign of recovery'.

*   *   *

The journey began badly. At three o'clock in the morning, very agitated, Rimbaud is already demanding to be dressed and driven to the station at Voncq, about three kilometres away from Roche. The train is due at 6.30 a.m. But the servants take too long to prepare the carriage. On the way, the horse – 'out of sorts from the early start', thinks Isabelle, with an empathy her brother did not share – dug his heels in and refused to budge. 'Arthur takes off his belt and brandishes it at the wretched creature, but to no avail.'

The journey is winding and in parts precipitous. The station is down below Roche, in the Aisne valley. They arrive two minutes too late. The train has left.

He is 'very downcast'. He hesitates a moment, almost preferring to wait there for the next train, rather than undergoing the agony of another carriage-ride. But the chilly morning fog makes him shiver. They decide to go back to the house.

The next train is due at 12.40 p.m. All morning he is very over-excited. We must leave now, at any cost: 'Quick! Quick!' He refuses all offers of food, says Isabelle. 'He has only one idea: to leave.'

The carriage is brought, but now his excitement fades. He gazes around him and begins to cry. He says: 'Can I not find a stone to rest my head on, and a place to die?' Isabelle sees in his face 'the resignation of a martyr'.

'He holds us close to his heart, holds us in his thin arms, and he weeps . . .'

They are at the station once more; they sit and wait under a chestnut tree. Beneath it there's a little flower-bed planted by the station master – a few drooping marguerites and dahlias, bordered by a little circle of sand. 'Arthur comments on this, with a flash of his former wit.'

The station at Voncq still stands, long disused, among waist-high yellow grass, a stone's throw from the Aisne river:

Clear water like the salt of childhood tears, like the whiteness of women's bodies against the sun . . . ['Memory']

The shutters lean drunkenly, the lath shows through above the little *guichet*. There's a slate on the wall, where announcements would have been chalked. Later visitors have scored their names and dates – Barbara, Henk, et al. Perhaps they came here by chance, a boat moored at the lock nearby, but at least one was a pilgrim and has scratched the words, *LA LIBERTÉ LIBRE* . . .

The railway-track runs off to a distant greyish vanishing-point, past the copses and fields and the big poplars muffled in mistletoe.

The whistle blows; the train arrives. Arthur is hoisted aboard in his wheelchair, not without suffering, and settles painfully into the cushions they have brought. The jolting of the train is cruel to him. He grips the stump of his leg in both hands. 'Oh the pain, the pain,' he says, over and over again. He tries leaning, he tries standing, he tries sitting: none of these positions works for him. He suffers dreadful pain in his back, his sides, his shoulders, his arms, above all his right shoulder and armpit, where the crutch has hurt him, and the stump of his leg.

They change trains at Amagne. He is taken in a wheelchair to the waiting room.

The journey resumes. 'He is seated on the red cushion. He has put his suitcase next to him and he rests his right arm on it. His bernous and a rug make it a little softer for supporting his bad arm. His left elbow leans against the sill of the carriage window.'

People join the train: a family on a Sunday outing. They are loud and careless and cluttered with baskets, but the sight of this haggard figure propped in the corner silences them.

> Broken with fatigue he falls into a somnolent torpor. He sleeps, but what a strange sleep it is. His eyes are open, his mouth is a grimace of unspeakable suffering. The fever hollows his cheeks and spreads a burning flush over them. His poor hands, bloodless and thin, rock inertly to the rhythm of the train. He seems very, very sick.

On the northern outskirts of Paris there's an August fête on. 'Everyone's hurrying there, flying along to it. What a sense of life is there. But he, Arthur, the indefatigable and ever-curious traveller, lies insensible from suffering, lies immobile in the corner of the stifling railway carriage.'

The train pulls into Paris: the Gare de l'Est, the station where Verlaine had come in search of him, and had missed him in the crowd. They had planned to stay the night. ('After so many years living an almost savage existence, Paris would be the place for him to see once more the civilized world,' Isabelle says primly.) But as they cross the city, the rain starts and the cab shakes terribly, and instead Rimbaud orders the coachman to drive directly to the 'Gare du P-L-M' [i.e. Paris–Lyon–Marseille].

His former haunts go by, but 'on that Sunday there is scarcely anyone to be seen on the boulevards and streets. The pavements shine in the rain. The gutters babble sadly. The shops are all shut. All is gloomy. Arthur, prostrate, looks feverishly out through the window of the cab.'

At the Gare de Lyon he waits impatiently for the express to Marseille. 'He has an instant of extraordinary and heartbreaking gaiety, occasioned by seeing the uniform of an officer . . .'

He takes another *soporifique* but knows it will not work.

Around eleven o'clock that night the porters carry him aboard the train, as gently as they can, and 'stretch the unfortunate traveller down in the *wagon-lit* we have reserved'.

As the train pulls out, the shabby, grey outskirts of southern Paris, the flat fields that today are littered with hangar-like hypermarkets and skateboard parks, are covered in darkness. Isabelle hopes the softness of the bed and the effects of the *soporifique* will make it easier for him to sleep. But nothing makes it easier. Through the night the torture continues. The carriage is stifling and gets hotter as they travel south.

'Anger, hunger, weakness and suffering kindled in him an intense fever; delirium held sway; and throughout that frightful night when the express train carried Arthur Rimbaud to Marseille, his companion, kneeling and cramped in that narrow space, witnessed the most dreadful paroxysm of despair and torture imaginable.' (This begins like a lost fragment from the *Season in Hell*, then breaks against the poignant bathos of the schoolgirl-diary third person, where she calls herself 'his companion'.)

In 1891 the express from Paris to Marseille took over eighteen hours. They left Paris at 11 p.m., and arrived at Marseille 'towards evening' the next day (i.e. in late August, about 6.00 p.m.) Nowadays the TGV, travelling at up to 300 km per hour, covers the distance in less than four hours: a bland, gliding journey.

They were at Lyon at sunrise. The sun 'made the golden stars on the bridge over the Rhône sparkle'. At last Rimbaud fell into 'a kind of comatose oblivion', though sometimes nightmares woke him, bathed in sweat and babbling senselessly on his 'narrow couch'.

'The ankylosis grows more marked', Isabelle notes solemnly. Ankylosis or anchylosis: 'the formation of a stiff joint by consolidation of the articulating surfaces' – another of these grand medical terms that uselessly surround Rimbaud's last months. Isabelle must have got this word from someone, perhaps from the family doctor in Roche, perhaps from the sufferer himself.

Through the morning of 24 August, the train trundles south through the Rhône valley: dark cypress, parched grass, granite bluffs, umbrella pines, white walls, orange tiles. The heat mounts. 'The narrow compartment becomes an infernal prison from which there was no means of escape.'

They pass through Arles, scene of another 'hell'. It was here, in 1888, that Van Gogh quarrelled with Gauguin, and threatened him with a razor, and later, in remorse, cut off his own ear. He was placed in an asylum at St-Rémy, and shot himself, at the scene of his painting *Cornfield with Flight of Birds*, on 27 July 1890. He was thirty-seven years old, as Rimbaud was when he died. That Van Gogh painting of the pair of boots always makes me think of Rimbaud:

> *I plucked like lyres the elastic of my wounded shoes, one foot close to my heart* . . . ['My Gypsy Life']

The train hauls through the long vistas of the Camargue, threads along the complex coastline of the Bouches-du-Rhône, and finally pulls into the Gare St-Charles, perched high above the precipitate heights and depths of Marseille, the gateway to Africa.

Here Isabelle concludes her account: 'On our arrival, Arthur was transported to the Conception, where he had himself registered under the name of "Jean Rimbaud". He would never again leave that hospital room alive.'

One notes the final enfeebled veiling, the last alias: this is not Arthur Rimbaud, this is somebody else.

* * *

On 22 September Isabelle writes to her mother. This is what the doctors have told her, apparently verbatim: 'The poor fellow is going, little by little: his life is a matter of days, of a few months at the most. If some dangerous complication arises, which could happen at any time, he would certainly not survive it. As for recovery, there is no hope whatsoever; he will not recover. We believe his condition to be a transmission, through the bone marrow, of the cancerous condition which necessitated the amputation.'

This is what they have told her privately. 'To him they say the opposite, holding out hopes and lies of a full recovery.'

A day in the death: an extract from Isabelle's diary, Sunday, 4 October 1891. She enters his room at 7.00 a.m. He sleeps with his eyes open, his breath short and fast. His eyes are sunk in heavy black shadows.

'He says *bonjour* to me, as he does every morning. He asks me how I am, if I have slept well, etc.'

He starts telling her certain 'improbable things' that have happened in the hospital overnight. (This appears to be some kind of repeated fantasy or *idée fixe*, for she says: 'Every morning, and at several other times of the day, he tells the same absurd story.') He accuses the nurses and sisters of 'abominable things which could not possibly be true'. Isabelle tells him he must have been dreaming. 'He refuses to be persuaded, and treats me as if I were an idiot.'

The nurse brings him his cup of black coffee; Isabelle helps him to drink it. The nurse also brings Isabelle a bowl of warm milk. She has a bad cough.

A hospital orderly called Eugène brings the 'electrical apparatus. There follows a painful fifteen-minute session of shock-treatment for his right arm, now almost paralysed. The hand twitches, clenches, but when the clamps are removed it is once more lifeless.

While Isabelle is at Mass someone brings the articulated false leg Rimbaud wanted, in a special case, but he has no money to pay the five-franc carriage fee. Later, Isabelle goes to the hospital office to settle up the bill. The young man in charge mistakes her talk of a case to mean a coffin, and offers his condolences.

At eleven o'clock, she tries to get him to eat. She chooses – an unexpected nugget of biographical detail – the menu he likes best: semolina broth; kidney and fried potatoes; omelette; fruit (grapes and a pear); and a slice of cake.

He does not eat it.

At 12.30 the postman, 'impatiently awaited', brings no letters. They are also expecting to see Maurice Riès, but he does not come. Isabelle thinks this is perhaps a good thing. Arthur is too ill to 'deal in any commercial operation'. Outside the little room, beyond the confines of the bed, with its rounded metal headboard and its institutional blanket, the world goes on. The weather is 'radiantly beautiful'. There have been rainstorms, but 'after them the mistral blows for a day and a night and then the sun returns even more brilliant than before'.

There are 'avalanches of fruit of all kinds' on sale in the markets.

In a nearby room, the room which Rimbaud had when they operated on him in May, is a Spanish family. The old man has been operated on for a hernia. He is there with his nephew, an officer in the Legion of Honour, and the nephew's wife who is a good Mass-goer and has become a friend of Isabelle's. They do not speak a word of French, however. In another room is a young French engineer, back from Madagascar, in delirium. They hear his shouts and moans; he is badly treated by the nurses; it would be the same for Arthur if she were not there.

Rimbaud wakes, sees the brilliant sun outside the window, the sun he loved, 'the god of fire', and cries in despair to Isabelle: 'I am going under the earth, but you, you will walk in the sun.'

At five o'clock in the afternoon, *la visite*. The doctors make their rounds, speak their 'pretty words'. They do not fool her. And then, at 5.30, the lighting of the candles, and the long evening begins. 'He will delay, minute by minute, the moment of my leaving', and when it comes 'he will wish me *adieu*' as if he would be dead by the morning.

'It is like this every evening . . .'

*   *   *

As Rimbaud lies dying, 'his life passes in a sort of continual dream'. The dream includes that strangely touching hallucination Isabelle reports in her letter of 28 October: 'Sometimes he calls me Djami.'

> We are at Harar, we are always leaving for Aden, we must find camels, organize the caravan; he walks very easily with his new artificial leg . . . Quick, quick, they are waiting for us. We must pack up our bags and go . . .

Djami 'keeps coming into his dream', she says, and with him the lost world of action and movement, of impatience and freedom: 'always leaving'. It is perhaps at this time that Rimbaud makes the legacy, charging Isabelle to get money to Djami, 750 thalers, by sure and certain means: his only bequest.

It is also at this time, if Isabelle is to be believed, that Rimbaud made his death-bed conversion to the Catholic faith. It is unsatisfactory that she is the sole authority for this. Locked into this long, traumatic vigil in Marseille, and deeply pious herself, one wonders how much of this is her 'dream': her brother *saved*!

On Sunday, 25 October, she relates, Rimbaud admitted the priest to his room. (This was one of the hospital's 'almoners', Canon Chaulier or Abbé Suche: they had tried to minister to him before but had been 'badly received'.) The priest now heard his confession. 'Your brother has faith, my child,' he tells her as he leaves. 'He has a faith such as I have never seen before.'

She finds Rimbaud no longer agitated, but to her eyes quite altered: 'serenely sad'. There follows this dialogue.

He says, 'Your blood and mine are the same. Do you believe?'

'Yes, I believe. Many wiser than me have believed, and do believe. And now I am sure. I have the proof. It is this!' (Meaning, presumably, her brother's conversion.)

He replies bitterly: 'Yes, they say they believe, they make everyone think they are converted, but that's only to make people read what they write. It's a speculation.' This curious comment seems to look back at Verlaine, the prison-convert, spouting 'the vulgarities of our Loyola'. The way the sentence runs it seems that 'speculation' is a pun on the philosophical and financial meanings of the word.

Isabelle hesitates, then replies in kind. 'Oh no, they would earn much more by blaspheming!'

He looks at her for a long time. 'We should have the same soul because we have the same blood. So you do believe?'

'Yes, I believe. One *must* believe.'

'We must prepare the room, then. We must get everything ready. He is coming back with the sacraments.'

Since then, says Isabelle – she is writing three days later – 'he has not once blasphemed'. He prays. 'Yes, him: he prays!'

But he did not, it seems, take communion that Sunday. Isabelle says the priest 'could not' give him the sacrament:

> At first he [the priest] feared it would agitate him too much. Then, because Arthur was spitting all the time, and could not bear anything in his mouth, we feared an involuntary profanity. And he became sad, thinking he had been forgotten, but made no complaint.

It is curiously unconvincing – that a priest would refuse him the host for fear of upsetting him, or because he might cough it back out. The matter rests in doubt. Later [letter to Berrichon, 30 December 1896] Isabelle says Rimbaud made a second confession and at the end received 'extreme unction'; and later still [*Rimbaud Catholique*, 1914] she imbued certain passages of his poetry with a retrospective glow of faith; but the account above is the only contemporary source for Rimbaud's return to the Christian fold, his effacement of the '*merde à Dieu*' scratched on the town-benches of Charleville.

His biographer Petitfils comments: 'he was not in the strict sense converted; he did not go very far down the path of belief; it was in returning back up the path of unbelief that he made his longest journey.' And Jules Borelli, writing to Starkie in 1936, strikes a balance: 'As he died, he repeated, *Allah kerim*; and he thought, *Ave crux spes unica*.' (Borelli was not, of course, present. He means that Rimbaud prayed, but not to the God of any one faith.)

*   *   *

Rimbaud's last recorded words take the form of a letter: the medium which fills the bulk of his *Œuvres Complètes*. It was addressed to the Messageries Maritimes steamship company in Marseille. It was dictated to Isabelle on 9 November 1891, the day before his death. It reads:

ONE LOT: A SINGLE TUSK
ONE LOT: TWO TUSKS
ONE LOT: THREE TUSKS
ONE LOT: FOUR TUSKS
ONE LOT: TWO TUSKS

To the Director

Dear Sir:

I have come to enquire if I have anything left on account with you. I wish to change today my booking on this ship whose name I don't even know, but anyway it must be the ship from Aphinar. There are shipping lines going all over the place, but helpless and unhappy as I am, I can't find a single one – the first dog you meet in the street will tell you this. Send me the prices of the ship from Aphinar to Suez. I am completely paralysed, so I wish to embark in good time. Please let me know when I should be carried aboard . . .

In this last delirious memorandum, Rimbaud is in Africa once more. There is business to attend to; consignments of ivory to be noted in the ledger. The face at his bedside is Djami's, the illiterate scribe who must write all this down, who weeps as he writes. And there is a journey to go on. Where or what Aphinar is no one is sure. The phrase he uses is *le service d'Aphinar*, which seems to mean 'the ship from Aphinar' but could equally mean 'the Aphinar shipping line', so one cannot be quite sure if Aphinar is a place or a company, or even a particular captain. One cannot even be sure that 'Aphinar' is what Rimbaud said: it is only Isabelle's transcription. Was it rather

Al Finar, the Arab word for 'lighthouse', and was this phantom ship which he wished to board 'in good time' the one that would carry him away from the light and into darkness?

We have no answer to this or to any other question arising from this most hermetic of Rimbaldien texts. The answer is known to the dogs in the street but they cannot, after all, tell us.

He died the following morning, Tuesday 10 November, at about ten o'clock. Isabelle would later say: 'He died like a saint.' It is certainly a moment of deliverance, an end to the martyrdom, but if there is a faith in which he lived and for which he died it was not Isabelle's God, nor indeed Djami's Allah, but his own unswerving doctrine of freedom.

The body was removed to the hospital chapel, was prepared according to the provisions of 'Funerals 6th Class' – a coffin of oak and lead, a plaque of copper – and was released for transportation back up to Charleville. Rimbaud had expressed to Isabelle a wish to be buried at Aden, 'because the cemetery there is next to the sea', but he knew this would be opposed by La Mother and so had 'renounced' the idea. The funeral took place, on 14 November, under the grey skies of Europe. The service was conducted by Abbé Gillet, who had known him as a boy. The organist, one Létrange, played the *Dies Irae*. Many years later he recalled how quickly Madame Rimbaud had the funeral arranged. 'I hardly had time to get dressed,' he said. 'I wondered who this dead man was who was in such a hurry.'

He was buried in the family vault, beside his sister Vitalie, beneath the memorial which says *'Priez pour lui'*, in the cemetery now looked over by the apartment-blocks of a Charleville suburb. The only mourners at the graveside were Isabelle and Madame Rimbaud. It was as he had written, the metaphor made fact: *'La Mother m'a mis là dans un triste trou.'*

* * *

Rimbaud's death was in this way – as his African life had been – something hidden, private, fiercely unannounced. No death-notice was printed, either in Charleville or elsewhere. A few people saw the cortège filing up the rue Flandres to the cemetery; a few people in Marseille knew that the end had come, among them probably

Maurice Riès, and so, through him, the news would soon have reached Aden and Harar.

It was not until 29 November, two weeks after the funeral, that a notice appeared in the *Courrier des Ardennes*: two and a half columns, headed 'Arthur Rimbaud', and signed 'L.P.'. This was Louis Pierquin, who had known Rimbaud quite well in Charleville and had followed his career with interest. He describes Rimbaud as 'one of the leading poets' of the Parnassian school of the 1870s; mentions but cannot remember the title of a 'slim volume printed at Brussels' [i.e. *A Season in Hell*]; and refers the reader to the poems gathered by Verlaine in *Les Poètes Maudits*. 'For the last fifteen years or so,' Pierquin continues, 'we lost all trace of him':

> His vagabond temperament and his unquiet spirit drove him off across Europe, all of whose languages he knew, always weary, never finding a place to repose in . . . Tortured by this predisposition always to seek the beyond [*l'au-delà*], he ended up devoted exclusively to this way of thought, and lost himself there.

And so the news gets out, and the epitaphs and tributes start to roll in. Verlaine had in fact already written an epitaph, in 1889, reacting to a stronger-than-usual rumour of Rimbaud's death out there in the *au-delà* –

> . . . *Dead! You?*
> *You, the god among demi-gods?*
> *The people who say this are mad.*
> *You, my great and radiant sin,*
> *The story of my past still burning*
> *In my veins and in my brain* . . .
> ['Læti et Errabundi', 1889]

After this, his reception of the news of Rimbaud's actual death is curiously anti-climactic. He is in Paris, working – ironically – on a new edition of the *Illuminations*. On 7 December he writes to his colleague Vanier: 'What about the preface for the Rimbaud (dead I hear)?' And the following day: 'Have received confirmation of the death of Rimbaud.' He stirred himself soon enough to another epitaph, which epitomises Rimbaud as 'the white negro, the splendidly civilized, carelessly civilizing savage', but it rings rather hollow, and one is left with that first parenthetic reaction – 'dead I hear' – and its implied sense of irrelevance: that Rimbaud's African life is now, already, no more than an editorial footnote to Rimbaud the poet.

Another early notice, from his old employer Alfred Bardey, redresses the balance a little (though not, of course, to any lasting effect). It was a letter to the Société de Géographie, curiously misdated 24 October (another premature epitaph). It was probably written on 24 December, and was read at a Society meeting on 22 January 1892:

> I have learned of the death of M. Arthur Rimbaud. He is better known in France as a decadent poet than as a traveller, but under this latter title he also deserves to be remembered . . .

> His first goal was to acquire through commerce the small fortune necessary for his independence. But either compulsion or habit, or that peculiar attraction which makes those who visit new countries return there to stay, often until death catches them up, made him decide to remain for good in East Africa. Because of his love of the unknown, and because of his personality, he avidly absorbed the essential qualities [*choses intellectuelles*] of the regions in which he travelled. He learned languages to the point where he could freely converse in each region; and he assimilated himself, as much as possible, to the manners and customs of the native people.

> He was one of the first pioneers at Harar, and all who have known him over the last eleven years will tell you that he was an honest, capable and courageous man.

These are among the first of the tributes to Rimbaud, already partitioning him into these twin guises of radiant sinner and hardbitten pioneer, but it was perhaps the very first, unprinted, unintended epitaph that is the most fitting. Within hours or perhaps minutes of his death in Marseille, a clerk filled out the particulars, with a scratchy pen, in the hospital register. This desperately brief synopsis is perhaps the one of which Rimbaud himself might have approved. It gives his profession as 'trader', and for his address it says simply '*de passage*' – in transit.

This is his true epitaph. He is the man in transit, the nomad or bedouin, the tramper of the highway. He is, to an extraordinarily intense degree, just passing through. And even now, a century later, standing at his graveside in a Charleville suburb, I do not feel I am

at his resting-place at all, but knocking at the door of yet another
empty inn, enquiring pointlessly for Monsieur Rimbaud, who has
gone off 'trafficking in the unknown', and has left to posterity no
forwarding address.

SOURCES

I. Rimbaud's writings

The French edition I have used for both the poems and the letters is the *Œuvres Complètes*, edited by Antoine Adam (Bibliothèque de la Pléiade, Gallimard, Paris, 1972). There are more recent collections of the poems (e.g. *Œuvres Poetiques Complètes*, ed. Alain Blottière, Laffont, Paris, 1980), but for the letters the Pléiade edition is by far the most comprehensive. It includes all the letters from and to Rimbaud which I cite in the text. (Letters about him are generally from other sources, as listed below in Sources 2.)

All translations are my own. In the case of the poems, I have consulted other English translations, principally Wallace Fowlie's (*Complete Works*, Chicago, 1966). Other available translations are by Paul Schmidt (*Complete Works*, New York, 1976; London, 1988); by Louise Varese (*A Season in Hell*, New York, 1945) and *Illuminations*, New York, 1947; by Oliver Bernard (*Selected Poems*, Penguin, Harmondsworth, 1990); and by various poets in *Rimbaud Centenary*, ed. Bernard Samuels (Plymouth Arts Centre, Plymouth, 1991).

2. *Memoirs of Rimbaud in Africa*

The following is an alphabetical list of primary sources relating to Rimbaud in Africa. All of them contain personal recollections of him, though with the usual uncertainties of anecdotal transmission. In many cases they are reminiscences written down several decades after the event; there was a spate of brief memoirs in the 1930s, as the last of Rimbaud's colleagues neared the end of their lives. Other than brief extracts, none of these sources has been translated into English. Short references are to books listed in Sources 3.

Alfred Bardey

1. *Barr-Adjam: Souvenirs d'Afrique Orientale, 1880–87*, edited and introduced by Joseph Tubiana (Centre Nationale de la Recherche Scientifique, Paris, 1981). This is Bardey's journal of his years in East Africa, with his own later annotations and intercalations, perhaps as late as *c.* 1930. He died in 1934. The typescript was made public by Bardey's great-niece. Madeleine Lombard-Gérin.

2. Letter to the Société de Géographie, Paris, written at Aden, *c.* 20 December 1891

(misdated 20 October 1891), and read at the Society's meeting, 22 January 1892. Published in *Comptes-rendus de la Société de, Géographie* (Paris, 1892).

3. Letter to Paterne Berrichon, 10 July 1897, in Berrichon, pp. 182–3.

4. Letters to Paterne Berrichon, 1897–1901, in Henri de Bouillane de Lacoste and Henri Matarasso, 'Nouveaux documents sur Rimbaud', *Mercure de France*, 15 May 1939.

5. Speech at unveiling of the Rimbaud statue, Charleville, 21 July 1901, in *Le Sagittaire*, August 1901.

6. Letter to M. de B–, 15 April 1923, published by 'P.P.' [Pascal Pia] in *Carrefour*, 2 November 1949.

7. Reminiscences, c. 1929, in Jean-Paul Vaillant, 'Le Vrai Visage de Rimbaud l'Africain' (*Mercure de France*, 1 January 1930).

Jules Borelli

1. *L'Éthiopie Méridionale: Journal de mon Voyage aux Pays Amhara, Oromo et Sidama* (Maison Quantin, Paris, 1890). Contains journal-entries relating to Rimbaud in 1887–8, and contemporary maps and engravings of Ethiopia.

2. Letter to Paterne Berrichon, c. 1897, in Berrichon, pp. 183–4.

3. Letter to Enid Starkie, c. 1936, in Starkie (1), pp. 152–3.

4. Letters to André Tian, 28 and 31 March 1939, in Matucci, pp. 114–17.

Capt. Antonio Cecchi

Report from Italian Consulate General, Aden, 22 May 1888, and English translation [June 1888]. In Public Record Office, FO 78/4167; transcribed in Matucci, pp. 108–111.

E. Dufaud *et al*

Memoir based on recollections of Rimbaud gathered by an anonymous French traveller in East Africa between 1906 and 1925, and particularly in the Obock area in c. 1911–13. His sources are listed as follows: M. and Mme E. Dufaud, hoteliers at Obock; Athanase Righas, hotelier at Djibouti, and his brother Vlakos; M. Marignac, French businessman in Obock: M. Kalos, Greek businessman in Obock; police authorities at Obock; Ato Joseph, Ethiopian consul at Djibouti; Negradas Aile-Gorguis, Ethiopian Minister of War at Addis Ababa; Hadji Bedros, Armenian, clockmaker to Emperor Menelik at Addis Ababa; Abo Samuel, Abyssinian priest in Harar. Their individual contributions to the memoir are not specified but can in some cases be surmised (e.g. the reference to Rimbaud's *hôtelière* is presumably to Mme Dufaud, the only female listed.) First published in an obscure French periodical. *Bulletin de la Société des Naturalistes et Archéologues du Nord de la Meuse*, Longuyon, 1934, it was republished ('presque de l'inédit') by Pierre Petitfils, 'Des Souvenirs Inconnus sur Rimbaud', *Mercure de France*, 1 January 1955.

Dr L. Faurot

Le Voyage au Golfe de Tajoura (Paris, 1888).

Ugo Ferrandi

1. *Lettere dell' Harar* (Milan, 1896).

2. Letter to Ottone Schanzer, 7 August 1923, in *Les Nouvelles Littéraires*, Paris, 20 October 1923.

3. MS journal: extracts relating to Rimbaud in *La Table Ronde*, January 1950.

Françoise Grisard

Letter to Paterne Berrichon, 22 July 1897, in Berrichon, pp. 158–59. Bardey's former housekeeper in Aden, Grisard wrote in reply to Berrichon's request for information about Rimbaud's Abyssinian mistress. She was by then living in Marseille, where she worked as a laundry-woman. Her husband was a driver and mechanic for the Messageries Maritimes.

G. L. Guigniony

He was a young employee of Armand Savouré. His reminiscences, which may or may not be first hand, are in Pierre Ripert, 'En Marge du Symbolisme', *Marseille*, No. 18, July-September 1952.

Alfred Ilg

As far as is known, Ilg left no memoir or impressions of Rimbaud. Some letters between them, owned by Henri Matarasso, were published in the 1930s, but the full correspondence appears in *Arthur Rimbaud, Correspondance, 1888–91*, introduced and edited by Jean Voellmy (Gallimard, Paris, 1965). The letters are incorporated into the Pléiade *Œuvres Complètes*.

Mgr André Jarosseau, Bishop of Harar

1. Interview with Evelyn Waugh, 1930; in Waugh (1), pp. 78–9.

2. Reminiscences, in Henri d'Acrémont, 'En Abyssinie sur les Traces de Rimbaud' (*Revue Hebdomadaire*, 27 August 1932).

3. Reminiscences, in Henriette Célarie, 'À Propos de Rimbaud: Souvenirs d'Éthiopie' (*Le Temps*, 10 June 1933).

4. Letter to Enid Starkie, 22 September 1936, in Starkie (1), p. 153.

5. Letter to André Tian, 30 May 1939, in *Le Feu*, Sept-Oct 1941.

6. Reminiscences, in Jean and Jérôme Tharaud, 'Rimbaud à Harrar' (*Candide*, 19 November 1941)

7. Anecdotal evidence (gathered in Harar after Jarosseau's death) in Max Guineheuf, 'Rimbaud et Mgr Jarosseau', *Mercure de France*. April 1948.

Pierre Mille

Mille was *chef de cabinet* to Rimbaud's former schoolfellow Paul Bourde when the latter was Secretary-General of Madagascar. He did not know Rimbaud personally, but gathered reminiscences of him from unnamed 'traders' in and around Djibouti in 1896: see *L'Age Nouveau*, No. 1, 1929; *L'Action Française*, 20 November 1938.

Maurice Riès

1. Letter to Émile Deschamps, 15 March 1929, in Pléiade *Œuvres Complètes*, p. 815.
2. Letter to André Tian, 12 May 1939. In Matucci, p. 121.

Luigi Robecchi-Brichetti

1. *Nell' Harar* (Galli di Chiesa, Milan, 1898).
2. 'Rimbaud: Ricordo di uno Soggiorno nell'Harar', *Bolletino della Societa Geografica Italiana* Series 3. No. 4, 1891.

Athanase Righas

See Dufaud above.

Ottoman Righas

1. Reminiscences recorded by M. Laminne, 'Hunter in Ethiopia', in a letter to Paterne Berrichon, 24 January 1912 (Bibliothèque Charleville-Mézières). Extracts quoted in Borer (1), p. 374.

Ottorino Rosa

1. *L'Impero del Leone di Giuda* (Brescia, Lunghi, 1913; 2nd edn 1980). Contains brief comments about Rimbaud in Aden in *c*. 1882, and photographs of Rimbaud's Abyssinian mistress [photo 142, page 207] and his last house in Harar [photo 73, p. 145].
2. MS notes on Rimbaud, *c*. 1930, in French and Italian. Extracts published by Lidia Herling Croce, 'Rimbaud à Chypre, à Aden et au Harar: Documents Inédits', *Études Rimbaldiennes*, No. 3, 1972.

Armand Savouré

1. Letter to Frédéric Rimbaud, Addis Ababa, 12 April 1897; facsimile in Borer *et al*, pp. 72–75.
2. Letter to Georges Maurevert, Grasse, 3 April 1930; facsimile in Borer *et al*, p. 76.

Edouardo Scarfoglio

Abissinia, 1888–1896 (Rome, 1938). This includes articles written in Harar and Djibouti, 1888–91, containing brief notices of Rimbaud and his circle. Scarfoglio was foreign correspondent of the *Corriere di Napoli* (he wrote under the nom de plume of 'Tartarin', a character in the stories of Alphonse Daudet).

André Tian

1. 'La Verité sur Arthur Rimbaud en Abyssinie', *Le Feu*, Aix-en-Provence, June-July 1941. A defence of his father, César Tian, and of Rimbaud, against Enid Starkie's slave-dealing allegations.
2 Letter to *Les Nouvelles Littéraires*, 13 Febuary 1947.
3. 'À Propos de Rimbaud', *Mercure de France*, 1 October 1954.

3. Secondary Sources

Arnoult, Pierre: *Rimbaud* (Albin Michel, Paris, 1943; revised ed. 1955)

Beachey, R. W.: 'The Arms Trade in East Africa in the late Nineteenth Century' (*Journal of African History* 3, 1962)

Bernoville, Gaetan: *Mgr Jarosseau et la Mission des Gallas* (Albin Michel, Paris, 1950)

Berrichon, Paterne [i.e. Pierre Dufour]: *La Vie de Jean-Arthur Rimbaud* (Mercure de France, Paris, 1897)

Borer, Alain: (1) *Rimbaud en Abyssinie* (Le Seuil, Paris, 1984; US ed., trans. Rosmarie Waldrop, Morrow, New York, 1991)

Borer, Alain: (2) *Rimbaud d'Arabie (Le Seuil, Paris, 1981)*

Borer, Alain: (3) *Rimbaud: L'Heure de la Fuite* (Gallimard, Paris, 1991)

Borer, Alain, Soupault, Philippe and Aeschbacher, Arthur: *Un Sieur Rimbaud se disant Négociant* (Lachenal & Ritter, Paris, 1983)

Burton, Sir Richard: *First Footsteps in East Africa* [1856], ed. Gordon Waterfield (Routledge, London, 1966)

Camus, Albert: *L'Homme revolté* (Gallimard, Paris, 1951)

Carré, Jean-Marie: (1) *Les Deux Rimbaud* (Les Cahiers Libres, Paris, 1928)

Carré, Jean-Marie: (2) 'Arthur Rimbaud en Éthiopie', *Revue de France*, 1 June 1935.

Colban, Jean-Claude, and Blottière, Alain: 'Rimbaud en Éthiopie', *Réalités*, July 1977

Delahaye, Ernest: (1) *Rimbaud: L'Artiste et l'Être Moral* (Messein, Paris, 1923)

Delahaye, Ernest: (2) *Souvenirs familiers à propos de Rimbaud, Verlaine et Germain Nouveau* (Messein, Paris, 1925)

Demais, Louis-Charles: 'Arthur Rimbaud à Java' (*Bulletin de la Société d'Études Indochinoises*, 12, 1967)

Étiemble, René: *Le Mythe de Rimbaud*, 2 vols (Gallimard, Paris, 1952–4; new ed., 1968–70)

Forbes, Duncan: (1) *The Heart of Ethiopia* (Robert Hale, London, 1972)

Forbes, Duncan: (2) *Rimbaud in Ethiopia* (Volturna Press, Hythe, 1979)

Foucher, Père Émile: 'L'Arrivée d'Arthur Rimbaud à Harar' (*Missions-Messages*, November-December 1980)

Fouchet, Max-Pol: 'Avec Rimbaud à Harar' (*Les Nouvelles Littéraires*, 14 May 1970)

Fowlie, Wallace: *Rimbaud and Jim Morrison* (Duke University Press, Durham, North Carolina, 1994)

Hanson, Jean and Vernon: *Verlaine, Prince of Poets* (Chatto & Windus, London, 1958)

Izambard, Georges: *Rimbaud tel que je l'ai connu* (Mercure de France, Paris, 1946)

Keller, Conrad: *Alfred Ilg: sein Leben und sein Wirken* (Leipzig, 1918)

Klein, Melanie: *Love, Guilt and Reparation* (Hogarth Press, London, 1975)

Lipski, George A.: *Ethiopia* (Human Relations Area Files, New Haven, Conn., 1962)

Marsden-Smedley, Philip: *A Far Country: Travels in Ethiopia* (Century, London, 1990)

Martin, Auguste: 'Documents inédits tirés des archives de la Préfecture de Police (*Nouvelle Revue Française*, 1 February 1943)

Matarasso, Henri and Petitfils, Pierre: *Album Rimbaud* (Gallimard, Paris, 1967)

Matucci, Mario: *Le dernier visage de Rimbaud en Afrique* (Edizioni Sensoni, Firenze, 1962)

Mauté, Mathilde (formerly Mme Verlaine): *Mémoires de ma Vie* (Flammarion, Paris, 1935)

McLynn, Frank: *Hearts of Darkness: The European Exploration of Africa* (Hutchinson, London, 1992)

Miller, Henry: *The Time of the Assassins* (P. J. Oswald, Paris, 1950)

Milliex, Roger: 'Le Premier Séjour d'Arthur Rimbaud à Chypre' (*Kupriakai Spoudai*, Nicosia, 1965)

Monfried, Henri de: *Le Radeau de la Méduse* (Bernard Grasset, Paris, 1958)

d'Orléans, Prince Henri: *Une Visite à l'Empereur Menelick* (Librairie Dentu, Paris, 1898)

Pankhurst, Dr Richard (ed.): *Ethiopian Royal Chronicles* (Institute of Ethiopian Studies, Addis Ababa, 1967)

Petitfils, Pierre: *Rimbaud* (Julliard, Paris, 1982)

Raimondi, Giuseppe: 'Rimbaud Mercante in Africa' (*Civiltà delle Macchine*, September 1954)

Rimbaud, Isabelle: *Reliques* (Mercure de France, Paris, 1921)

Selassie, Emperor Haile: *My Life and Ethiopia's Progress*, trans. Edward Ullendorff (Oxford University Press, Oxford, 1978)

Starkie, Enid: (1) *Arthur Rimbaud in Abyssinia* (Clarendon Press, Oxford, 1937)

Starkie, Enid: (2) *Arthur Rimbaud* (Faber, London, 1938; revised ed, 1947)

Starkie, Enid: (3) 'Sur les Traces de Rimbaud' (Mercure de France, 1 May 1947)

Steinmetz, Jean-Luc: *Arthur Rimbaud: Une Question de Présence* (Tallendier, Paris, 1991)

Thompson, Virginia, and Adloff, Richard: *Djibouti and the Horn of Africa* (Stanford University Press, Stanford, Ca, 1968)

Trampant, Jacques: *Djibouti Hier de 1887 à 1939* (Hatier, Paris, 1990)

Tubiana, Joseph: 'Le Patron de Rimbaud' (in Bardey, *Barr-Adjam*, pp. v-lvii)

Underwood, V. P.: (1) *Verlaine et l'Angleterre* (Nizet, Paris, 1956)

Underwood, V.P.: (1) *Rimbaud et l'Angleterre* (Nizet, Paris, 1978)

Vaillant, Jean-Paul: (1) *Rimbaud tel qu'il fut* (Le Rouge et le Noir, Paris, 1930)

Vaillant, Jean-Paul: (2) 'Abdoh Rinb – Rimbaud Serviteur de Dieu', *Le Figaro Littéraire*, 16 October 1954.

Verlaine, Paul: (1) *Œuvres Poetiques Complètes* (Gallimard, Paris, 1954)

Verlaine, Paul: (2) *Correspondence*, ed A. van Bever, 3 vols (Messein, Paris, 1922)

Waugh, Evelyn: (1) *Remote People* (Duckworth, London, 1931; pbk, Penguin, Harmondsworth, 1985)

Waugh, Evelyn: (2) *Waugh in Abyssinia* (Longmans, London, 1938)

1. Illustrations

Photographs and documents relating to Rimbaud are reproduced by kind permission of the Musée Arthur Rimbaud and Bibliothèque Municipale, Charleville-Mézières. The photograph of César Tian's office in Aden is published here for the first time. It is from a collection of photographs formerly belonging to Tian's great-nephew, Jean Malo-Renault, and purchased by the Biblothèque Municipale in 1995. I am grateful to the librarian, M. Gérard Martin, for showing me this collection. The drawing of Communards by Félix Regamey first appeared in the *Illustrated London News*, January 1872. The postcard photograph of Roche was supplied by Mme Maryse Aubry. Photographs of Harar and Djibouti by Ron Orders. Photographs of Aden and Marseille by the author.

'STRINGY KIDS':

A Personal Note

THIS BOOK IS dedicated to the memory of my friend Kevin Stratford, who first introduced me to the poetry of Rimbaud. I had certainly heard of Rimbaud before that, but like many who knew the name I hadn't actually read him. I think I first heard of Rimbaud in 1966, when I was sixteen, and what I heard about him was that he was Bob Dylan's favourite poet. I can now document this with reference to an interview with Dylan on a San Francisco television station, KQED, on 3 December 1965:

Interviewer: What poets do you dig?

Dylan: Rimbaud, W. C. Fields, the trapeze family in the circus, Smokey Robinson, Allen Ginsberg, Charlie Rich . . .

I believe this was Dylan's first public utterance on the subject, though how I got to hear of it, five thousand miles away in a Buckinghamshire boarding school, I have no idea. Not, I suspect, via the usual channels of wisdom – Radio Luxemburg, *Record Mirror*, etc. – but more probably from my school-friend Charles 'Chip' Graham, a Dylanologist *avant la lettre*, an A. J. Weberman in metaphorical short pants, who seemed to be plugged deeper and quicker than anyone else into the mysteries of 'Pop' (as it still was) and of Dylan in particular.

Whatever the source, I have it firmly in my memory that this mysterious name Rimbaud was in the air as I sat up illicitly at dawn listening to 'Visions of Johanna' and 'Sad-Eyed Lady of the Lowlands' and other archetypal songs from what is now thought of as Dylan's 'Early Electric' period.

Had I read my Rimbaud then I would have known how profoundly those songs were steeped in his influence. Reference is often made to 'A Hard Rain', written in 1962 in response to the Cuban missile crisis, as Dylan's first great 'Symbolist' song. ('Symbolist' in the literary history sense: the school of *fin-de-siècle*

French poets like Mallarmé and Laforgue who took Rimbaud as their great precursor.) The folk-blues singer Dave van Ronk (from whom Dylan got 'House of the Rising Sun') recalls:

I once asked Bobby: 'Have you ever heard about Rimbaud?'

He said: 'Who?'

I repeated: 'Rimbaud. R-I-M-B-A-U-D. He's a French poet. You really ought to read him,' I said.

Bobby kind of twitched a little; he seemed to be thinking about it. He just said: 'Yeah, yeah.'

I raised Rimbaud with him a couple of times after that. Much later, I was up at his place. I always look at people's books. On his shelf I discovered a book of translations of French Symbolist poets that had obviously been thumbed through over a period of years! I think he probably knew Rimbaud backward and forward before I even mentioned him.

I didn't mention Rimbaud to him again until I heard his *A Hard Rain's A-Gonna Fall*, his first symbolist venture. I said to Bob: 'You know that song of yours is heavy in symbolism, don't you?'

He said: 'Huh?'

But to me the song which heralds Rimbaud's influence on Dylan is 'Chimes of Freedom' (1964) with its political message of compassion for the 'luckless and forsaken' wrapped up in a hallucinatory sort of landscape, 'a wild cathedral evening' through which the poet stumbles 'spellbound and swallowed'. Lines from this song seem to me the beginning of Dylan's great lyric soaring, and they seem to me very Rimbaud:

> *Even though a cloud's white curtain*
> *In a far off corner flared*
> *And the hypnotic splattered mist was*
> *Slowly lifting . . .*

And there can be few more gnomic summaries of Rimbaud's life than the line 'Condemned to drift or else be kept from drifting'.

(Rimbaud uses exactly this phrase about himself – '*condamné à errer*' – in a letter from Africa.) From there one goes on to 'It's Alright Ma' and 'It's All Over Now Baby Blue' and 'Desolation Row', and most especially to 'Like a Rolling Stone', which is always said to be about the waif-like Warhol acolyte Edie Sedgwick, but seems also to be a reading of Rimbaud's nomadic life:

> *When you ain't got nothing,*
> *You got nothing to lose.*
> *You're invisible now*
> *You got no secrets to conceal.*
> *How does it feel*
> *To be on your own,*
> *A complete unknown,*
> *With no direction home,*
> *Like a rolling stone . . .*

It was at this time, in late 1965, that Dylan was playing San Francisco, and gave that interview naming Rimbaud as his favourite poet. San Francisco was the home of the Beat Poets. Dylan's triumphant concert dates there that winter have something of the air of Rimbaud setting feathers flying among the poets of Paris in the early 1870s. At the first Berkeley concert, all the Beat luminaries were there – Laurence Ferlinghetti, Allen Ginsberg, Ken Kesey, etc. – in the front row. The journalist Ralph Gleason recalls their mix of fascination and discomfiture:

> The San Francisco poets freaked out when they saw this Dylan thing happening. I thought Larry [Ferlinghetti] was a tragic figure that weekend, a shaken and embittered man. You know: What is that stringy kid doing up there with his electric guitar? I mean: I'm a major poet, and this kid has thirty-five hundred kids in this hall. And Larry's been mumbling to himself ever since.

This seems precisely parallel to Rimbaud in Paris in 1871: 'that stringy kid' outplaying them at their own game; the new voice that makes the others seem suddenly old.

And so from Dylan it went on into the more satanic, strung-out side of the Sixties: to Jim Morrison ('Cancel my subscription to the Resurrection'), and to Cammell and Roeg's *Performance*, and to the *évènements* of 1968, when the students tore up the cobblestones of

Paris under Rimbaldien placards proclaiming LA LIBERTÉ LIBRE and CHANGER LA VIE! All this gave Rimbaud a status of 'rock & roll hero' not usually accorded to dead French poets, and he remains indelibly associated in my mind with these helter-skelter years: *les nerfs vont vite chasser*, your nerve-ends gallop off hunting.

It was in 1968 that I met Kevin Stratford, at Cambridge. He was already a very good poet, and continued to be a poet long after the rest of us callow littérateurs had buckled down to more profitable métiers. A selection of his poems, *Songs of the Adept*, is published by Carcanet Press. He was perhaps more Rimbaldien than any of the more obvious candidates among my acquaintance at that time. Not that he was a showily romantic sort of figure: he was a Yorkshireman, from Dewsbury; his father Arthur worked on the buses. There was always an aspect of grittiness in him, for all the brilliant flights of his mind.

At Cambridge we edited a poetry magazine called *Pawn* together, one issue of which came trendily on loose pages inside a large white envelope. Kevin later instituted a phantom school of poetry called Totalism which met on Thursday evenings (in emulation of Mallarmé's *jeudis soirs*), in theory to read poems and discuss the universe but more often to get stoned and listen to records. Another member was Peter Ackroyd. I remember him reading a poem which began: 'Simon Stylites has piles'.

Kevin introduced me to Rilke and Frank O'Hara; to Mahler and Charlie Parker; to Baudelaire and Rimbaud. I can't think that I introduced him to anything, though he was impressed by some obscure Otis Redding imports I had.

He died in 1984 at the age of thirty-five (even younger than Rimbaud). I had not seen him much, perhaps a couple of times in the last five years, but I dreamed of him the night he died. His last years were dogged by illness; he refused a liver transplant that may or may not have saved him. There was always something otherworldly and gentle about him, despite the gruff ironic Yorkshirisms and the sometimes barbed mischievousness. I think of his startling blue eyes and his thin pale fingers holding, slightly concave about the knuckles, a Players No. 6 cigarette, as he expounded in his darting quicksilver style on anything from Heidegger to Hedley Verity.

I still have the little Livre de Poche edition of Rimbaud he gave me, signing himself 'Le Bateleur', the conjuror, a reference to the

Tarot card of that ilk. It has accompanied me on my Rimbaud travels – to Charleville and Paris and Marseille, to Alexandria and Aden and Harar – and now, belatedly, I place this other book beside it in memory of Kevin and of those stringy teenage kids that we all once were.

For 'belatedly', of course, read 'too late'.

INDEX